lonely planet

GERMAN

Travel Phrasebook & Dictionary

Credits

Production Editor Vicky Smith
Language Writers Gunter Muehl, Birgit Jordan, Mario Kaiser

Thanks

Sofie Andersen, Marc Backwell, Fergal Condon, Gwen Cotter, Kellie Langdon, Saralinda Turner, Clifton Wilkinson

Published by Lonely Planet Global Limited
CRN 554153

Digital Depot, Roe Lane off Thomas Street, Dublin
D08 TCV4, Ireland (EU authorised representative)

9th Edition – Sep 2026
ISBN 978 1 80653 152 3

Cover Image Brandenburger Gate, SAHACHATZ/Shutterstock; Pretzel; Bavarian beer, Food Impressions/Shutterstock
Printed in China 10 9 8 7 6 5 4 3 2 1

Contact lonelyplanet.com/contact

Look out for the following icons throughout the book:

'Shortcut' Phrase
Easy-to-remember alternative to the full phrase

Q&A Pair
'Question-and-answer' pair – we suggest a response to the question asked

Look for
Phrases you may see on signs, menus etc

Listen for
Phrases you may hear from officials, locals etc

LANGUAGE TIP

An insight into the German language

CULTURE TIP

An insight into the local culture

How to read the phrases:

- Coloured words and phrases throughout the book are phonetic guides to help you pronounce the German phrases.
- Lists of phrases with tinted background are options you can choose to complete the phrase above them.

These abbreviations will help you choose the right words and phrases in this book:

f	feminine	m	masculine	n	neuter
inf	informal	pl	plural	sg	singular
lit	literal	pol	polite		

CONTENTS

ABOUT GERMAN 6

Learn about German, build your own sentences and pronounce words correctly.

Introduction 6

Top Phrases 8

Pronunciation.......................... 10

Grammar.................................. 14

TRAVEL PHRASES

Ready-made phrases for every situation – buy a ticket, book a hotel and much more.

BASICS.......................... 27

Understanding...................... 28

Numbers & Amounts........... 30

Time & Dates 32

PRACTICAL 37

Transport.............................. 38

Border Crossing.................... 51

Directions............................. 53

Accommodation.................. 56

Shopping 69

Communications................. 79

Money & Banking................. 86

Business.....90
Sightseeing.....92
Seniors & Travellers with Disabilities.....97
Travel with Children.....99

SOCIAL.....101
Meeting People.....102
Interests.....114
Feelings & Opinions.....119
Going Out.....124
Romance.....129
Beliefs & Culture.....134
Sports.....136
Outdoors.....142

SAFE TRAVEL.....147
Emergencies.....148
Police.....150
Health.....152

FOOD.....161
Eating Out.....162
Self-Catering.....179
Vegetarian & Special Meals.....184

MENU DECODER.....187

Dishes and ingredients explained – order with confidence and try new foods.

TWO-WAY DICTIONARY.....197

Quick reference vocabulary guide – 3500 words to help you communicate.

English–German Dictionary.....197
German–English Dictionary.....233

INDEX.....267

INTRO

German

DEUTSCH/DOYTCH

Who Speaks German?

Why Bother

Don't be put off by the fact that German tends to join words together to express a single notion – it's not hard to tell parts of words, and you'll have fun recognising 'the Football World Cup qualifying match' hidden within *Fussballweltmeisterschaftsqualifikationsspiel*!

Distinctive Sounds

The ü (pronounced as 'e' with rounded lips), plus the throaty kh (like in the Scottish *loch* or the name Bach) and r (a bit like gargling).

100 MILLION speak German as their first language

80 MILLION speak German as a second language

German in the World

It's not usually described as romantic, but its role in science has long been recognised, and the German language lays claim to some of the most famous works ever printed – just think of the influence of Goethe, Nietzsche, Freud and Einstein.

German in Germany

The *Gesellschaft für deutsche Sprache* (Society for German Language) publishes an *Unwort des Jahres* (Unword of the Year) – an unloved word that dominated the media. The 2025 'unword' was *Sondervermögen* ('special funds'), criticised for its use as a euphemism for taking on debt.

False Friends

Warning: many German words look like English words but have a different meaning altogether, eg *Chef* shef is boss, not chef (which is *Koch* kokh in German).

Language Family

West Germanic – close relatives include English, Dutch, Afrikaans, Frisian and Yiddish.

Must-Know Grammar

German words can have a number of different endings, depending on their role in the sentence. There's also a formal and informal word for 'you' (*Sie* zee and *du* doo respectively).

Donations to English

Numerous – you may recognise *kindergarten*, *kitsch*, *waltz*, *hamburger*, *poodle* ...

5 Phrases TO LEARN BEFORE YOU GO

01 Do you accept credit cards?

Nehmen Sie Kreditkarten?

nay·men zee kre·*deet*·kar·ten

Cash is still king in Germany, so don't assume you'll be able to pay by credit card – it's best to enquire first.

02 Which beer would you recommend?

Welches Bier empfehlen Sie?

vel·khes beer emp·*fay*·len zee

Who better to ask for advice on beer than the Germans, whether at a beer garden, hall, cellar or on a brewery tour?

03 Can I get this without meat?

Kann ich das ohne Fleisch bekommen?

kan ikh das *aw*·ne flaish be·*ko*·men

The land of *Wurst* has embraced vegetarianism over the last decade, but you may still struggle to find options in smaller towns.

04 A (non)smoking table, please.

Einen (Nicht)rauchertisch, bitte.

ai·nen (*nikht*·)*row*·kher·tish *bi*·te

Germany has only partial smoking bans, so choose where to sit in cafes, bars and restaurants.

05 Do you run original versions?

Spielen auch Originalversionen?

shpee·len owkh o·ri·gi·*nahl*·fer·zi·*aw*·nen

Cinemas often run movies dubbed into German – look for a cinema that runs subtitled original versions.

10 Phrases TO SOUND LIKE A LOCAL

Hey!	Hey!	hei
Great!	Toll	tol
Cool!	Spitze!	*shpi*·tse
No problem.	Kein Problem.	kain pro·*blaym*
Sure.	Klar!	klahr
Maybe.	Vielleicht.	fi·*laikht*
No way!	Auf keinen Fall!	owf *kai*·nen fal
It's OK.	Alles klar.	a·les klahr
What a pity!	Schade!	*shah*·de
Doesn't matter.	Macht nichts.	makht nikhts

GERMAN

Pronunciation

VOWEL SOUNDS

As in English, vowels can be pronounced short or long, to give different meanings (compare 'ship' and 'sheep'). Vowels are pronounced crisply and cleanly with your mouth tenser than in English, eg *Tee* (tea) is pronounced tay, not *tay*·ee.

SYMBOL	ENGLISH EQUIVALENT	GERMAN EXAMPLE	TRANSLITERATION
a	run	hat	hat
ah	rather	habe	*hah*·be
ai	aisle	mein	main
air	hair	Bär	bair
aw	saw	Boot	bawt
ay	say	leben	*lay*·ben
e	red	Bett, Männer	bet, *me*·ner
ee	bee	fliegen	*flee*·gen
er	teacher	schön	shern
i	bit	mit	mit
o	pot	Koffer	*ko*·fer
oo	moon	Schuhe	*shoo*·e
ow	house	Haus	hows
oy	boy	Leute, Häuser	*loy*·te, *hoy*·zer
u	foot	unter	*un*·ter
ü	ee with rounded lips	zurück	tsu·*rük*

CONSONANT SOUNDS

All German consonant sounds exist in English, except for the kh and r sounds, so all you need is a little practice.

SYMBOL	ENGLISH EQUIVALENT	GERMAN EXAMPLE	TRANSLITERATION
b	big	Bett	bet
ch	chili	Tschüss	chüs
d	din	dein	dain
f	fun	vier	feer
g	go	gehen	*gay*·en
h	hit	helfen	*hel*·fen
k	kick	kein	kain
kh	Bach	Sprache	*shprah*·khe
l	loud	laut	lowt
m	man	Mann	man
n	no	nein	nain
ng	sing	singen	*zing*·en
p	pig	Preis	prais
r	run	Reise	*rai*·ze
s	so	heiß	hais
sh	show	schön	shern
t	tin	Tag	tahk
ts	hits	Zeit	tsait
v	van	wohnen	*vaw*·nen
y	yes	ja	ya
z	zoo	sitzen	*zi*·tsen
zh	pleasure	Garage	ga·*rah*·zhe

The kh sound is generally like the 'ch' in 'Bach' or the Scottish *loch*, pronounced at the back of the throat. After the vowels e and i it's pronounced more forward in your mouth, almost like a sh sound. A kh sound, however, will always get you by. In this book we've used one symbol for both sounds to simplify things.

The r sound is pronounced at the back of the throat, almost like saying a g sound, but with some friction - a bit like gargling.

WORD STRESS

Stress in German is straightforward - almost all German words are pronounced with stress on the first syllable. There are just a couple of things to watch out for.

Some prefixes aren't stressed, like *ver-* in the verb *verstehen* fer·*shtay*·en (understand). Also, words borrowed from other languages often keep their original stress, and words like *Organisation* or·ga·ni·sa·*tsyawn* (organisation) and *Student* shtu·*dent* (student) may have the stress on a different syllable than in English.

While these are handy rules of thumb, you can always rely on our coloured pronunciation guides which show the stressed syllable in italics.

INTONATION

German intonation is quite similar to that of English. If you're asking a question, your voice goes up at the end, just like in English: *Bist du fertig?* bist du *fer*·tikh (Are you ready?) or *Tee?* tay (Tea?). If you start with a question word, however, your voice falls, also like in English: *Woher kommst du?* vo·*hair* komst du (Where are you from?).

Note that, like in English, a rise in intonation can indicate that the speaker hasn't finished. For example, if someone asks you where you're from, you can say *Melbourne ... eine Stadt ... in Australien* *mel*·bawn ... *ai*·ne shtat ... in ow·*stra*·*li*·en (Melbourne ... a city ... in Australia), rising on the first two parts, and everyone will wait with bated breath!

READING & WRITING

The relationship between German sounds and the characters that represent them in writing is consistent, so once you become familiar with them, you should be able to pronounce a new word without a hitch. The examples in the tables on pages 10 and 11 show the correspondence between the sounds (in the first column) and how they're typically spelt (in the third column). However, there are a few points worth noting:

- The letter *ß* stands for *ss* (but the rules for whether you use *ß* or *ss* are even confusing to Germans themselves).
- Unlike in English, the *k* is pronounced in words that begin with *kn*, such as *Knödel* kner·del.
- The letters *sp* and *st* at the start of a word are pronounced like shp and sht, eg *Sport* (sport) is pronounced shport.
- Final *d, g,* and *b* are 'unvoiced', ie pronounced more like t, k and p, eg *Geld* (money) is pronounced gelt.

Don't be intimidated by the length of some words. Unlike English, which often uses a number of separate words to express a single notion, German tends to join words together. After a while you'll start to recognise parts of words. For example, *Haupt-* howpt means 'main', so *Hauptpost* *howpt*·post for 'main post office', and *Hauptstadt* *howpt*·shtat is 'main city', ie 'capital'.

~ GERMAN ALPHABET ~

A a ah	**B b** bay	**C c** tsay
D d day	**E e** ay	**F f** ef
G g gay	**H h** hah	**I i** ee
J j yot	**K k** kah	**L l** el
M m em	**N n** en	**O o** aw
P p pay	**Q q** koo	**R r** er
S s es	**T t** tay	**U u** oo
V v fow	**W w** vay	**X x** iks
Y y *üp*·si·lon	**Z z** tset	

GERMAN Grammar

This chapter is designed to explain the main grammatical structures you need to make your own sentences. Look under each heading – listed in alphabetical order – for information on functions which these grammatical categories express in a sentence. For example, demonstratives are used for giving instructions. A glossary of grammatical terms is included at the end of the chapter to help you.

ADJECTIVES & ADVERBS

Describing People/Things • Doing Things

Adjectives don't change their form if they come after 'be' in a sentence. However, if they come before a noun, adjectives have either 'strong' endings (if used without an article) or 'weak' endings (if used with an article). Strong endings change to match the gender, number and case of the noun, but weak endings don't indicate this. See also **articles**, **case** (p16), **gender** (p18) and **plurals** (p21).

My meal is cold.	Mein Essen ist kalt. (lit: my-nom-n-sg meal is cold) main e·sen ist kalt
cold meal	kaltes Essen (lit: cold-nom-n-sg meal) *kal*·tes e·sen
the cold meal	das kalte Essen (lit: the-nom-n-sg cold meal) das *kal*·te e·sen

	WEAK ENDINGS				STRONG ENDINGS			
	m sg	f sg	n sg	pl	m sg	f sg	n sg	pl
nom	-e	-e	-e	-en	-er	-e	-es	-e
acc	-en	-e	-e	-en	-en	-e	-es	-e
dat	-en	-en	-en	-en	-em	-er	-em	-en
gen	-en	-en	-en	-en	-en	-er	-en	-er

Most adjectives in German can also be used as adverbs in their basic form (with no endings), and they usually come towards the end of the sentence.

a quiet restaurant	ein ruhiges Restaurant (lit: a-nom-n-sg quiet-nom-n-sg restaurant) ain *roo*·ikh·es res·to·*rang*
I work quietly.	Ich arbeite ruhig (lit: I work quiet) ikh *ar*·bai.te *roo*·ikh

ARTICLES

Naming People/Things

German has various forms of both the definite article (ie 'the' in English) and the indefinite article (ie 'a' or 'an' in English), depending on the gender, number and case of the noun (see **case**, p16, **gender**, p18, and **plurals**, p21). If you just use the nominative (dictionary form), you'll still be understood.

DEFINITE ARTICLE ('THE')

	m sg	f sg	n sg	pl
nom	der dair	die dee	das das	die dee
acc	den dayn	die dee	das das	die dee
dat	dem daym	der dair	dem daym	den dayn
gen	des des	der dair	des des	der dair

~ INDEFINITE ARTICLE ('A/AN') ~

	m sg	f sg	n sg	pl
nom	ein ain	eine *ai*·ne	ein ain	keine * *kai*·ne
acc	einen *ai*·nen	eine *ai*·ne	ein ain	keine *kai*·ne
dat	einem *ai*·nem	einer *ai*·ner	einem *ai*·nem	keinen *kai*·nen
gen	eines *ai*·nes	einer *ai*·ner	eines *ai*·nes	keiner *kai*·ner

**kein* kain is the negative indefinite article meaning 'no'

BE

Describing People/Things • Making Statements

Just like in English, the verb *sein* zain (be) has different forms depending on the subject of the sentence. For information on negative forms, see **negatives** (p20).

~ SEIN (BE) – PRESENT TENSE ~

I	**am**	ich	bin	ikh	bin
you sg inf	**are**	du	bist	doo	bist
you sg pol	**are**	Sie	sind	zee	zind
he/she/it	**is**	er/sie/es	ist	air/zee/es	ist
we	**are**	wir	sind	veer	zind
you pl inf	**are**	ihr	seid	eer	zait
you pl pol	**are**	Sie	sind	zee	zind
they	**are**	sie	sind	zee	zind

CASE

Doing Things • Giving Instructions • Indicating Location • Naming People/Things • Possessing

German has a system of four cases (shown through word endings) which are used to indicate the 'role' of certain words in a sentence and their relationship to other words (ie whether it's the subject, direct or indirect object). Pronouns, adjectives and articles all take different endings for case, while nouns take case endings only in a few instances – a noun's case is generally indicated by the article or adjective accompanying it (see **adjectives & adverbs**, p14, and **articles**, p15).

The word lists, **menu decoder** (p187) and **dictionaries** (p197) in this book provide words in the nominative case – you can just use this case, even if another case would be grammatically correct in a sentence, and you'll still be understood. The main functions of the four cases in German are explained below. See also **prepositions** (p23).

– CASE –

NOMINATIVE nom – shows the subject of a sentence

The tour guide is handsome.	Der Reiseführer ist schön. (lit: the-nom tour-guide-nom is handsome) dair *rai*·ze·fü·rer ist shern

ACCUSATIVE acc – shows the direct object of a sentence

I love the tour guide.	Ich liebe den Reiseführer. (lit: I love the-acc tour-guide-acc) ikh *lee*·be dayn *rai*·ze·fü·rer

DATIVE dat – shows the indirect object of a sentence

I gave my ticket to the tour guide.	Ich habe dem Reiseführer meine Fahrkarte gegeben. (lit: I have the-dat tour-guide-dat my-acc ticket-acc given) ikh *hah*·be daym *rai*·ze·fü·rer *mai*·ne *fahr*·kar·te ge·*gay*·ben

GENITIVE gen – shows possession

What's the tour guide's name?	Wie ist der Name des Reiseführers? (lit: how is the-nom name-nom the-gen tour-guide-gen) vee ist dair *nah*·me des *rai*·ze·fü·rers

DEMONSTRATIVES

Giving Instructions • Indicating Location • Pointing Things Out

The easiest way to point something out in German is to use *das ist* das ist (this/that is) and *das sind* das zint (these/those are).

That's my bag; those are her suitcases.	Das ist meine Tasche; das sind ihre Koffer. (lit: that is my-nom-f-sg bag; those are her-nom-m-pl suitcases) das ist *mai*·ne *ta*·she; das zint *ee*·re *ko*·fer

The demonstrative *dieser dee*·zer (this) changes to match the noun's gender, number and case (see **case**, p16, **gender** and **plurals**, p21). The table below shows all the forms – they follow the same pattern as the definite article (see **articles**, p15).

- DEMONSTRATIVES -

	m sg	f sg	n sg	pl
nom	dieser *dee*·zer	diese *dee*·ze	dieses *dee*·zes	diese *dee*·ze
acc	diesen *dee*·zen	diese *dee*·ze	dieses *dee*·zes	diese *dee*·ze
dat	diesem *dee*·zem	dieser *dee*·zer	diesem *dee*·zem	diesen *dee*·zen
gen	dieses *dee*·zes	dieser *dee*·zer	dieses *dee*·zes	dieser *dee*·zer

GENDER

Naming People/Things

In German, all nouns (words which denote a thing, person or idea) have masculine, feminine or neuter gender. You can recognise the noun's gender by the article, demonstrative, possessive or any other adjective accompanying the noun, as they change form to agree with the noun's gender (see **adjectives & adverbs**, p14, **articles**, p15, **demonstratives**, **possessives**, p22). The gender of words is also indicated in the dictionary, but here are some general rules:

- nouns ending in *-er, -ig* or *-ing* are generally masculine
- nouns ending in *-in, -heit* or *-keit* are generally feminine
- nouns which refer to young people and animals are neuter

The gender of words is indicated with m (masculine), f (feminine) and n (neuter) throughout this phrasebook where relevant. See also the box **M Before F** (p131).

HAVE

Possessing

Possession can be indicated in various ways in German (see also **possessives**, p22). One way is with the verb *haben* *hah*·ben (have), which is shown below. For negative forms, see **negatives** (p20).

~ HABEN (HAVE) – PRESENT TENSE ~

I	**have**	ich	habe	ikh	*hah*·be
you sg inf	**have**	du	hast	doo	hast
you sg pol	**have**	Sie	haben	zee	*hah*·ben
he/she/it	**has**	er/sie/es	hat	air/zee/es	hat
we	**have**	wir	haben	veer	*hah*·ben
you pl inf	**have**	ihr	habt	eer	hapt
you pl pol	**have**	Sie	haben	zee	*hah*·ben
they	**have**	sie	haben	zee	*hah*·ben

NEGATIVES

Negating

To make a negative statement in German, just add the word *nicht* nikht (not) after the verb, or after the object if included.

I don't smoke.	Ich rauche nicht. (lit: I smoke not) ikh *row*·khe nikht
I don't love you.	Ich liebe dich nicht. (lit: I love you-acc-sg-inf not) ikh *lee*·be dikh nikht

In sentences with the indefinite article *ein* ain (a/an) or no article, the negative article *kein* kain is used instead of *nicht*.

I see a taxi.	Ich sehe ein Taxi. (lit: I see a-acc-n-sg taxi) ikh *zay*·e ain *tak*·si
I don't see a taxi.	Ich sehe kein Taxi. (lit: I see no-acc-n-sg taxi) ikh *zay*·e kain *tak*·si

PERSONAL PRONOUNS

Making Statements • Naming People/Things

Personal pronouns ('I', 'you' etc) change their form in German for person, number and case (see **case**). It's similar in English, which has 'I' and 'me' as the subject and object pronouns.

There are two forms of the second-person singular pronoun (ie 'you') in German. Use the polite form *Sie* zee when talking to anyone you don't know well, and the informal forms *du* du (singular) and *ihr* eer (plural) only with people you know well or who are younger than you. Phrases in this book use the form of 'you' that is appropriate to the situation. Where both forms are used, they are indicated by pol and inf.

- PERSONAL PRONOUNS -

	nom		acc		dat		gen	
I	ich	ikh	mich	mikh	mir	meer	meiner	*mei*·ner
you sg inf	du	du	dich	dikh	dir	deer	deiner	*dai*·ner
you sg pol	Sie	zee	Sie	zee	Ihnen	ee·nen	Ihrer	ee·rer
he	er	air	ihn	een	ihm	eem	seiner	*zai*·ner
she	sie	zee	sie	zee	ihr	eer	ihrer	ee·rer
it	es	es	es	es	ihm	eem	seiner	*zai*·ner
we	wir	veer	uns	uns	uns	uns	unser	*un*·zer
you pl inf	ihr	eer	euch	oykh	euch	oykh	euer	o·yer
you pl pol	Sie	zee	Sie	zee	Ihnen	ee·nen	Ihrer	ee·rer
they	sie	zee	sie	zee	ihnen	ee·nen	ihrer	ee·rer

PLURALS

Naming People/Things

The most common ways of forming plurals in German:

- no plural endings and often an umlaut added over the vowel, mostly for masculine nouns ending in a consonant: *Spiegel* *shpee*·gel (mirror), *Spiegel* *shpee*·gel (mirrors); *Boden* *baw*·den (soil), *Böden* *ber*·den (soils)
- adding -e and often an umlaut over the vowel for nouns ending in a consonant, mostly single-syllable masculine nouns: *Tag* tahk (day), *Tage* *tah*·ge (days); *Zug* tsook (train), *Züge* *tsoo*·ge (trains)
- adding *-er* and often an umlaut over the vowel, mostly for single-syllable neuter nouns: *Bild* bilt (picture), *Bilder* *bil*·der (pictures); *Blatt* blat (leaf), *Blätter* *ble*·ter (leaves)

- adding *-s* to all nouns ending in a vowel, except those ending in *-e*, and to English loanwords: *Auto* ow·to (car), *Autos* ow·tos (cars); *Park* park (park), *Parks* parks (parks)
- adding *-n* to nouns ending in *-e*, and adding *-en* to almost all feminine nouns: *Junge* yung·e (boy), *Jungen* yung·en (boys); *Frau* frow (woman), *Frauen* frow·en (women)

POSSESSIVES

Possessing

A common way of indicating possession is by using possessive adjectives before the noun they refer to. Like other adjectives, they agree with the noun in gender, number and case (see also **case**, p16, **gender**, p18, and **plurals**, p21). The table below shows only the nominative case, singular forms; for other cases and for plural see **demonstratives** (p18), as they follow the same pattern.

- POSSESSIVE ADJECTIVES -

	m sg		f sg		n sg	
my	mein	main	meine	*mai*·ne	mein	main
your sg inf	dein	dain	deine	*dai*·ne	dein	dain
your sg pl	Ihr	eer	Ihre	ee·re	Ihr	eer
his	sein	zain	seine	*zai*·ne	sein	zain
her	ihr	eer	ihre	ee·re	ihr	eer
its	sein	zain	seine	*zai*·ne	sein	zain
our	unser	*un*·zer	unsere	*un*·ze·re	unser	*un*·zer
your pl inf	euer	o·yer	eure	oy·re	euer	o·yer
your pl pol	Ihr	eer	Ihre	ee·re	Ihr	eer
their	ihr	eer	ihre	ee·re	ihr	eer

PREPOSITIONS

Giving Instructions • Indicating Location • Pointing Things Out

Like English, German uses prepositions to explain where things are in time or space. All prepositions in German require the noun to be in a certain case (see **case**, p16), most frequently the dative.

- PREPOSITIONS -

after	nach	nakh	**from**	von	fon
at (time)	um	um	**in (place)**	in	in
before	vor	fawr	**to**	zu	tsoo

QUESTIONS

Asking Questions • Negating

The easiest way of forming 'yes/no' questions is to add *nicht wahr* nikht var (literally 'not true') to the end of a statement, similar to 'isn't it?' in English. You can also turn a statement into a question by putting the verb before the subject of the sentence.

The hotel is nearby, isn't it?	Das Hotel ist nahe, nicht wahr? (lit: the-nom-n-sg hotel is near not true) das ho·*tel* ist *nah*·e nikht var
Is the hotel nearby?	Ist das Hotel nahe? (lit: is the-nom-n-sg hotel near) ist das ho·*tel* *nah*·e

As in English, there are question words (see the table on p24) for more specific questions. They go at the start of the sentence, followed by the verb.

- QUESTION WORDS -

how	wie	vee	**where**	wo	vaw
what	was	vas	**who**	wer	vair
when	wann	van	**why**	warum	va·*rum*

VERBS

Doing Things

Most German verbs are regular, with the infinitive ending in -*(e)n*. Tenses are formed by adding various endings for each person to the verb stem (the dictionary form without the -*(e)n*). See also **be** (p16), **have** (p19) and **negatives** (p20).

- PRESENT TENSE – SAGEN (SAY) -

I	**say**	ich	sage	ikh	*zah*·ge
you sg inf	**say**	du	sagst	doo	zahkst
you sg pol	**say**	Sie	sagen	zee	*zah*·gen
he/she/it	**says**	er/sie/es	sagt	air/zee/es	zahkt
we	**say**	wir	sagen	veer	*zah*·gen
you pl inf	**say**	ihr	sagt	eer	zahkt
you pl pol	**say**	Sie	sagen	zee	*zah*·gen
they	**say**	sie	sagen	zee	*zah*·gen

- PAST TENSE – SAGEN (SAY) -

I	**said**	ich	sagte	ikh	*zahk*·te
you sg inf	**said**	du	sagtest	doo	*zahk*·test
you sg pol	**said**	Sie	sagten	zee	*zahk*·ten
he/she/it	**said**	er/sie/es	sagte	air/zee/es	*zahk*·te
we	**said**	wir	sagten	veer	*zahk*·ten
you pl inf	**said**	ihr	sagtet	eer	*zahk*·tet
you pl pol	**said**	Sie	sagten	zee	*zahk*·ten
they	**said**	sie	sagten	zee	*zahk*·ten

For the future tense, use the construction '*werden* + infinitive' (like 'going to ...' in English). The verb *werden* *vair*·den (lit: 'become') changes form for each person as shown in the table below.

I'm going to travel to Berlin.	Ich werde nach Berlin fahren. (lit: I am-going-to to Berlin travel) ikh *vair*·de nakh ber·*leen* *fah*·ren

FUTURE TENSE

I	**am going to**	ich	werde	ikh	*vair*·de
you sg inf	**are going to**	du	wirst	doo	virst
you sg pol	**are going to**	Sie	werden	zee	*vair*·den
he/she/it	**is going to**	er/sie/es	wird	air/zee/es	virt
we	**are going to**	wir	werden	veer	*vair*·den
you pl inf	**are going to**	ihr	werdet	eer	*vair*·det
you pl pol	**are going to**	Sie	werden	zee	*vair*·den
they	**are going to**	sie	werden	zee	*vair*·den

WORD ORDER

Making Statements

In a straightforward German statement, the verb is the second element, usually following the subject of the sentence. So, if the sentence starts with an adverb such as 'tomorrow', the order of the subject and the verb is reversed to keep the verb as the second element. See also **negatives** (p20) and **questions** (p23).

I'm going to Berlin.	Ich gehe nach Berlin. (lit: I go to Berlin) ikh *gay*·e nakh ber·*leen*
Tomorrow I'm going to Berlin.	Morgen gehe ich nach Berlin. (lit: tomorrow go I to Berlin) *mawr*·gen *gay*·e ikh nakh ber·*leen*

– GRAMMAR GLOSSARY –

adjective	a word that describes something – 'German beer is up there with the world's **best**'
adverb	a word that explains how an action is done – 'it **supposedly** doesn't give you a hangover'
article	the words 'a', 'an' and 'the'
case (marking)	word ending which tells us the role of a thing or person in the sentence
demonstrative	a word that means 'this' or 'that'
direct object	the thing or person in the sentence that has the action directed to it – 'most visitors just drink **it**'
gender	classification of *nouns* into classes (like masculine, feminine and neuter), requiring other words (eg *adjectives*) to belong to the same class
indirect object	the person or thing in the sentence that is the recipient of the action – 'others go to **breweries**'
infinitive	dictionary form of a *verb* – '**to learn** about beer'
noun	a thing, person or idea – 'and its **production**'
number	whether a word is singular or plural – '**breweries** use four **ingredients**: **malt**, **yeast**, **hops**, **water**'
personal pronoun	a word that means 'I', 'you' etc
possessive adjective	a word that means 'my', 'your' etc
possessive pronoun	a word that means 'mine', 'yours' etc
preposition	a word like 'for' or 'before' in English
subject	the thing or person in the sentence that does the action – '**monasteries** still produce beer too'
tense	form of a *verb* that tells you whether the action is in the present, past or future – eg 'drink' (present), 'drank' (past), 'will drink' (future)
verb	a word that tells you what action happened – 'many people **visit** them on brewery tours'
verb stem	part of a *verb* that doesn't change – eg '**taste**' in '**tast**ing' and '**tast**ed'

BASICS

UNDERSTANDING 28

NUMBERS & AMOUNTS 30

TIME & DATES 32

Understanding

KEY PHRASES

Do you speak English?	Sprechen Sie Englisch? pol Sprichst du Englisch? inf	*shpre*·khen zee *eng*·lish shprikhst doo *eng*·lish
I don't understand.	Ich verstehe nicht.	ikh fer·*shtay*·e nikht
What does ... mean?	Was bedeutet ...?	vas be·*doy*·tet...

Q **Do you speak English?**	Sprechen Sie Englisch? pol *shpre*·khen zee *eng*·lish Sprichst du Englisch? inf shprikhst doo *eng*·lish
Q **Does anyone speak English?**	Spricht hier jemand Englisch? shprikht heer *yay*·mant *eng*·lish
A **I speak a little (German).**	Ich spreche ein bisschen (Deutsch). ikh *shpre*·khe ain *bis*·khen (doytsh)
Q **Do you understand (me)?**	Verstehen Sie (mich)? fer·*shtay*·en zee (mikh)
A **I (don't) understand.**	Ich verstehe (nicht). ikh fer·*shtay*·e (nikht)
I'd like to practise German.	Ich möchte Deutsch üben. ikh *merkh*·te (doytsh) *ü*·ben

☑ LANGUAGE TIP: BEING POLITE

There are two forms of the second-person singular pronoun 'you'. Use the polite *Sie* zee with anyone you don't know well, and only use the informal *du* doo with people you know very well. All the phrases in this chapter use *Sie* unless indicated.

What does 'Kugel' mean?	Was bedeutet 'Kugel'? vas be·*doy*·tet *koo*·gel
How do you pronounce this?	Wie spricht man dieses Wort aus? vee shprikht man *dee*·zes vort ows
How do you say 'ticket' in German?	Wie sagt man 'ticket' auf Deutsch? vee zagt man *ti*·ket owf doytsh
How do you write 'Schweiz'?	Wie schreibt man 'Schweiz'? vee shraipt man shvaits
Could you please repeat that?	Könnten Sie das bitte wiederholen? *kern*·ten zee das *bi*·te vee·der·*haw*·len
Could you please write it down?	Könnten Sie das bitte aufschreiben? *kern*·ten zee das *bi*·te *owf*·shrai·ben
Could you please speak more slowly?	Könnten Sie bitte langsamer sprechen? *kern*·ten zee *bi*·te *lang*·za·mer *shpre*·khen

✂ **Slowly, please!** Langsamer, bitte! *lang*·za·mer *bi*·te

Numbers & Amounts

KEY PHRASES

How much?	Wieviel?	vee·*feel*
How many?	Wie viele?	vee *fee*·le

CARDINAL NUMBERS

0	null	nul
1	eins	ains
2	zwei	tsvai
3	drei	drai
4	vier	feer
5	fünf	fünf
6	sechs	zeks
7	sieben	*zee*·ben
8	acht	akht
9	neun	noyn
10	zehn	tsayn
11	elf	elf
12	zwölf	zverlf
13	dreizehn	*drai*·tsayn
14	vierzehn	*feer*·tsayn
15	fünfzehn	*fünf*·tsayn
16	sechzehn	*zeks*·tsayn
17	siebzehn	*zeep*·tsayn
18	achtzehn	*akht*·tsayn
19	neunzehn	*noyn*·tsayn
20	zwanzig	*tsvan*·tsikh

21	einundzwanzig	*ain*·unt·tsvan·tsikh
22	zweiundzwanzig	*tsvai*·unt·tsvan·tsikh
30	dreißig	*drai*·tsikh
40	vierzig	*feer*·tsikh
50	fünfzig	*fünf*·tsikh
60	sechzig	*zekh*·tsikh
70	siebzig	*zeep*·tsikh
80	achtzig	*akht*·tsikh
90	neunzig	*noyn*·tsikh
100	hundert	*hun*·dert
1000	tausend	*tow*·sent
1,000,000	eine Million	*ai*·ne mil·*yawn*

ORDINAL NUMBERS

1st	erste	*ers*·te
2nd	zweite	*tsvai*·te
3rd	dritte	*dri*·te

AMOUNTS

How much?	Wieviel?	vee·*feel*
How many?	Wie viele?	vee *fee*·le
a quarter	ein Viertel	ain *fir*·tel
a third	ein Drittel	ain *dri*·tel
a half	eine Hälfte	ai·*ne helf*·te
all/none	alles/nichts	*a*·les/nikhts
less/more	weniger/mehr	*vay*·ni·ger/mair
(just) a little	(nur) ein bisschen	(noor) ain *bis*·khen
much/a lot	viel	feel
some/many	einige/viele	*ai*·ni·ge/*fee*·le

For other useful amounts, see **self-catering** (p181).

Time & Dates

KEY PHRASES

What time is it?	Wie spät ist es?	vee shpayt ist es
At what time?	Um wie viel Uhr?	um vee feel oor
What date?	Welches Datum?	*vel*·khes *dah*·tum

TELLING THE TIME

Many German-speaking countries use 24-hour time, particularly in written language. To denote the time between noon and midnight, you can also use *nachmittags* *nahkh*·mi·tahks for times between noon and 6pm, and *abends* *ah*·bents for times from 6pm to midnight.

Q **What time is it?**	Wie spät ist es? vee shpayt ist es
A **It's (10) o'clock.**	Es ist (zehn) Uhr. es ist (tsayn) oor
A **It's 2.12pm.**	Es ist 14:12. es ist *feer*·tsayn oor tsverlf
Q **At what time?**	Um wie viel Uhr? um vee feel oor
A **At ...**	Um ... um ...
Quarter past (one).	Viertel nach (eins). *fir*·tel nahkh (ains)
Twenty past (one).	Zwanzig nach (eins). *tsvan*·tsikh nahkh (ains)

Half past one.	Halb zwei. (lit: half two) halp tsvai
Twenty to (one).	Zwanzig vor (eins). *tsvan*·tsikh fawr (ains)
Quarter to (one).	Viertel vor (eins). *fir*·tel fawr (ains)
6am	sechs Uhr vormittags zeks oor *fawr*·mi·tahks
6pm	sechs Uhr nachmittags/ abends zeks oor *nahkh*·mi·tahks/ *ah*·bents

THE CALENDAR

Monday	Montag m	*mawn*·tahk
Tuesday	Dienstag m	*deens*·tahk
Wednesday	Mittwoch m	*mit*·vokh
Thursday	Donnerstag m	*do*·ners·tahk
Friday	Freitag m	*frai*·tahk
Saturday	Samstag m	*zams*·tahk
Sunday	Sonntag m	*zon*·tahk

January	Januar m	*yan*·u·ahr
February	Februar m	*fay*·bru·ahr
March	März m	merts
April	April m	a·*pril*
May	Mai m	mai
June	Juni m	*yoo*·ni
July	Juli m	*yoo*·li
August	August m	ow·*gust*

September	September m	zep·*tem*·ber
October	Oktober m	ok·*taw*·ber
November	November m	no·*vem*·ber
December	Dezember m	de·*tsem*·ber
summer	Sommer m	*zo*·mer
autumn/fall	Herbst m	herpst
winter	Winter m	*vin*·ter
spring	Frühling m	*frü*·ling

What date?	Welches Datum? *vel*·khes *dah*·tum
Q **What date is it today?**	Der Wievielte ist heute? dair *vee*·feel·te ist *hoy*·te
A **It's (18 October) today.**	Heute ist (der 18 Oktober). *hoy*·te ist (dair *akh*·tsayn·te ok·*taw*·ber)

PRESENT

now	jetzt	yetst
right now	jetzt gerade	yetst ge·*rah*·de
today	heute	*hoy*·te
tonight	heute Abend	*hoy*·te *ah*·bent
this afternoon	heute Nachmittag	*hoy*·te *nahkh*·mi·tahk
this morning	heute Morgen	*hoy*·te *mor*·gen
this week	diese Woche	*dee*·ze *vo*·khe
this month	diesen Monat	*dee*·zen *maw*·nat
this year	dieses Jahr	*dee*·zes yahr

PAST

day before yesterday	vorgestern	*fawr*·ges·tern
last night	vergangene Nacht	fer·*gang*·e·ne nakht
last week	letzte Woche	*lets*·te *vo*·khe
last month	letzten Monat	*lets*·ten *maw*·nat
last year	letztes Jahr	*lets*·tes yahr
since (May)	seit (Mai)	zait (mai)
a while ago	vor einer Weile	fawr *ai*·ner *vai*·le
(half an) hour ago	vor einer (halben) Stunde	fawr *ai*·ner (*hal*·ben) *shtun*·de
(three) days ago	vor (drei) Tagen	fawr (drai) *tah*·gen
(five) years ago	vor (fünf) Jahren	fawr (fünf) *yah*·ren
yesterday	gestern	*ges*·tern
yesterday afternoon	gestern Nachmittag	*ges*·tern *nahkh*·mi·tahk
yesterday evening	gestern Abend	*ges*·tern *ah*·bent
yesterday morning	gestern Morgen	*ges*·tern *mor*·gen

FUTURE

day after tomorrow	übermorgen	*ü*·ber·mor·gen
in (six) days	in (sechs) Tagen	in (zeks) *tah*·gen
in (five) minutes	in (fünf) Minuten	in (fünf) mi·*noo*·ten
next month	nächsten Monat	*naykhs*·ten *maw*·nat

next week	nächste Woche	*naykhs*·te *vo*·khe
next year	nächstes Jahr	*naykhs*·tes yahr
tomorrow	morgen	*mor*·gen
tomorrow afternoon	morgen Nachmittag	*mor*·gen *nahkh*·mi·tahk
tomorrow evening	morgen Abend	*mor*·gen *ah*·bent
tomorrow morning	morgen früh	*mor*·gen frü
until (June)	bis (Juni)	bis (*yoo*·ni)
within a month	in einem Monat	in *ai*·nem *maw*·nat
within an hour	in einer Stunde	in *ai*·ner *shtun*·de

DURING THE DAY

It's early.	Es ist früh.	es ist frü
It's late.	Es ist spät.	es ist shpayt

afternoon	Nachmittag m	*nahkh*·mi·tahk
dawn	Dämmerung f	*de*·me·rung
day	Tag m	tahk
evening	Abend m	*ah*·bent
midday	Mittag m	*mi*·tahk
midnight	Mitternacht f	*mi*·ter·nakht
morning	Morgen m	*mor*·gen
night	Nacht f	nakht
noon	Mittag m	*mi*·tahk
sunrise	Sonnenaufgang m	*zo*·nen·owf·gang
sunset	Sonnen-untergang m	*zo*·nen·un·ter·gang

PRACTICAL

TRANSPORT	38
BORDER CROSSING	51
DIRECTIONS	53
ACCOMMODATION	56
SHOPPING	69
COMMUNICATIONS	79
MONEY & BANKING	86
BUSINESS	90
SIGHTSEEING	92
SENIORS & TRAVELLERS WITH DISABILITIES	97
TRAVEL WITH CHILDREN	99

Transport

KEY PHRASES

What time's the next bus?	Wann fährt der nächste Bus?	van fairt dair *naykhs*·te bus
A ticket to (Berlin).	Eine Fahrkarte nach (Berlin).	*ai*·ne *fahr*·kar·te nahkh (ber·*leen*)
Can you tell me when we get to (Kiel)?	Könnten Sie mir bitte sagen, wann wir in (Kiel) ankommen?	*kern*·ten zee meer *bi*·te *zah*·gen van veer in (keel) *an*·ko·men
Please take me to (this address).	Bitte bringen Sie mich zu (dieser Adresse).	*bi*·te *bring*·en zee mikh tsoo (*dee*·zer a·*dre*·se)

GETTING AROUND

What time does the plane leave?	Um wieviel Uhr geht der Flug? um vee·*feel* oor gayt dair flook
What time does the bus/train leave?	Wann fährt der Bus/Zug ab? van fairt dair bus/tsook ap
What time does it arrive?	Wann kommt es an? van komt es an
What time's the first bus?	Wann fährt der erste Bus? van fairt dair *ers*·te bus
What time's the last bus?	Wann fährt der letzte Bus? van fairt dair *lets*·te bus

LISTEN FOR

Es ist ausgebucht.	es ist *ows*·ge·bookht It's full.
... ist gestrichen.	... ist ge·*shtri*·khen ... is cancelled.
... hat Verspätung.	... hat fer·*shpay*·tung ... is delayed.
Dieser Halt ist ...	*dee*·zer halt ist ... This stop is ...
Der nächste Halt ist ...	dair *nairkh*·ste halt ist ... The next stop is ...

What time's the next bus?	Wann fährt der nächste Bus? van fairt dair *naykhs*·te bus
How long will it be delayed?	Wie lange hat es Verspätung? vee *lang*·e hat es fer·*shpay*·tung
Is this seat free?	Ist dieser Platz frei? ist *dee*·zer plats frai

Is it free? | Ist hier frei? | ist heer frai

That's my seat.	Dieses ist mein Platz. *dee*·zes ist main plats
Can you tell me when we get to (Kiel)?	Könnten Sie mir bitte sagen, wann wir in (Kiel) ankommen? *kern*·ten zee meer *bi*·te *zah*·gen van veer in (keel) *an*·ko·men
I want to get off here.	Ich möchte hier aussteigen. ikh *merkh*·te heer *ows*·shtai·gen

Can we take public transport?	Können wir öffentlichen Verkehrsmitteln nehmen? *ker*·nen veer *er*·fent·li·khen fair·*kairs*·mi·teln nay·men
I'd prefer to walk there.	Ich gehe lieber zu Fuß dahin. ikh *gay*·e *lee*·ber tsoo foos dah·*hin*

BUYING TICKETS

Where can I buy a ticket?	Wo kann ich eine Fahrkarte kaufen? vaw kan ikh *ai*·ne *fahr*·kar·te *kow*·fen
Do I need to book?	Muss ich einen Platz reservieren lassen? mus ikh *ai*·nen plats re·zer·*vee*·ren *la*·sen
A ... ticket to (Berlin).	Eine ... nach (Berlin). *ai*·ne ... nahkh (ber·*leen*)

1st-class	Fahrkarte erster Klasse	*fahr*·kar·te *ers*·ter *kla*·se
2nd-class	Fahrkarte zweiter Klasse	*fahr*·kar·te *tsvai*·ter *kla*·se
child's	Kinderfahrkarte	*kin*·der·fahr·kar·te
one-way	einfache Fahrkarte	*ain*·fa·khe *fahr*·kar·te
return	Rückfahrkarte	*rük*·fahr·kar·te
student's	Studentenfahrkarte	shtu·*den*·ten·fahr·kar·te

Buying a Ticket

WHAT TIME IS THE NEXT ...?
Wann fährt der/das nächste ... ab? m/n
van fairt dair/das *naykhs*·te ... ap

BOAT
Boot n
bawt

BUS
Bus m
bus

TRAIN
Zug m
tsook

ONE ... TICKET, PLEASE.
Eine .... bitte.
ai·ne ... bi·te

ONE-WAY
einfache Fahrkarte
ain·fa·khe *fahr*·kar·te

RETURN
Rückfahrkarte
rük·fahr·kar·te

I'D LIKE A/AN ... SEAT.
Ich hätte gern einen ...
ikh *he*·te gern *ai*·nen ...

AISLE
Platz am Gang
plats am gang

WINDOW
Fensterplatz
fens·ter·plats

WHICH PLATFORM DOES IT DEPART FROM?
Auf welchem Bahnsteig fährt es ab?
owf *vel*·khem *bahn*·shtaik fairt es ap

Two (return tickets), please.	Zwei (Rückfahrkarten) bitte. tsvai (*rük*·fahr·kar·ten) *bi*·te
I'd like an aisle seat.	Ich hätte gern einen Platz am Gang. ikh *he*·te gern *ai*·nen plats am gang
I'd like a window seat.	Ich hätte gern einen Fensterplatz. ikh *he*·te gern *ai*·nen *fens*·ter·plats
How long does the trip take?	Wie lange dauert die Fahrt? vee *lang*·e *dow*·ert dee fahrt
Is it a direct route?	Ist es eine direkte Verbindung? ist es *ai*·ne di·*rek*·te fer·*bin*·dung
Can I get a stand-by ticket?	Kann ich ein Standby-Ticket bekommen? kan ikh ain stend·*bai*·ti·ket be·*ko*·men
day ticket	Tageskarte f *tah*·ges·kar·te
weekly ticket	Wochenkarte f *vo*·khen·kar·te
ticket for multiple trips	Mehrfachfahrkarte f *mair*·fakh·fahr·kar·te
I'd like to ... my ticket, please.	Ich möchte meine Fahrkarte bitte ... ikh *merkh*·te *mai*·ne *fahr*·kar·te *bi*·te ...

cancel	zurückgeben	tsu·*rük*·gay·ben
change	ändern lassen	*en*·dern *la*·sen
collect	abholen	ab·*ho*·len
confirm	bestätigen lassen	be·*shtay*·ti·gen *la*·sen

LANGUAGE TIP: TICKET TYPES

German distinguishes between different types of journeys, depending on the transport used: *Fahrt* fahrt for a journey by road or rail; *Flug* flook for a journey by plane. This is reflected in the names of the tickets used: *Fahrkarte* *fahr*·kar·te for a train/bus/underground ticket; *Flugticket* *flook*·ti·ket for a plane ticket. This chapter uses *Fahrkarte*, so make sure you use the right word when buying tickets.

LUGGAGE

My luggage has been damaged.	Mein Gepäck ist beschädigt. main ge·*pek* ist be·shay·dikht
My luggage has been stolen.	Mein Gepäck ist gestohlen worden. main ge·*pek* ist ge·*shtaw*·len *vor*·den
My luggage hasn't arrived.	Mein Gepäck ist nicht angekommen. main ge·*pek* ist nikht *an*·ge·ko·men
I'd like a luggage locker.	Ich hätte gern ein Gepäckschließfach. ikh *he*·te gern ain ge·*pek*·shlees·fakh

BUS

Which bus goes to (Cologne)?	Welcher Bus fährt nach (Köln)? *vel*·kher bus fairt nakh (kerln)
Which bus goes to (the station)?	Welcher Bus fährt (zum Bahnhof)? *vel*·kher bus fairt (tsum *bahn*·hawf)

☑ LANGUAGE TIP: TALKING ABOUT DESTINATIONS

German uses two different words for the English word 'to'. With place names, use *nach* nakh, eg 'to Salzburg' is *nach Salzburg* nakh *zalts*·boorg. For all other destinations, use *zum/zur/zum* tsum/tsur/tsum with masculine/feminine/neuter nouns. For example, 'to the station' is *zum Bahnhof* m tsum *bahn*·hawf; 'to the youth hostel' is *zur Jugendherberge* f tsur *yoo*·gent·her·ber·ge; and 'to the city centre' is *zum Stadtzentrum* n *tsum shtat*·tsen·trum.

Bus number ...	Bus Nummer ... bus *nu*·mer ...
Where's the bus stop?	Wo ist die Bushaltestelle? vo ist dee *bus*·hal·te·shte·le
What's the next stop?	Welches ist der nächste Halt? *vel*·khes ist dair *naykh*·ste halt
I'd like to get off (at Alexanderplatz).	Ich möchte (am Alexanderplatz) aussteigen. ikh *merkh*·te (am a·lek·*san*·der·plats) *ows*·shtai·gen

For bus numbers, see **numbers & amounts** (p30).

TRAIN

What station is this?	Welcher Bahnhof ist das? *vel*·kher *bahn*·hawf ist das
What's the next station?	Welches ist der nächste Bahnhof? *vel*·khes ist dair *naykhs*·te *bahn*·hawf

Where's the nearest metro station?	Wo ist der nächste U-Bahnhof? vaw ist dair *naykhs*·te *oo*·bahn·hawf
Which line goes to (Potsdamer Platz)?	Welche Linie geht zum (Potsdamer Platz)? *vel*·khe *lee*·ni·e gayt tsum (pots·*dah*·mer plats)
Does this train stop at (Freiburg)?	Hält dieser Zug in (Freiburg)? helt *dee*·zer tsook in (*frai*·boorg)
Do I need to change trains?	Muss ich umsteigen? mus ikh *um*·shtai·gen
Which carriage is 1st class?	Welcher Wagen ist erste Klasse? *vel*·kher *vah*·gen ist *ers*·te *kla*·se

Wo is der nächste U-Bahnhof?

vaw ist dair *naykhs*·te oo·bahn·hawf

Where's the nearest metro station?

Which carriage is for Munich?	Welcher Wagen geht nach München? *vel*·kher *vah*·gen gayt nahkh *mün*·khen
underground	U-Bahn f *oo*·bahn
underground station	U-Bahnhof m *oo*·bahn·hawf
urban railway	S-Bahn f *es*·bahn

BOAT

Are there life jackets?	Gibt es Schwimmwesten? gipt es *shvim*·ves·ten
What's the sea like today?	Wie ist das Meer heute? vee ist das mair *hoy*·te
I feel seasick.	Ich bin seekrank. ikh bin *zay*·krangk

TAXI

I'd like a taxi at (9am).	Ich hätte gern ein Taxi für (neun Uhr). ikh *he*·te gern ain *tak*·si für (noyn oor)
Where's the taxi stand?	Wo ist der Taxenstand? vaw ist dair *tak*·sen·shtant
Are you available?	Sind Sie frei? zint zee frai
How much is it to ...?	Was kostet es bis ...? vas *kos*·tet es bis ...

Please take me to (this address).	Bitte bringen Sie mich zu (dieser Adresse). *bi*·te *bring*·en zee mikh tsoo (*dee*·zer a·*dre*·se)
To ...	Zu ... *tsoo ...*
Please slow down.	Fahren Sie bitte langsamer. *fah*·ren zee *bi*·te *lang*·za·mer
Please wait here.	Bitte warten Sie hier. *bi*·te *var*·ten zee heer
Stop at the corner.	Halten Sie an der Ecke. *hal*·ten zee an dair *e*·ke
Stop here.	Halten Sie hier. *hal*·ten zee heer

For more phrases, see **directions** (p53) and **money & banking** (p86).

CAR & MOTORBIKE

I'd like to hire a/an ...	Ich möchte ein ... mieten. ikh *merkh*·te ain ... *mee*·ten

4WD	Allradfahrzeug	*al*·raht·fahr·tsoyk
automatic	Fahrzeug mit Automatik	*fahr*·tsoyk mit ow·to·*mah*·tik
car	Auto	*ow*·to
manual	Fahrzeug mit Schaltung	*fahr*·tsoyk mit *shal*·tung
motorbike	Motorrad	*maw*·tor·raht

How much is it per day/week?	Wie viel kostet es pro Tag/Woche? vee feel *kos*·tet es praw tahk/*vo*·khe

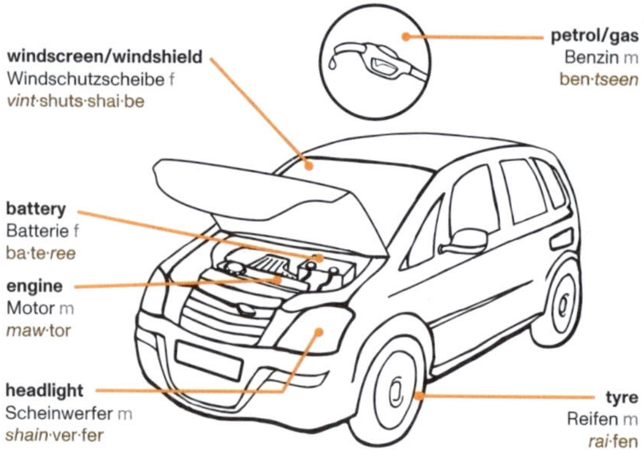

Does that include insurance/mileage?	Ist eine Versicherung/ Kilometerzahl inbegriffen? ist *ai*·ne fer·*zi*·khe·rung/ kee·lo·*may*·ter·tsahl *in*·be·gri·fen
Does this road go to ...?	Führt diese Straße nach ...? fürt *dee*·ze *shtrah*·se nahkh ...
What's the speed limit?	Was ist die Höchstgeschwindigkeit? vas ist dee *herkhst*·ge·shvin·dikh·kait
(How long) Can I park here?	(Wie lange) Kann ich hier parken? (vee *lang*·e) kan ikh heer *par*·ken
Where do I pay?	Wo muss ich bezahlen? vaw mus ikh be·*tsah*·len

LOOK FOR

Einfahrt	*ain*·fahrt	Entrance
Ausfahrt	*ows*·fahrt	Exit
Einfahrt Verboten	*ain*·fahrt fer·*baw*·ten	No Entry
Einbahnstraße	*ain*·bahn·shtrah·se	One Way
Parkverbot	*park*·fer·bawt	No Parking
Stopp	shtop	Stop
Mautstelle	*mowt*·shte·le	Toll

Where's a petrol/gas station?	Wo ist eine Tankstelle? vaw ist *ai*·ne *tangk*·shte·le
I need a mechanic.	Ich brauche einen Mechaniker. ikh *brow*·khe *ai*·nen me·*khah*·ni·ker
My car/motorbike has broken down (at ...).	Ich habe (in ...) eine Panne mit meinem Auto/Motorrad. ikh *hah*·be (in ...) *ai*·ne *pa*·ne mit *mai*·nem *ow*·to/*maw*·tor·raht
I had an accident.	Ich hatte einen Unfall. ikh *ha*·te *ai*·nen *un*·fal
I have a flat tyre.	Ich habe eine Reifenpanne. ikh *hah*·be *ai*·ne *rai*·fen·pa·ne
I've run out of petrol/gas.	Ich habe kein Benzin mehr. ikh *hah*·be kain ben·*tseen* mair
Can you fix it?	Können Sie es reparieren? *ker*·nen zee es re·pa·*ree*·ren

BICYCLE

Where can I hire a bicycle?	Wo kann ich ein Fahrrad mieten? vaw kan ikh ain *fahr*·raht *mee*·ten
How much is it per day?	Wie viel kostet es für einen Tag? vee feel *kos*·tet es für *ai*·nen tahk
How much is it per hour?	Wie viel kostet es für eine Stunde? vee feel *kos*·tet es für *ai*·ne *shtun*·de
Where can I buy a secondhand bike?	Wo kann ich ein gebrauchtes Fahrrad kaufen? vaw kan ikh ain ge·*browkh*·tes *fahr*·raht *kow*·fen
I have a puncture.	Ich habe einen Platten. ikh *hah*·be *ai*·nen *pla*·ten
I'd like to have my bicycle repaired.	Ich möchte mein Fahrrad reparieren lassen. ikh *merkh*·te main *fahr*·raht re·pa·*ree*·ren *la*·sen
Can I take my bike on the train?	Kann ich mein Fahrrad im Zug mitnehmen? kan ikh main *fahr*·raht im tsook *mit*·nay·men
Can we get there by bike?	Können wir mit dem Fahrrad dahin kommen? *ker*·nen veer mit daym *fahr*·raht dah·*hin* *ko*·men
Are there cycling paths?	Gibt es Fahrradwege? geept es *fahr*·raht·vay·ge
Is there bicycle parking?	Gibt es Fahrrad-Parkplätze? geept es *fahr*·raht·park·ple·tse

For phrases on access for travellers with disabilities, see **seniors & travellers with disabilities** (p97).

Border Crossing

KEY PHRASES

I'm here for (four) days.	Ich bin hier für (vier) Tage.	ikh bin heer für (feer) *tah*·ge
I'm staying at the ...	Ich übernachte im ...	ikh *oo*·ber·*nakh*·te im ...
I have nothing to declare.	Ich habe nichts zu verzollen.	ikh *hah*·be nikhts tsoo fer·*tso*·len

PASSPORT CONTROL

I'm here ... Ich bin hier ...
ikh bin heer ...

in transit	auf der Durchreise	owf dair *durkh*·rai·ze
on business	auf Geschäftsreise	owf ge·*shefts*·rai·ze
on holiday	im Urlaub	im *oor*·lowp
to study	zum Studieren	tsum shtu·*dee*·ren

I'm here for (four) days. Ich bin hier für (vier) Tage.
ikh bin heer für (feer) *tah*·ge

I'm here for (three) weeks. Ich bin hier für (drei) Wochen.
ikh bin heer für (drai) *vo*·khen

I'm here for (two) months. Ich bin hier für (zwei) Monate.
ikh bin heer für (tsvai) *maw*·na·te

I'm going to (Salzburg).	Ich gehe nach (Salzburg). ikh *gay*·e nahkh (*zalts*·burg)
I'm staying at the ...	Ich übernachte im ... ikh *oo*·ber·*nakht*·er im ...

AT CUSTOMS

I have nothing to declare.	Ich habe nichts zu verzollen. ikh *hah*·be nikhts tsoo fer·*tso*·len
I have something to declare.	Ich habe etwas zu verzollen. ikh *hah*·be *et*·vas tsoo fer·*tso*·len
I didn't know I had to declare it.	Ich wusste nicht, dass ich das verzollen muss. ikh *vus*·te nikht das ikh das fer·*tso*·len mus
That's (not) mine.	Das ist (nicht) meins. das ist (nikht) mains

For phrases on payments and receipts, see **money & banking** (p86).

LISTEN FOR

Ihren Reisepass, bitte.	*ee*·ren *rai*·ze·pas *bi*·te Your passport, please.
Ihr Visum, bitte.	eer *vee*·zum *bi*·te Your visa, please.
Reisen Sie allein?	*rai*·zen zee a·*lain* Are you travelling on your own?
Reisen Sie in einer Gruppe?	*rai*·zen zee in *ai*·ner *gru*·pe Are you travelling in a group?
Reisen Sie mit Ihrer Familie?	*rai*·zen zee mit *ee*·rer fa·*mee*·li·e Are you travelling with your family?

Directions

KEY PHRASES

Where's (a bank)?	Wo ist (eine Bank)?	vaw ist (*ai*·ne bangk)
What's the address?	Wie ist die Adresse?	vee ist dee a·*dre*·se
How far is it?	Wie weit ist es?	vee *vait* ist es

Where's (a bank)?	Wo ist (eine Bank)? vaw ist (*ai*·ne bangk)
I'm looking for (the cathedral).	Ich suche (den Dom). ikh *zoo*·khe (dayn dawm)
How can I get there?	Wie kann ich da hinkommen? vee kan ikh dah *hin*·ko·men
Can you show me (on the map)?	Können Sie es mir (auf der Karte) zeigen? *ker*·nen zee es meer (owf dair *kar*·te) *tsai*·gen
What's the address?	Wie ist die Adresse? vee ist dee a·*dre*·se
Turn left/right.	Biegen Sie links/rechts ab. *bee*·gen zee lingks/rekhts ap
Turn at the corner.	Biegen Sie an der Ecke ab. *bee*·gen zee an dair *e*·ke ap
Turn at the traffic lights.	Biegen Sie bei der Ampel ab. *bee*·gen zee bai dair *am*·pel ap

It's ...	Es ist ... es ist ...

behind ...	hinter ...	*hin*·ter ...
far away	weit weg	vait vek
here	hier	heer
in front of ...	vor ...	fawr ...
left	links	lingks
near	nahe	*nah*·e
next to ...	neben ...	*nay*·ben ...
on the corner	an der Ecke	an dair e·ke
opposite ...	gegenüber ...	gay·gen·*ü*·ber ...
right	rechts	rekhts
straight ahead	geradeaus	ge·rah·de·*ows*
there	dort	dort

north/south	Norden m/Süden m *nor*·den/*zü*·den
east/west	Osten m/Westen m *os*·ten/*ves*·ten
How far is it?	Wie weit ist es? vee *vait* ist es
by bus	mit dem Bus mit daym *bus*
by taxi	mit dem Taxi mit daym *tak*·si
by train	mit dem Zug mit daym *tsook*
on foot	zu Fuß tsoo *foos*

It's (10) metres.	Es ist (10) Meter entfernt. es ist (tsayn) *may*·ter ent·*fernt*
It's (five) minutes.	Es ist (fünf) Minuten entfernt. es ist (fünf) mi·*noo*·ten ent·*fernt*
avenue	Allee f a·*lay*
lane	Gasse f *ga*·se
square	Platz m plats
street	Straße/Weg f/m *shtrah*·se/vayk

Accommodation

KEY PHRASES

Where's a hotel?	Wo ist ein Hotel?	vaw ist ain ho·*tel*
How much is it per night?	Wie viel kostet es pro Nacht?	vee feel *kos*·tet es praw nakht
Is breakfast included?	Ist das Frühstück inklusive?	ist das *frü*·shtük in·kloo·*zee*·ve
What time is checkout?	Wann muss ich auschecken?	van mus ikh *ows*·che·ken

FINDING ACCOMMODATION

Where's a/an ...? Wo ist ...? vaw ist ...

bed & breakfast	eine Pension	*ai*·ne pahng·*zyawn*
camping ground	ein Campingplatz	ain *kem*·ping·plats
guesthouse	eine Pension	*ai*·ne pahng·*zyawn*
hotel	ein Hotel	ain ho·*tel*
youth hostel	eine Jugendherberge	*ai*·ne *yoo*·gent·her·ber·ge

Can you recommend somewhere (cheap/ nearby)? Können Sie etwas (Günstiges/ in der Nähe) empfehlen? *ker*·nen zee *et*·vas (*gün*·sti·ges/ in dair *nay*·e) emp·*fay*·len

For responses, see **directions** (p53).

LISTEN FOR

Es tut mir Leid, wir haben keine Zimmer frei.	es toot meer lait veer *hah*·ben *kai*·ne *tsi*·mer frai	I'm sorry, we're full.
Für wie viele Nächte?	für vee *fee*·le *nekh*·te	For how many nights?

BOOKING AHEAD & CHECKING IN

I'd like to book a room, please.	Ich möchte bitte ein Zimmer reservieren. ikh *merkh*·te *bi*·te ain *tsi*·mer re·zer·*vee*·ren
Are there rooms?	Gibt es freie Zimmer? gipt es *fra*·ye *tsi*·mer
I have a reservation.	Ich habe eine Reservierung. ikh *hah*·be *ai*·ne re·zer·*vee*·rung
For (three) nights/weeks.	Für (drei) Nächte/Wochen. für (drai) *nekh*·te/*vo*·khen
From (2 July) to (6 July).	Vom (2. Juli) bis zum (6. Juli). vom (*tsvai*·ten *yoo*·li) bis tsum (*zeks*·ten *yoo*·li)
Is breakfast included?	Ist das Frühstück inklusive? ist das *frü*·shtük in·kloo·*zee*·ve
Do you have wi-fi?	Gibt es hier WLAN? geept es heer *vay*·lahn

How much is it per night/ person?	Wie viel kostet es pro Nacht/Person? vee feel *kos*·tet es praw nakht/ per·*zawn*
How much is it per week?	Wie viel kostet es pro Woche? vee feel *kos*·tet es praw *vo*·khe
Do you have a double room?	Haben Sie ein Doppelzimmer mit einem Doppelbett? *hah*·ben zee ain *do*·pel·tsi·mer mit *ai*·nem *do*·pel·bet

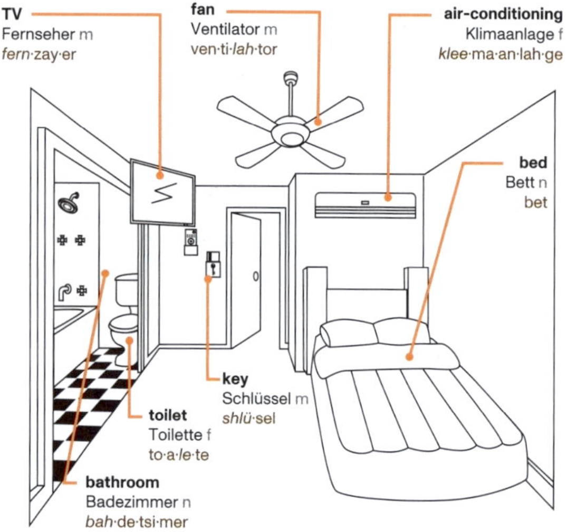

Finding a Room

DO YOU HAVE A ... ROOM?
Haben Sie ein ...?
hah·ben zee ain ...

DOUBLE
Doppelzimmer
do·pel·tsi·mer

SINGLE
Einzelzimmer
ain·tsel·tsi·mer

HOW MUCH IS IT PER ...?
Wie viel kostet es pro ...?
vee feel *kos*·tet es praw ...

NIGHT
Nacht
nakht

PERSON
Person
per·*zawn*

IS BREAKFAST INCLUDED?
Ist das Frühstück inklusive?
ist das *frü*·shtük in·kloo·*zee*·ve

CAN I SEE THE ROOM?
Kann ich es sehen?
kan ikh es *zay*·en

I'LL TAKE IT.
Ich nehme es.
ikh *nay*·me es

I WON'T TAKE IT.
Ich nehme es nicht.
ikh *nay*·me es nikht

Do you have a single room?	Haben Sie ein Einzelzimmer? *hah*·ben zee ain *ain*·tsel·tsi·mer
Do you have a twin room?	Haben Sie ein Doppelzimmer mit zwei Einzelbetten? *hah*·ben zee ain *do*·pel·tsi·mer mit tsvai ain·tsel·be·ten
Can I see it?	Kann ich es sehen? kan ikh es *zay*·en
It's fine. I'll take it.	Es ist gut, ich nehme es. es ist goot ikh *nay*·me es

For methods of payment, see **money & banking** (p86).

REQUESTS & QUERIES

When/Where is breakfast served?	Wann/Wo gibt es Frühstück? van/vaw gipt es *frü*·shtük
Please wake me at (seven).	Bitte wecken Sie mich um (sieben) Uhr. *bi*·te *ve*·ken zee mikh um (*zee*·ben) oor
There's no need to change my sheets/towels.	Sie brauchen meine Bettwäsche/Handtücher nicht zu wechseln. zee *brow*·khen *mai*·ne *bet*·ve·she/*han*·tü·kher nikht tsoo *ve*·kseln
Can I use (the internet)?	Kann ich (das Internet) benutzen? kan ikh (das *in*·ter·net) be·*nu*·tsen
Can I use (the laundry)?	Kann ich (eine Waschmaschine) benutzen? kan ikh (*ai*·ne *vash*·ma·shee·ne) be·*nu*·tsen

Do you have a ...?	Haben Sie ...?	*hah*·ben zee ...

laundry service	einen Wäscheservice	*ai*·nen *ve*·she·ser·vis
lift/elevator	einen Aufzug	*ai*·nen *owf*·tsook
safe	einen Safe	*ai*·nen sayf
swimming pool	ein Schwimmbad	ain *shvim*·baht

Do you arrange tours here?
Arrangieren Sie hier Touren?
a·rang·*zhee*·ren zee heer *too*·ren

Can I leave a message for someone?
Kann ich eine Nachricht für jemanden hinterlassen?
kan ikh *ai*·ne *nahkh*·rikht für *yay*·man·den hin·ter·*la*·sen

Is there a message for me?
Haben Sie eine Nachricht für mich?
hah·ben zee *ai*·ne *nahkh*·rikht für mikh

Can I get another ...?
Kann ich noch einen/eine/ein ... bekommen? m/f/n
kan ikh nokh *ai*·nen/*ai*·ne/ain ... be·*ko*·men

blanket	Decke f	*de*·ke
pillow	Kopfkissen n	*kopf*·ki·sen
pillowcase	Kopfkissenbezug m	*kopf*·ki·sen·be·tsook
towel	Handtuch n	*hant*·tookh

Could I have my key, please?	Könnte ich bitte meinen Schlüssel haben? *kern*·te ikh *bi*·te *mai*·nen *shlü*·sel *hah*·ben	
Could I have a receipt, please?	Könnte ich bitte eine Quittung haben? *kern*·te ikh *bi*·te *ai*·ne *kvi*·tung *hah*·ben	
I'm locked out of my room.	Ich habe mich aus meinem Zimmer ausgesperrt. ikh *hah*·be mikh ows *mai*·nem *tsi*·mer *ows*·ge·shpert	
There's no hot water.	Es gibt kein warmes Wasser. es geept kain *var*·mes *va*·ser	
(This sheet) isn't clean.	(Dieses Bettlaken) ist nicht sauber. (*dee*·zes *bet*·lah·ken) ist nikht *zow*·ber	
It's too ...	Es ist zu ... es ist tsoo ...	

cold	kalt	kalt
dark	dunkel	*dung*·kel
light/bright	hell	hel
noisy	laut	lowt
small	klein	klain

The ... doesn't work.	... funktioniert nicht. ... fungk·tsyaw·*neert* nikht

air-conditioning	Die Klimaanlage	dee *klee*·ma·an·lah·ge
fan	Der Ventilator	dair ven·ti·*lah*·tor
heater	Das Heizgerät	das *haits*·ge·rayt
toilet	Die Toilette	dee to·a·*le*·te

ANSWERING THE DOOR

Who is it?	Wer ist da? vair ist dah
Just a moment.	Einen Augenblick, bitte! *ai*·nen ow·gen·*blik bi*·te
Come in.	Herein! he·*rain*
Come back later, please.	Kommen Sie bitte später noch einmal. *ko*·men zee *bi*·te *shpay*·ter nokh *ain*·mahl

CHECKING OUT

What time is checkout?	Wann muss ich auschecken? van mus ikh *ows*·che·ken
How much extra to stay until (six o'clock)?	Was kostet es extra, wenn ich bis (sechs Uhr) bleiben möchte? vas *kos*·tet es *eks*·tra ven ikh bis (zeks oor) *blai*·ben *merkh*·te
I'm leaving now.	Ich reise jetzt ab. ikh *rai*·ze yetst ap
Can you call a taxi for me (for 11 o'clock)?	Können Sie mir (für 11 Uhr) ein Taxi rufen? *ker*·nen zee meer (für elf oor) ain *tak*·si *roo*·fen
Can I leave my bags here until (tonight)?	Kann ich meine Taschen bis (heute Abend) hier lassen? kan ikh *mai*·ne *ta*·shen bis (*hoy*·te *ah*·bent) heer *la*·sen

Could I have my deposit, please?	Könnte ich bitte meine Anzahlung haben? *kern*·te ikh *bi*·te *mai*·ne *an*·tsah·lung *hah*·ben
Could I have my passport, please?	Könnte ich bitte meinen Pass haben? *kern*·te ikh *bi*·te *mai*·nen *pas hah*·ben
Could I have my valuables, please?	Könnte ich bitte meine Wertsachen haben? *kern*·te ikh *bi*·te *mai*·ne *vert*·za·khen *hah*·ben
I had a great stay, thank you.	Es hat mir hier sehr gut gefallen. es hat meer heer zair goot ge·*fa*·len
I'll recommend it to my friends.	Ich werde Sie weiterempfehlen. ikh *ver*·de zee *vai*·ter·emp·fay·len

CAMPING

Can I camp here?	Kann ich hier zelten? kan ikh heer *tsel*·ten
Where's the nearest camp site?	Wo ist der nächste Zeltplatz? vaw ist dair *naykhs*·te *tselt*·plats
Do you have ...?	Haben Sie ...? *hah*·ben zee ...

electricity	Strom	shtrawm
shower facilities	Duschen	*doo*·shen
a site	einen Stellplatz	*ai*·nen *shtel*·plats
tents for hire	Zelte zu vermieten	*tsel*·te tsoo fer·*mee*·ten

Is the water drinkable?	Kann man das Wasser trinken? kan man das *va*·ser *tring*·ken
Who do I ask to stay here?	Wen muss ich fragen, wenn ich hier zelten möchte? vayn mus ikh *frah*·gen ven ikh heer *tsel*·ten *merkh*·te
How much do you charge ...?	Wie viel berechnen Sie ...? vee feel be·*rekh*·nen zee ...

for a car	für ein Auto	für ain *ow*·to
for a caravan	für einen Wohnwagen	für *ai*·nen *vawn*·vah·gen
for a tent	für ein Zelt	für ain tselt
per person	pro Person	praw per·*zawn*

gas cylinder	Gasflasche f *gahs*·fla·she
mallet	Holzhammer m *holts*·ha·mer
peg	Hering m *hay*·ring
rope	Seil n zail
sleeping bag	Schlafsack m *shlahf*·zak
spade	Spaten m *shpah*·ten
tent	Zelt n tselt
torch/flashlight	Taschenlampe f *ta*·shen·lam·pe

RENTING

I'm here about the ... for rent.	Ich komme wegen des/der/ des zu vermietenden ... m/f/n ikh *ko*·me *vay*·gen des/dair/ des tsoo fer·*mee*·ten·den ...

apartment	Wohnung f	*vaw*·nung
cabin	Hütte f	*hü*·te
holiday apartment	Ferienwohnung f	*fay*·ri·en·vaw·nung
house	Haus n	hows
room	Zimmer n	*tsi*·mer
villa	Villa f	*vi*·la

furnished	möbliert mer·*bleert*
partly furnished	teilmöbliert *tail*·mer·bleert
unfurnished	unmöbliert *un*·mer·bleert
Do you have a/an ... for rent?	Haben Sie ... zu vermieten? *hah*·ben zee ... tsoo fer·*mee*·ten
How much is it for (one) week?	Was kostet es für (eine) Woche? vas *kos*·tet es für (*ai*·ne) *vo*·khe
How much is it for (two) months?	Was kostet es für (zwei) Monate? vas *kos*·tet es für (tsvai) *maw*·na·te

I want to rent it from (2 July) to (6 July).	Ich möchte es vom (2. Juli) bis zum (6. Juli) mieten. ikh *merkh*·te es fom (*tsvai*·ten *yoo*·li) bis tsum (*zeks*·ten *yoo*·li) *mee*·ten
How many rooms does it have?	Wie viele Zimmer hat es? vee *fee*·le *tsi*·mer hat es
Is there a deposit/bond?	Gibt es eine Kaution? gipt es *ai*·ne kow·*tsyawn*
Are bills extra?	Kommen noch Nebenkosten dazu? *ko*·men nokh *nay*·ben·kos·ten da·*tsoo*
Who is my contact person?	Wer ist meine Kontaktperson? vair ist *mai*·ne kon·*takt*·per·zawn

Wann muss ich auschecken?

van mus ikh *ows*·che·ken

What time is checkout?

STAYING WITH LOCALS

Can I stay at your place?	Kann ich bei Ihnen/dir übernachten? pol/inf kan ikh bai *ee*·nen/deer ü·ber·*nakh*·ten
I have my own sleeping bag.	Ich habe meinen eigenen Schlafsack. ikh *hah*·be *mai*·nen *ai*·ge·nen shlahf·zak
Is there anything I can do to help?	Kann ich Ihnen/dir irgendwie helfen? pol/inf kan ikh *ee*·nen/deer *ir*·gent·vee *hel*·fen
Can I bring anything for the meal?	Kann ich etwas für das Essen mitbringen? kan ikh *et*·vas für das *e*·sen *mit*·bring·en
Can I do the dishes?	Kann ich abwaschen? kan ikh *ap*·va·shen
Can I set/clear the table?	Kann ich den Tisch decken/abräumen? kan ikh dayn tish *de*·ken/*ap*·roy·men
Thanks for your hospitality.	Vielen Dank für Ihre/deine Gastfreundschaft. pol/inf *fee*·len dangk für *ee*·re/*dai*·ne *gast*·froynt·shaft

To compliment your host's cooking, see **eating out** (p170).

Shopping

KEY PHRASES

I'd like to buy ...	Ich möchte ... kaufen.	ikh *merkh*·te ... *kow*·fen
Can you show it to me?	Können Sie es mir zeigen?	*ker*·nen zee es meer *tsai*·gen
Can I try it on?	Kann ich es anprobieren?	kan ikh es *an*·pro·bee·ren
How much is this?	Wie viel kostet das?	vee feel *kos*·tet das

LOOKING FOR ...

Where's (a/the supermarket)?	Wo ist (ein/der Supermarkt)? vaw ist (ain/dair *zoo*·per·markt)
Where can I buy (locally produced goods/ souvenirs)?	Wo kann ich (lokal produzierte Waren/ Andenken) kaufen? vaw kan ikh (lo·*kal* pro·du·*tseer*·te *vah*·ren/ *an*·deng·ken) *kow*·fen

For phrases on getting there, see **directions** (p53), and for additional shops and services, see the **dictionary** (p197).

MAKING A PURCHASE

I'd like to buy ...	Ich möchte ... kaufen. ikh *merkh*·te ... *kow*·fen
I'm just looking.	Ich schaue mich nur um. ikh *show*·e mikh noor um

LISTEN FOR

Kann ich Ihnen helfen?	kan ikh *ee*·nen *hel*·fen Can I help you?
Möchten Sie noch etwas?	*merkh*·ten zee nokh *et*·vas Would you like anything else?
Nein, (haben wir) leider nicht.	nain (*hah*·ben veer) *lai*·der nikht No, we don't have any.

What is this made of?	Woraus ist das gemacht? vaw·*rows* ist das ge·*makht*
How much is this?	Wie viel kostet das? vee feel *kos*·tet das

How much?	Das kostet?	das *kos*·tet

Can you write down the price?	Können Sie den Preis aufschreiben? *ker*·nen zee dayn prais *owf*·shrai·ben
Do you have any others?	Haben Sie noch andere? *hah*·ben zee nokh *an*·de·re
Can I look at it?	Können Sie es mir zeigen? *ker*·nen zee es meer *tsai*·gen
Do you accept credit/debit cards?	Nehmen Sie Kreditkarten/Debitkarten? *nay*·men zee kre·*deet*·kar·ten/ *day*·bit·kar·ten
Could I have a bag, please?	Könnte ich eine Tüte bekommen? *kern*·te ikh *ai*·ne *tü*·te be·*ko*·men

Making a Purchase

I'D LIKE TO BUY …
Ich möchte … kaufen.
ikh *merkh*·te … *kow*·fen

HOW MUCH IS IT?
Wie viel kostet das?
vee feel *kos*·tet das

OR

CAN YOU WRITE DOWN THE PRICE?
Können Sie den Preis aufschreiben?
ker·nen zee dayn prais *owf*·shrai·ben

DO YOU ACCEPT CREDIT CARDS?
Nehmen Sie Kreditkarten?
nay·men zee kre·*deet*·kar·ten

COULD I HAVE A …, PLEASE?
Könnte ich eine … bekommen?
kern·te ikh *ai*·ne … be·*ko*·men

RECEIPT
Quittung
kvi·tung

BAG
Tüte
tü·te

Could I have a receipt, please?	Könnte ich eine Quittung bekommen? *kern*·te ikh *ai*·ne *kvi*·tung be·ko·men
Receipt, please.	Eine Quittung, bitte. *ai*·ne *kvi*·tung *bi*·te
Could I have it wrapped, please?	Könnte ich es eingepackt bekommen? *kern*·te ikh es *ain*·ge·pakt be·*ko*·men
I don't need a bag, thanks.	Ich brauche keine Tüte, danke. ikh *brow*·khe *kai*·ne *tü*·te *dang*·ke
Does it have a guarantee?	Gibt es darauf Garantie? gipt es da·*rowf* ga·ran·*tee*
Can I have it sent overseas?	Kann ich es ins Ausland verschicken lassen? kan ikh es ins *ows*·lant fer·*shi*·ken *la*·sen
Can I pick it up later?	Kann ich es später abholen? kan ikh es *shpay*·ter *ap*·haw·len
It's faulty/broken.	Es ist fehlerhaft/kaputt. es ist *fay*·ler·haft/ka·*put*
I'd like my change, please.	Ich möchte bitte mein Wechselgeld. ikh *merkh*·te *bi*·te main *vek*·sel·gelt
I'd like my money back, please.	Ich möchte bitte mein Geld zurückhaben. ikh *merkh*·te *bi*·te main gelt tsu·*rük*·hah·ben

LISTEN FOR

Ausverkauf m	*ows*·fer·kowf	sale
Nepp m	nep	rip-off
Schnäppchen n	*shnep*·khen	bargain
Sonderangebote n pl	*zon*·der·an·ge·baw·te	specials

I'd like to return this, please.	Ich möchte bitte dieses zurückgeben. ikh *merkh*·te *bi*·te *dee*·zes tsu·*rük*·gay·ben

BARGAINING

That's too expensive.	Das ist zu teuer. das ist tsoo *toy*·er
Can you lower the price?	Können Sie mit dem Preis runtergehen? *ker*·nen zee mit dem prais *run*·ter·gay·en
Do you have something cheaper?	Haben Sie etwas Günstigeres? *hah*·ben zee *et*·vas *gün*·sti·ge·res
I'll give you ...	Ich gebe Ihnen ... ikh *gay*·be *ee*·nen ...

BOOKS & READING

Is there a/an (English-language) section?	Gibt es eine Abteilung (für englische Bücher)? gipt es *ai*·ne ap·*tai*·lung (für *eng*·li·she *bü*·kher)
Is there a/an (English-language) bookshop?	Gibt es einen Buchladen (für englische Bücher)? gipt es *ai*·nen *bookh*·lah·den (für *eng*·li·she *bü*·kher)

Do you have Lonely Planet guidebooks?	Haben Sie Lonely-Planet-Reiseführer? *hah*·ben zee *lohn*·li·*ple*·net·*rai*·ze·fü·rer
I'm looking for something by (Hermann Hesse).	Ich suche nach etwas von (Hermann Hesse). ikh *zoo*·khe nahkh *et*·vas fon (*her*·man *he*·se)

CLOTHES

Can I try it on?	Kann ich es anprobieren? kan ikh es *an*·pro·bee·ren
My size is ...	Ich habe Größe ... ikh *hah*·be *grer*·se ...
It doesn't fit.	Es passt nicht. es past nikht
small/medium/large	klein/mittelgroß/groß klain/*mi*·tel·graws/graws

For clothes items see the **dictionary (p197)**, and for sizes see **numbers & amounts** (p30).

MUSIC

I'd like headphones.	Ich hätte gern Kopfhörer. ikh *he*·te gern *kopf*·her·rer
Can you recommend any local bands?	Können Sie mir lokale Bands empfehlen? *ker*·nen zee meer lo·*ka*·le bands emp·*fay*·len
What's their best album?	Was ist ihr bestes Album? vas ist *ee*·re *bes*·tes al·bum
Can I listen to this?	Kann ich mir das anhören? kan ikh meer das *an*·her·ren

PHOTOGRAPHY

Can you print digital photos?	Können Sie digitale Fotos drucken? *ker*·nen zee dee·gee·*tah*·le *faw*·tos *dru*·ken
Do you have (batteries) for this camera?	Haben Sie (Akkus) für diese Kamera? *hah*·ben zee (a·koos) für *dee*·ze *ka*·me·ra
Do you have (memory cards) for this camera?	Haben Sie (Speicherkarten) für diese Kamera? *hah*·ben zee (*shpai*·kher·kar·ten) für *dee*·ze *ka*·me·ra

Kann ich es anprobieren?
kan ikh es *an*·pro·bee·ren
Can I try it on?

I need a cable to connect my camera to a computer.	Ich brauche ein Kabel, um meine Kamera an einem Computer anzuschließen. ikh *brow*·khe ain *kah*·bel um *mai*·ne *ka*·me·ra an *ai*·nem kom·*pyoo*·ter *an*·tsoo·shlee·sen
I need a cable to recharge this battery.	Ich brauche ein Ladekabel für diesen Akku. ikh *brow*·khe ain *lah*·de·kah·bel für *dee*·zen a·koo
I need a passport photo taken.	Ich möchte ein Passfoto machen lassen. ikh *merkh*·te ain *pas*·faw·to *ma*·khen *la*·sen
digital camera	Digitalkamera f dee·gee·*tahl*·kah·me·ra
disposable camera	Wegwerfkamera f *vek*·verf·kah·me·ra

CULTURE TIP: SOUVENIRS

Austria	chocolates *(Pralinen* n pl pra·*lee*·nen*)*, fruit brandies (*Obstler* m *awpst*·ler)
Bavarian Forest	crystal glassware (*Kristallglas* n kris·*tal*·glahs)
Black Forest	cuckoo clocks, dolls (*Puppe* f *pu*·pe), fruit brandies
Harz Mountains	puppets (*Puppe* f *pu*·pe), marionettes (*Marionette* f ma·ri·o·*ne*·te), glassware (*Glaswaren* pl *glahs*·vah·ren)
Lübeck	marzipan (*Marzipan* n *mar*·tsi·pahn)
Meissen	modern and antique porcelain (*Porzellan* n por·tse·*lahn*)
Nuremberg	tin toys (*Blechspielzeug* n *blekh*·shpeel·tsoyk), gingerbread (*Lebkuchen* m *layp*·koo·khen)
Rhine and Moselle Rivers	white wines (*Weißwein* m *vais*·vain)
Rothenburg ob der Tauber	wooden toys (*Holzspielzeug* n *holts*·shpeel·tsoyk), Christmas decorations (*Weihnachtsschmuck* m *vai*·nakhts·shmuk)
Switzerland	cuckoo clocks (*Kuckucksuhr* f *ku*·kuks·oor), chocolate (Schokolade f sho·ko·*lah*·de), cow bells (*Kuhglocke* f *koo*·glo·ke)
Thuringia	wooden figures (*Holzfigur* f *holts*·fi·goor), Christmas decorations

REPAIRS

Can I have my ... repaired here?	Kann ich hier mein ... reparieren lassen? kan ikh heer main ... re·pa·*ree*·ren *la*·sen
When will my shoes be ready?	Wann sind meine Schuhe fertig? van zint *mai*·ne *shoo*·e *fer*·tikh
When will my backpack be ready?	Wann ist mein Rucksack fertig? van ist main *ruk*·zak *fer*·tikh
When will my mobile/cell phone be ready?	Wann ist mein Handy fertig? van ist main *hen*.di *fer*·tikh
When will my (sun)glasses be ready?	Wann ist meine (Sonnen)Brille fertig? van ist *mai*·ne (*zo*·nen·)*bri*·le *fer*·tikh

Communications

KEY PHRASES

What's your phone number?	Wie ist Ihre/deine Telefonnummer? pol/inf	vee ist ee·re/ *dai*·ne te·le·*fawn*·nu·mer
I'd like to check my email.	Ich möchte meine E-Mails checken.	ikh *merkh*·te *mai*·ne ee·mayls *che*·ken
I'd like a SIM card for your network.	Ich hätte gern eine SIM-Karte für Ihr Netz.	ikh *he*·te gern *ai*·ne *zim*·kar·te für eer nets

POST OFFICE

I want to send a parcel.	Ich möchte ein Paket senden. ikh *merkh*·te ain pa·*kayt* *zen*·den
I want to send a postcard.	Ich möchte eine Postkarte senden. ikh *merkh*·te *ai*·ne *post*·kar·te *zen*·den
I want to buy an envelope.	Ich möchte einen Umschlag kaufen. ikh *merkh*·te *ai*·nen *um*·shlahk *kow*·fen
I want to buy a stamp.	Ich möchte eine Briefmarke kaufen. ikh *merkh*·te *ai*·ne *breef*·mar·ke *kow*·fen

LISTEN FOR

Einschreiben n	*ain*·shrai·ben	registered mail
Expresspost f	eks·*pres*·post	express mail
Inlands-	*in*·lants·	domestic
international	in·ter·na·tsyo·*nahl*	international
Luftpost f	*luft*·post	airmail
Postfach n	*post*·fakh	PO box
Postleitzahl f	*post*·lait·tsahl	postcode
Schiffspost f	*shifs*·post	sea mail
zerbrechlich	tser·*brekh*·likh	fragile
Zollerklärung f	*tsol*·er·klair·rung	customs declaration

Please send it by (airmail) to ...	Bitte schicken Sie das per (Luftpost) nach ... *bi*·te *shi*·ken zee das per (*luft*·post) nahkh ...
It contains ...	Es enthält ... es ent·*helt* ...
Is there any mail for me?	Ist Post für mich da? ist post für mikh dah

PHONE

Q **What's your phone number?**	Wie ist Ihre/deine Telefonnummer? pol/inf vee ist *ee*·re/*dai*·ne te·le·*fawn*·nu·mer
A **The number is ...**	Die Nummer ist ... dee *nu*·mer ist ...

LANGUAGE TIP: PHONE NUMBERS

To avoid confusion with *drei* drai (three) on the phone, Germans use *zwo* tsvoh instead of *zwei* tsvai, for 'two' (see also **numbers & amounts**, p30).

I want to make a call to (Singapore).	Ich möchte nach (Singapur) telefonieren. ikh *merkh*·te nahkh (*zing*·a·poor) te·le·fo·*nee*·ren
I want to make a local call.	Ich möchte ein Ortsgespräch führen. ikh *merkh*·te ain *orts*·gesh·prairkh *fü*·ren
I want to make a reverse charges/collect call.	Ich möchte ein R-Gespräch führen. ikh *merkh*·te ain *air*·ge·shpraykh *fü*·ren
I'd like to know the number for ...	Ich möchte gerne die Nummer für ... wissen. ikh *merkh*·te gern dee *nu*·mer für ... *vi*·sen
What's the area/country code for ...?	Was ist die Vorwahl für ...? vas ist dee *fawr*·vahl für ...
It's engaged.	Es ist besetzt. es ist be·*zetst*

LISTEN FOR

Tut mir Leid, Sie haben die falsche Nummer.	toot meer lait zee *hah*·ben dee *fal*·she *nu*·mer Sorry, wrong number.
Wer ist am Apparat?	vair ist am a·pa·*raht* Who's calling?
Mit wem möchten Sie sprechen?	mit vaym *merkh*·ten zee *shpre*·khen Who do you want to speak to?
Einen Augenblick, bitte.	*ai*·nen ow·gen·*blik* *bi*·te One moment, please.
Es tut mir Leid, (er/sie) ist nicht hier.	es toot meer lait (air/zee) ist nikht heer I'm sorry, (he/she) is not here.

The connection's bad.	Die Verbindung ist schlecht. dee fer·*bin*·dung ist shlekht
I've been cut off.	Ich bin unterbrochen worden. ikh bin un·ter·*bro*·khen *vor*·den
Can I speak to ...?	Kann ich mit ... sprechen? kan ikh mit ... *shpre*·khen
Can I leave a message?	Kann ich eine Nachricht hinterlassen? kan ikh *ai*·ne *nahkh*·rikht hin·ter·*la*·sen
My number is ...	Meine Nummer ist ... *mai*·ne *nu*·mer ist ...

Please tell him/her I called.	Bitte sagen Sie ihm/ihr, dass ich angerufen habe. *bi*·te *zah*·gen zee eem/eer das ikh *an*·ge·roo·fen *hah*·be
I'll call back later.	Ich rufe später nochmal an. ikh *roo*·fe *shpay*·ter *nokh*·mahl an
What time should I call?	Wann kann ich am besten anrufen? van kan ikh am *bes*·ten *an*·roo·fen

MOBILE/CELL PHONE

I'd like a ...	Ich hätte gern ... ikh *he*·te gern ...

charger for my phone	ein Ladegerät für mein Handy	ain *lah*·de·ge·rayt für main *hen*·di
SIM card for your network	eine SIM-Karte für Ihr Netz	*ai*·ne *zim*·kar·te für eer nets

What are the rates?	Wie hoch sind die Gebühren? vee hawkh zint dee ge·*bü*·ren

INTERNET

Is there wi-fi here?	Gibt es hier WLAN? geept es heer *vay*·lahn
Can I connect my laptop here?	Kann ich meinen Laptop hier anschließen? kan ikh *mai*·nen *lep*·top heer *an*·shlee·sen
How much per page?	Was kostet es pro Seite? vas *kos*·tet es praw *zai*·te
I'd like to ...	Ich möchte ... ikh *merkh*·te ...

check my email	meine E-Mails checken	*mai*·ne *ee*·mayls *che*·ken
download my photos	meine Fotos herunterladen	*mai*·ne *faw*·tos he·*run*·ter·lah·den
use a printer	einen Drucker benutzen	*ai*·nen *dru*·ker be·*nu*·tsen
use a scanner	einen Scanner benutzen	*ai*·nen *ske*·ner be·*nu*·tsen

Do you have PCs/Macs?	Haben Sie PCs/Macs? *hah*·ben zee pay·*tsays*/meks
Do you have headphones (with a microphone)?	Haben Sie Kopfhörer (mit einem Mikrofon)? *hah*·ben zee *kopf*·her·rer (mit *ai*·nem *mee*·kro·fawn)
How do I log on?	Wie logge ich mich ein? vee *law*·ge ikh mikh ain
What's the password?	Wie lautet das Passwort? vee *low*·tet das *pas*·vort

Can I connect my ... to this computer?	Kann ich ... an diesen Computer anschließen? kan ikh ... an *dee*·zen kom·*pyoo*·ter *an*·shlee·sen

camera	meine Kamera	*mai*·ne *kah*·me·ra
mobile/cell phone	meinen Handy	*mai*·nen *hen*·di
USB flash drive (memory stick)	meinen USB-Stick	*mai*·nen oo·es·*bay*·shtik

It's crashed.	Es ist abgestürzt. es ist *ap*·ge·shtürtst
I've finished.	Ich bin fertig. ikh bin *fer*·tikh

Money & Banking

KEY PHRASES

How much is it?	Wie viel kostet es?	vee feel *kos*·tet es
Where's the nearest ATM?	Wo ist der nächste Geldautomat?	vaw ist dair *naykhs*·te *gelt*·ow·to·maht
What's the exchange rate?	Wie ist der Wechselkurs?	vee ist dair *vek*·sel·kurs

PAYING THE BILL

Q **How much is it?**	Wie viel kostet es? vee feel *kos*·tet es
A **It's free.**	Das ist umsonst. das ist um·*zonst*
A **It costs (30) euros.**	Das kostet (30) Euro. das *kos*·tet (*drai*·tsikh) *oy*·ro
Can you write down the price?	Können Sie den Preis aufschreiben? *ker*·nen zee dayn prais *owf*·shrai·ben
There's a mistake in the bill.	Da ist ein Fehler in der Rechnung. dah ist ain *fay*·ler in dair *rekh*·nung
Do you accept credit/ debit cards?	Nehmen Sie Kreditkarten/ Debitkarten? *nay*·men zee kre·*deet*·kar·ten/ *day*·bit·kar·ten

I'd like my change, please.	Ich möchte bitte mein Wechselgeld. ikh *merkh*·te *bi*·te main *vek*·sel·gelt
I'd like a receipt, please.	Ich möchte bitte eine Quittung. ikh *merkh*·te *bi*·te *ai*·ne *kvi*·tung
I'd like a refund, please.	Ich möchte bitte mein Geld zurückhaben. ikh *merkh*·te *bi*·te main gelt tsu·*rük*·hah·ben

AT THE BANK

Where's the nearest ATM?	Wo ist der nächste Geldautomat? vaw ist dair *naykhs*·te *gelt*·ow·to·maht
Where's the nearest foreign exchange office?	Wo ist die nächste Geldwechselstube? vaw ist dee *naykhs*·te *gelt*·vek·sel·shtoo·be

LISTEN FOR

Kann ich bitte einen Ausweis sehen?	kan ikh *bi*·te *ai*·nen *ows*·vais *zay*·en Can I see some ID, please?
Bitte unterschreiben Sie hier.	*bi*·te un·ter·*shrai*·ben zee heer Please sign here.
Es gibt da ein Problem mit Ihrem Konto.	es gipt dah ain pro·*blaym* mit *ee*·rem *kon*·to There's a problem with your account.
Ihr Konto ist überzogen.	eer *kon*·to ist ü·ber·*tsaw*·gen You're overdrawn.

What time does the bank open?	Wann macht die Bank auf? van makht dee bangk owf
Where can I ...?	Wo kann ich ...? vaw kan ikh ...
I'd like to ...	Ich möchte ... ikh *merkh*·te ...

arrange a transfer	einen Transfer tätigen	*ai*·nen trans·*fer* *tay*·ti·gen
change money	Geld umtauschen	gelt *um*·tow·shen
get a cash advance	eine Barauszahlung	*ai*·ne *bahr*·ows·tsah·lung
get change for this note	diesen Schein wechseln	*dee*·zen shain *vek*·seln
withdraw money	Geld abheben	gelt *ap*·hay·ben

What's the exchange rate?	Wie ist der Wechselkurs? vee ist dair *vek*·sel·kurs
What's the charge for that?	Wie hoch sind die Gebühren dafür? vee hawkh zint dee ge·*bü*·ren da·*für*
What's the commission?	Wie hoch ist die Kommission? vee hawkh ist dee ko·mi·*syawn*
The ATM took my card.	Der Geldautomat hat meine Karte einbehalten. dair *gelt*·ow·to·maht hat *mai*·ne *kar*·te *ain*·be·hal·ten
I've forgotten my PIN.	Ich habe meine Geheimnummer vergessen. ikh *hah*·be *mai*·ne ge·*haim*·nu·mer fer·*ge*·sen

LANGUAGE TIP: CURRENCIES

Talking about prices is really easy in German because you don't need to add a plural ending to the currency. Twenty dollars is simply *zwanzig Dollar* *tsvan*·tsikh *do*·lahr. Some more international currencies to get you started: *Euro* m *oy*·ro (euro); *Pfund* n pfunt (pound).

Can I use my credit card to withdraw money?	Kann ich mit meiner Kreditkarte Geld abheben? kan ikh mit *mai*·ner kre·*deet*·kar·te gelt *ap*·hay·ben
Has my money arrived yet?	Ist mein Geld schon angekommen? ist main gelt shawn *an*·ge·ko·men
How long will it take to arrive?	Wie lange dauert es, bis es da ist? vee *lang*·e *dow*·ert es bis es dah ist

Business

KEY PHRASES

I'm attending a conference.	Ich nehme an einer Konferenz teil.	ikh *nay*·me an *ai*·ner kon·fe·*rents* tail
I have an appointment with ...	Ich habe einen Termin bei ...	ikh *hah*·be *ai*·nen ter·*meen* bai ...
Can I have your business card?	Kann ich Ihre/ deine Karte bekommen? pol/inf	kan ikh *ee*·re/ *dai*·ne *kar*·te be·*ko*·men

I'm attending a conference.	Ich nehme an einer Konferenz teil. ikh *nay*·me an *ai*·ner kon·fe·*rents* tail
I'm attending a course/ meeting.	Ich nehme an einem Kurs/ Meeting teil. ikh *nay*·me an *ai*·nem kurs/ *mee*·ting tail
I'm visiting a trade fair.	Ich besuche eine Messe. ikh be·*zoo*·khe *ai*·ne *me*·se
I'm here for (three) days/ weeks.	Ich bin für (drei) Tage/Wochen hier. ikh bin für (drai) *tah*·ge/*vo*·khen heer
I'm with my colleague.	Ich bin mit meinem Kollegen hier. m ikh bin mit *mai*·nem ko·*lay*·gen heer Ich bin mit meiner Kollegin hier. f ikh bin mit *mai*·ner ko·*lay*·gin heer

CULTURE TIP: BODY LANGUAGE

Shaking hands is customary for both men and women in Germany, Austria and Switzerland. Always give a firm handshake and look people in the eye. Never keep your other hand in your pocket, as this is considered impolite.

I'm alone.	Ich bin allein. ikh bin a·*lain*
I'm staying at ...	Ich übernachte im ... ikh *oo*·ber·*nakh*·te im ...
I have an appointment with ...	Ich habe einen Termin bei ... ikh *hah*·be *ai*·nen ter·*meen* bai ...
Ⓠ **Can I have your business card?**	Kann ich Ihre/deine Karte bekommen? pol/inf kan ikh *ee*·re/*dai*·ne *kar*·te be·*ko*·men
Ⓐ **Here's my business card.**	Hier ist meine Karte. heer ist *mai*·ne *kar*·te
That went very well.	Das war sehr gut. das vahr zair goot
Thank you for your time.	Danke für Ihre/deine Zeit. pol/inf *dang*·ke für *ee*·re/*dai*·ne tsait
Thank you for your interest.	Danke für Ihr/dein Interesse. pol/inf *dang*·ke für eer/dain in·te·*re*·se
Shall we go for a drink/meal?	Sollen wir noch etwas trinken/essen gehen? *zo*·len veer nokh *et*·vas *tring*·ken/*e*·sen *gay*·en

See also the box **titles & addressing people** (p104).

Sightseeing

KEY PHRASES

I'd like a guide.	Ich hätte gern einen Reiseführer.	ikh *he*·te gern *ai*·nen *rai*·ze·fü·rer
Can I take photographs?	Kann ich fotografieren?	kan ikh fo·to·gra·*fee*·ren
What time does it open?	Wann macht es auf?	van makht es owf
I'd like to see ...	Ich möchte ... sehen.	ikh *merkh*·te ... *zay*·en

REQUESTS & QUERIES

I'd like an audio set.	Ich hätte gern einen Audioführer. ikh *he*·te gern *ai*·nen *ow*·di·o·fü·rer
I'd like a guide.	Ich hätte gern einen Reiseführer. ikh *he*·te gern *ai*·nen *rai*·ze·fü·rer
I'd like a (local) map.	Ich hätte gern eine Karte (von hier). ikh *he*·te gern *ai*·ne *kar*·te (fon heer)
Do you have information on (historical) sights?	Haben Sie Informationen über (historische) Sehenswürdigkeiten? *hah*·ben zee in·for·ma·*tsyaw*·nen *ü*·ber (his·*taw*·ri·she) *zay*·ens·vür·dikh·kai·ten

I'd like to see ...	Ich möchte ... sehen. ikh *merkh*·te ... *zay*·en
What's that?	Was ist das? vas ist das
How old is it?	Wie alt ist es? vee alt ist es
Can I take photographs (of you)?	Kann ich (Sie/du) fotografieren? pol/inf kan ikh (zee/doo) fo·to·gra·*fee*·ren
Could you take a photograph of me?	Könnten Sie ein Foto von mir machen? *kern*·ten zee ain *faw*·to fon meer *ma*·khen

Kann ich fotografieren?

kan ikh fo·to·gra·*fee*·ren

Can I take photographs?

GETTING IN

What time does it open/close?	Wann macht es auf/zu? van makht es owf/tsoo
Q **What's the admission charge?**	Was kostet der Eintritt? vas *kos*·tet dair *ain*·trit
A **It costs ...**	Er kostet ... air *kos*·tet ...
Is there a discount for ...?	Gibt es eine Ermäßigung für ...? gipt es *ai*·ne er·*may*·si·gung für ...

children	Kinder	*kin*·der
families	Familien	fa·*mee*·li·en
groups	Gruppen	*gru*·pen
older people	Senioren	zay·*nyaw*·ren
students	Studenten	shtu·*den*·ten

GALLERIES & MUSEUMS

Q **What kind of art are you interested in?**	Für welche Art von Kunst interessieren Sie sich? pol für *vel*·khe art fon kunst in·tre·*see*·ren zee zikh Für welche Art von Kunst interessierst du dich? inf für *vel*·khe art fon kunst in·tre·*seerst* doo dikh
A **I'm interested in ...**	Ich interessiere mich für ... ikh in·tre·*see*·re mikh für ...
A **I like the works of ...**	Ich mag die Werke von ... ikh mahk dee *ver*·ke fon ...
Q **What's in the collection?**	Was gibt es in der Sammlung? vas gipt es in dair *zam*·lung

It's a/an ... exhibition. | Es ist eine ...-Ausstellung.
es ist ai·ne ...·ows·shte·lung

It reminds me of ... | Es erinnert mich an ...
es er·i·nert mikh an ...

TOURS

Are there (organised) walking tours?	Gibt es (organisierte) Wandertouren? geept es (or·ga·ni·*zeer*·te) *van*·der·too·ren
I'd like to do cooking/ language classes.	Ich würde gerne eine Kochkurs/Sprachkurs machen. ikh *vür*·de gern *ai*·ne *kokh*·kurs/ *shprahkh*·kurs *ma*·khen
Can you recommend a ...?	Können Sie ein ... empfehlen? *ker*·nen zee ain ... emp·*fay*·len
When's the next ...?	Wann ist der/die nächste ...? m/f van ist dair/dee *naykhs*·te ...

boat trip	Bootsrundfahrt f	*bawts*·runt·fahrt
day trip	Tagesausflug m	*tah*·ges·ows·flook
excursion	Ausflug m	*ows*·flook
tour	Tour f	toor

Is (accommodation) included?	Ist (die Unterkunft) inbegriffen? ist (dee *un*·ter·kunft) *in*·be·gri·fen
Is (food) included?	Ist (das Essen) inbegriffen? ist (das *e*·sen) *in*·be·gri·fen

LOOK FOR

Ausgang	*ows*·gang	Exit
Damen	*dah*·men	Women
Eingang	*ain*·gang	Entrance
Geschlossen	ge·*shlo*·sen	Closed
Heiß	hais	Hot
Herren	*hair*·en	Men
Kalt	kalt	Cold
Kein Zutritt	kain *tsu*·trit	No Entry
Offen	*o*·fen	Open
Rauchen Verboten	*row*·khen fer·*baw*·ten	No Smoking
Toiletten/WC	to·a·*le*·ten/ vee·*tsee*	Toilets
Verboten	fer·*baw*·ten	Prohibited

Is (transport) included?	Ist (die Beförderung) inbegriffen? ist (dee be·*fer*·de·rung) *in*·be·gri·fen
How long is the tour?	Wie lange dauert die Führung? vee *lang*·e *dow*·ert dee *fü*·rung
Do I need to take ... with me?	Muss ich ... mitnehmen? mus ikh ... *mit*·nay·men
(Q) **What time should we be back?**	Wann sollen wir zurück sein? van *zo*·len veer tsu·*rük* zain
(A) **Be back here at (10) o'clock.**	Seien Sie um (zehn) Uhr zurück. *zai*·en zee um (tsayn) oor tsu·*rük*
I've lost my group.	Ich habe meine Gruppe verloren. ikh *hah*·be *mai*·ne *gru*·pe fer·*law*·ren

Seniors & Travellers with Disabilities

KEY PHRASES

I need assistance.	Ich brauche Hilfe.	ikh *brow*·khe *hil*·fe
Is there wheel-chair access?	Gibt es eine Rollstuhlrampe?	gipt es *ai*·ne *rol*·shtool·ram·pe
Are there toilets for people with a disability?	Gibt es barrierefreie Toiletten?	gipt es ba.ree.*er*.e.frai.ye to·a·*le*·ten

I have a disability.	Ich habe eine Behinderung. ikh *hah*·be *ai*·ne be·*hin*·der·ung
I need assistance.	Ich brauche Hilfe. ikh *brow*·khe *hil*·fe
Are guide dogs permitted?	Sind Blindenhunde erlaubt? zint *blin*·den·hun·de er·*lowpt*
Is there wheelchair access?	Gibt es eine Rollstuhlrampe? gipt es *ai*·ne *rol*·shtool·ram·pe
Are there parking spaces for people with a disability?	Gibt es Parkplätze für Menschen mit Behinderungen? geept es *park*·ple·tse für *men*·shen mit be·*hin*·der·ung·en
Is the bathroom accessible?	Ist das Bad behindertengerecht? ist das baht be·*hin*·der·ten·ge·rekht

Are there toilets for people with a disability?	Gibt es Toiletten für Menschen mit Behinderungen? gipt es to·a·*le*·ten für *men*·shen mit be·*hin*·der·ung·en
How wide are the doors?	Wie breit sind die Türen? vee brait sind dee *tü*·ren
How many steps are there?	Wieviele Stufen sind es? vee·*fee*·le *shtoo*·fen sind es
Is there a lift/elevator?	Gibt es einen Aufzug? gipt es *ai*·nen owf·*tsook*
Is there somewhere I can sit down?	Kann ich mich hier irgendwo hinsetzen? kan ikh mikh heer ir·gent·*vaw* *hin*·ze·tsen
Could you help me cross this street safely?	Könnten Sie mich sicher über diese Straße bringen? *kern*·ten zee mikh *zi*·kher *ü*·ber *dee*·ze *shtrah*·se *bring*·en
Could you call me an accessible taxi?	Könnten Sie mir ein behindertengerechtes Taxi rufen? *kern*·ten zee meer ain be·*hin*·der·ten·ge·*rekht*·es *tak*·si *roo*·fen
crutches	Krücke f pl *krü*·ke
guide dog	Blindenhund m *blin*·den·hunt
walking frame	Gehwagen/Gehstock m *gay*·vah·gen/*gay*·shtok
wheelchair	Rollstuhl m *rol*·shtool
wheelchair ramp	Rollstuhlrampe f *rol*·shtool·ram·pe
wheelchair space	Rollstuhlplatz m *rol*·shtool·plats

Travel with Children

KEY PHRASES

Are children allowed?	Sind Kinder erlaubt?	zint *kin*·der er·*lowpt*
Is there a child discount?	Gibt es eine Kinderermäßigung?	gipt es *ai*·ne *kin*·der·er·may·si·gung
Is there a baby change room?	Gibt es einen Wickelraum?	gipt es *ai*·nen *vi*·kel·rowm

Is there a/an...? Gibt es ...? gipt es ...

baby change room	einen Wickelraum	*ai*·nen *vi*·kel·rowm
babysitter	einen Babysitter	ai·nen *bay*·bi·si·ter
child discount	eine Kinder-ermäßigung	*ai*·ne *kin*·der·er·may·si·gung
child-minding service	einen Babysitter-Service	*ai*·nen *bay*·bi·si·ter·*ser*·vis
children's menu	eine Kinderkarte	*ai*·ne *kin*·der·kar·te
family discount	eine Familien-ermäßigung	*ai*·ne fa·*mee*·li·en·er·may·si·gung
highchair	einen Kinderstuhl	*ai*·nen *kin*·der·shtool

Is there a park/ playground?	Gibt es einen Park/Spielplatz?	gipt es *ai*·nen park/*shpeel*·plats
I need a ...	Ich brauche ...	ikh *brow*·khe ...

baby seat	einen Babysitz	*ai*·nen *bay*·bi·zits
child seat	einen Kindersitz	*ai*·nen *kin*·der·zits
cot	ein Kinderbett	ain *kin*·der·bet
potty	ein Kinder-töpfchen	ain *kin*·der·terpf·khen
stroller	einen Kinderwagen	*ai*·nen *kin*·der·vah·gen

Do you sell ...?	Verkaufen Sie ...?	fer·*kow*·fen zee ...

baby wipes	feuchte Tücher	*foykh*·te *tü*·kher
disposable nappies/diapers	Einweg-Windeln	*ain*·vek·vin·deln
milk formula	Muttermilchersatz	*mu*·ter·milkh·er·zats
painkillers for infants	Schmerzmittel für Kinder	*shmerts*·mi·tel für *kin*·der

Can I breastfeed here?	Kann ich meinem Kind hier stillen?	kan ikh *mai*·nem kint heer *shtil*·len
Are children allowed?	Sind Kinder erlaubt?	zint *kin*·der er·*lowpt*
Is this suitable for (three)-year-old children?	Ist das für (drei) Jahre alte Kinder geeignet?	ist das für (drai) *yah*·re *al*·te *kin*·der ge·*aig*·net

See also **health** (p152), **talking with children** (p111).

SOCIAL

MEETING PEOPLE	102
INTERESTS	114
FEELINGS & OPINIONS	119
GOING OUT	124
ROMANCE	129
BELIEFS & CULTURE	134
SPORTS	136
OUTDOORS	142

Meeting People

KEY PHRASES

My name is ...	Mein Name ist ... pol Ich heiße ... inf	mine *nah*·me ist ... ikh *hai*·se ...
I'm from ...	Ich komme aus ...	ikh *ko*·me ows ...
I work in ...	Ich arbeite ...	ikh *ar*·bai·te ...
I'm ... years old.	Ich bin ... Jahre alt.	ikh bin ... *yah*·re alt
And you?	Und Ihnen/dir? pol/inf	unt *ee*·nen/deer

BASICS

Yes./No.	Ja./Nein. yah/nain
Please.	Bitte. *bi*·te
Thank you.	Danke. *dang*·ke
Thank you very much.	Vielen Dank. *fee*·len dangk
You're (very) welcome.	Bitte (sehr). *bi*·te (zair)
Excuse me./Sorry.	Entschuldigung. ent·*shul*·di·gung
Don't worry.	Macht nichts. makht nikhts

GREETINGS

Hello. (all of Germany)	Guten Tag. *goo*·ten tahk
Hello. (southern Germany)	Grüß Gott. grüs got
Hello. (Switzerland)	Grüezi. *grü*·e·tsi
Hello. (Austria)	Servus. *zer*·vus
Good morning.	Guten Morgen. *goo*·ten *mor*·gen
Good day/afternoon.	Guten Tag. *goo*·ten tahk
Good evening.	Guten Abend. *goo*·ten *ah*·bent
Hi.	Hallo. *ha*·lo
See you later.	Bis später. bis *shpay*·ter
Good night.	Gute Nacht. *goo*·te nakht
Goodbye.	Auf Wiedersehen. owf *vee*·der·zay·en
Bye.	Tschüss./Tschau. chüs/chow
Q **How are you?**	Wie geht es Ihnen/dir? **pol/inf** vee gayt es *ee*·nen/deer
A **Fine. And you?**	Danke, gut. Und Ihnen/dir? **pol/inf** *dang*·ke goot unt *ee*·nen/deer

☑ LANGUAGE TIP: TITLES & ADDRESSING PEOPLE

In the past *Fräulein froy*·lain was used to address all unmarried women regardless of age, but today the term is only used to address female children or teenagers. All women should be addressed using *Frau* frow. There's no equivalent of the English 'Ms' – use *Frau*. The equivalents of Sir and Madam, *Mein Herr* main her and *Meine Dame mai*·ne *dah*·me, are very old-fashioned. If you want to include academic titles when addressing somebody, these are combined with *Herr* and *Frau*, eg *Frau Professor* frow *pro*·fe·sor or *Herr Doktor* her *dok*·tor.

Mr	Herr	her
Mrs	Frau	frow
Miss	Frau/Fräulein	frow/*froy*·lain

Ⓠ **What's your name?**	Wie ist Ihr Name? pol vee ist eer *nah*·me Wie heißt du? inf vee haist doo
Ⓐ **My name is ...**	Mein Name ist ... pol main *nah*·me ist ... Ich heiße ... inf ikh *hai*·se ...
I'm pleased to meet you.	Angenehm. *an*·ge·naym
I'd like to introduce you to ...	Darf ich Ihnen/dir ... vorstellen? pol/inf darf ikh ee·nen/dir ... *fawr*·shte·len

This is ...	Das ist ...	das ist ...

This is my ...	Das ist mein/meine/mein ... m/f/n das ist main/*mai*·ne/main ...

child	Kind n	kint
colleague	Kollege m Kollegin f	ko·*lay*·ge ko·*lay*·gin
friend	Freund(in) m/f	froynt/*froyn*·din
husband	Mann m	man
partner	Partner(in) m/f	*part*·ner/*part*·ne·rin
wife	Frau f	frow

MAKING CONVERSATION

Do you live here?	Wohnen Sie hier? pol *vaw*·nen zee heer Wohnst du hier? inf vawnst doo heer
Where are you going?	Wohin fahren Sie? pol *vaw*·hin *fah*·ren zee Wohin fährst du? inf *vaw*·hin fairst doo
What are you doing?	Was machen Sie? pol vas *ma*·khen zee Was machst du? inf vas makhst doo
Nice day, isn't it?	Schönes Wetter heute! *sher*·nes *we*·ter *hoy*·te
Terrible weather today!	Furchtbares Wetter heute! *furkht*·bah·res *we*·ter *hoy*·te
Q **Do you like it here?**	Gefällt es Ihnen/dir hier? pol/inf ge·*felt* es *ee*·nen/deer heer
A **I love it here.**	Mir gefällt es hier sehr gut. meer ge·*felt* es heer zair goot

What do you think (about ...)?	Was denken Sie (über ...)? pol vas *deng*·ken zee (*ü*·ber ...) Was denkst du (über ...)? inf vas dengkst doo (*ü*·ber ...)
That's (beautiful), isn't it?	Ist das nicht (schön)? ist das nikht (shern)
Q **Are you here on holiday?**	Sind Sie hier im Urlaub? pol zint zee heer im *oor*·lowp Bist du hier im Urlaub? inf bist doo heer im *oor*·lowp
A **I'm here ...**	Ich bin hier ... ikh bin heer ...

for a holiday	im Urlaub	im *oor*·lowp
on business	auf Geschäftsreise	owf ge·*shefts*·rai·ze
to study	zum Studieren	tsum shtu·*dee*·ren
with my family	mit meiner Familie	mit *mai*·ner fa·*mee*·li·e
with my partner	mit meinem Partner m mit meiner Partnerin f	mit *mai*·nem *part*·ner mit *mai*·ner part·ne·rin

Q **How long are you here for?**	Für wie lange sind Sie hier? pol für vee *lang*·e zint zee heer Für wie lange bist du hier? inf für vee *lang*·e bist doo heer
A **I'm here for (four) days/weeks.**	Ich bin für (vier) Tage/Wochen hier. ikh bin für (feer) *tah*·ge/*vo*·khen heer

NATIONALITIES

Q **Where are you from?**	Woher kommen Sie? pol *vaw*·hair *ko*·men zee Woher kommst du? inf *vaw*·hair komst doo
A **I'm from (Australia).**	Ich komme aus (Australien). ikh *ko*·me ows (ows·*trah*·li·en)
A **I'm from (the USA).**	Ich komme aus (den USA). ikh *ko*·me ows (dayn oo·es·*ah*)
A **I'm from (New Zealand).**	Ich komme aus (Neuseeland). ikh *ko*·me ows (noy·*zay*·lant)

For more countries, see the **dictionary** (p197).

Ist das nicht schön?

ist das nikht shern

That's beautiful, isn't it?

LISTEN FOR

Hi/Hey!	hai/hei	Hey!
Toll/Geil!/ Super!/Spitze!	tol/gail/*zoo*·per/ *shpi*·tse	Great!
Kein Problem.	kain pro·*blaym*	No problem.
Klar!	klahr	Sure.
Vielleicht.	fi·*laikht*	Maybe.
Auf keinen Fall!	owf *kai*·nen fal	No way!
Das ist OK.	das ist o·*kay*	It's OK.
Alles klar.	a·les klahr	I'm OK.
Das war nur ein Scherz!	das vahr noor ain sherts	Just joking!
Guck mal!	guk mahl	Look!
Hör mal!	her mahl	Listen!
Hör dir das an!	her deer das an	Listen to this!
Ich bin so weit.	ikh bin zaw vait	I'm ready.
Bist du so weit?	bist doo zaw vait	Are you ready?
Einen Augenblick.	*ai*·nen ow·gen·*blik*	Just a minute.

AGE

Q **How old are you?**	Wie alt sind Sie? pol vee alt zint zee Wie alt bist du? inf vee alt bist doo
A **I'm ... years old.**	Ich bin ... Jahre alt. ikh bin ... *yah*·re alt
Too old!	Zu alt! tsoo alt
I'm younger than I look.	Ich bin jünger als ich aussehe. ikh bin *yüng*·er als ikh *ows*·zay·e

Q **How old is your daughter?**	Wie alt ist Ihre/deine Tochter? pol/inf vee alt ist *ee*·re/*dai*·ne *tokh*·ter
Q **How old is your son?**	Wie alt ist Ihr/dein Sohn? pol/inf vee alt ist eer/dain zawn
A **He's/She's ... years old.**	Er/Sie ist ... Jahre alt. air/zee ist ... *yah*·re alt

For your age, see **numbers & amounts** (p30).

OCCUPATIONS & STUDIES

Q **What's your occupation?**	Was machen Sie beruflich? pol vas *ma*·khen zee be·*roof*·likh Was machst du beruflich? inf vas makhst doo be·*roof*·likh
A **I'm a ...**	Ich bin ein/eine ... m/f ikh bin ain/*ain*·e ...

farmer	Bauer m Bäuerin f	*bow*·er *boy*·e·rin
student	Student m Studentin f	shtu·*dent* shtu·*den*·tin
teacher	Lehrer m Lehrerin f	*lay*·rer *lay*·re·rin
writer	Schriftsteller m Schriftstellerin f	*shrift*·shte·ler *shrift*·shte·le·rin

I work in IT.	Ich arbeite in der IT-Branche. ikh *ar*·bai·te in dair ai·*tee*·brang·she
I work in sales and marketing.	Ich arbeite im Verkauf und Marketing. ikh *ar*·bai·te im fer·*kowf* unt *mar*·ke·ting

I'm retired.	Ich bin Rentner/Rentnerin. m/f ikh bin *rent*·ner/*rent*·ne·rin
I'm self-employed.	Ich bin selbstständig. ikh bin *zelpst*·shten·dikh
I'm unemployed.	Ich bin arbeitslos. ikh bin *ar*·baits·laws
Q **What are you studying?**	Was studieren Sie? pol vas shtu·*dee*·ren zee Was studierst du? inf vas shtu·*deerst* doo
A **I'm studying (engineering).**	Ich studiere (Ingenieurwesen). ikh shtu·*dee*·re (in·zhe·*nyer*·vay·zen)

For more occupations and fields of study, see the **dictionary** (p197).

FAMILY

Q **Do you have a ...?**	Haben Sie einen/eine ...? m/f pol *hah*·ben zee *ai*·nen/*ai*·ne ... Hast du einen/eine ...? m/f inf hast doo *ai*·nen/*ai*·ne ...
A **I (don't) have a ...**	Ich habe (k)einen/(k)eine ... m/f ikh *hah*·be (k)*ai*·nen/(k)*ai*·ne ...
Q **Do you live with (your parents)?**	Leben Sie bei (Ihren Eltern)? pol *lay*·ben zee bai (*ee*·ren el·tern) Lebst du bei (deinen Eltern)? inf laypst doo bai (*dai*·nen el·tern)
A **I live with my ...**	Ich lebe bei meinem/meiner/meinen ... m/f/pl ikh *lay*·be bai *mai*·nem/*mai*·ner/*mai*·nen ...
This is my ...	Das ist mein/meine ... m/f das ist main/*mai*·ne ...

Q **Are you married?**	Sind Sie verheiratet? pol zint zee fer·*hai*·ra·tet Bist du verheiratet? inf bist doo fer·*hai*·ra·tet
A **I'm married.**	Ich bin verheiratet. ikh bin fer·*hai*·ra·tet
A **I live with someone.**	Ich lebe mit jemandem zusammen. ikh *lay*·be mit *yay*·man·dem tsu·*za*·men
A **I'm separated.**	Ich bin getrennt. ikh bin ge·*trent*
A **I'm single.**	Ich bin Single. ikh bin *sing*·el

TALKING WITH CHILDREN

When's your birthday?	Wann hast du Geburtstag? van hast doo ge·*burts*·tahk
Do you go to school or kindergarten?	Gehst du in die Schule oder in den Kindergarten? gayst doo in dee *shoo*·le *aw*·der in dayn *kin*·der·gar·ten
What grade are you in?	In welcher Klasse bist du? in *vel*·kher *kla*·se bist doo
Do you learn English?	Lernst du Englisch? lernst doo *eng*·lish
I come from very far away.	Ich komme von sehr weit her. ikh *ko*·me fon zair vait hair

FAREWELLS

Tomorrow is my last day here.	Morgen ist mein letzter Tag hier. *mor*·gen ist main *lets*·ter tahk heer

Q **What's your...?**	Wie ist Ihre/deine ...? pol/inf vee ist *ee*·re/*dai*·ne ...
A **Here's my ...**	Hier ist meine ... heer ist *mai*·ne ...

address	Adresse	a·*dre*·se
email address	E-mail-Adresse	ee·mayl·a·dre·se
mobile/cell number	Handynummer	*hen*·di·nu·mer
work number	Nummer bei der Arbeit	*nu*·mer bai dair *ar*·bait

For more on addresses, see **directions** (p53).

Are you on (Facebook)?	Haben Sie (Facebook)? pol *hah*·ben zee (*fays*·buk) Hast du (Facebook)? inf hast doo (*fays*·buk)
Keep in touch!	Melden Sie sich doch mal! pol *mel*·den zee zikh dokh mahl Melde dich mal! inf *mel*·de dikh mahl
It's been great meeting you.	Es war schön, Sie/dich kennen zu lernen. pol/inf es vahr shern zee/dikh *ke*·nen tsoo *ler*·nen

WELL-WISHING

Bless you! (when sneezing)	Gesundheit! ge·*zunt*·hait
Bon voyage!	Gute Reise! *goo*·te *rai*·ze
Cheers!	Prost! prawst

LANGUAGE TIP: FALSE FRIENDS

Many German words look like English words but have a completely different meaning, so be careful! Here are a few examples:

blank blank	shiny (not 'blank', which is *leer* leer)
Chef shef	boss (not 'chef', which is *Koch* kokh)
komisch *kaw*·mish	strange (not 'comical', which is *lustig* *lus*·tikh)
Konfektion kon·fekt·*tsyawn*	ready-made clothes (not 'confectionery', which is *Konfekt* kon·*fekt*)
sensibel zen·*zee*·bel	sensitive (not 'sensible', which is *vernünftig* fer·*nünf*·tikh)
Tip tip	advance information (not a monetary tip, which is *Trinkgeld* *trink*·gelt)

Good luck!	Viel Glück! feel glük
Happy birthday!	Herzlichen Glückwunsch zum Geburtstag! *herts*·li·khen *glük*·vunsh tsum ge·*burts*·tahk
What a pity!	Schade! *shah*·de
Congratulations!	Gratuliere! gra·too·*lee*·re

Interests

KEY PHRASES

What do you do in your spare time?	Was machen Sie in Ihrer Freizeit? pol	vas *ma*·khen zee in *ee*·rer *frai*·tsait
	Was machst du in deiner Freizeit? inf	vas makhst doo in *dai*·ner *frai*·tsait
Do you like ...?	Mögen Sie ...? pol Magst du ...? inf	*mer*·gen zee ... mahkst doo ...
I (don't) like ...	Ich mag (keinen/keine) ... m/f	ikh mahk (*kai*·nen/*kai*·ne) ...

COMMON INTERESTS

Q **What do you do in your spare time?**	Was machen Sie in Ihrer Freizeit? pol vas *ma*·khen zee in *ee*·rer *frai*·tsait Was machst du in deiner Freizeit? inf vas makhst doo in *dai*·ner *frai*·tsait
Q **Do you like ...?**	Mögen Sie ...? pol *mer*·gen zee ... Magst du ...? inf mahkst doo ...
A **I (don't) like art.**	Ich mag (keine) Kunst. ikh mahk (*kai*·ne) kunst
A **I (don't) like sport.**	Ich mag (keinen) Sport. ikh mahk (*kai*·nen) shport

I like (cooking).	Ich (koche) gern. ikh (*ko*·khe) gern
I don't like (hiking).	Ich (wandere) nicht gern. ikh (*van*·de·re) nikht gern
And you?	Und Sie/du? pol/inf unt zee/doo

For more interests, see **sports** (p136) and the **dictionary** (p197).

MUSIC

Do you like to listen to music?	Hören Sie gern Musik? pol *her*·ren zee gern mu·*zeek* Hörst du gern Musik? inf herst doo gern mu·*zeek*
Do you like to dance?	Tanzen Sie gern? pol *tan*·tsen zee gern Tanzt du gern? inf tantst doo gern
Do you like to go to concerts?	Gehen Sie gern in Konzerte? pol *gay*·en zee gern in kon·*tser*·te Gehst du gern in Konzerte? inf gayst doo gern in kon·*tser*·te
Do you like to sing?	Singen Sie gern? pol *zing*·en zee gern Singst du gern? inf zingkst doo gern
Do you play an instrument?	Spielen Sie ein Instrument? pol *shpee*·len zee ain in·stru·*ment* Spielst du ein Instrument? inf shpeelst doo ain in·stru·*ment*

Which bands/ singers do you like?	Welche Bands/Sänger mögen Sie? pol *vel*·khe bents/*zeng*·er mer·gen zee Welche Bands/Sänger magst du? inf *vel*·khe bents/*zeng*·er mahkst doo
Which music do you like?	Welche Art von Musik mögen Sie? pol *vel*·khe art fon mu·*zeek* mer·gen zee Welche Art von Musik magst du? inf *vel*·khe art fon mu·*zeek* mahkst doo

classical music	klassische Musik f	*kla*·si·she mu·*zeek*
electronic music	elektronische Musik f	e·lek·*traw*·ni·she mu·*zeek*
metal	Metal m	*me*·tel
pop	Popmusik f	*pop*·mu·zeek
rock	Rockmusik f	*rok*·mu·zeek
traditional music	traditionelle Musik f	tra·di·tsyo·*ne*·le mu·*zeek*
world music	Weltmusik f	*velt*·mu·zeek

Planning to go to a concert? See **buying tickets** (p40) and **going out** (p124).

CINEMA & THEATRE

I feel like going to a film/play.	Ich hätte Lust, ins Kino/Theater zu gehen. ikh *he*·te lust ins *kee*·no/te·*ah*·ter tsoo *gay*·en
What's showing at the cinema/theatre tonight?	Was gibt es heute im Kino/Theater? vas gipt es *hoy*·te im *kee*·no/te·*ah*·ter
Is it in English?	Ist es auf Englisch? ist es owf *eng*·lish
Is it dubbed?	Ist er synchronisiert? ist air zün·kro·nee·*zeert*
Does it have subtitles?	Hat es Untertitel? hat es *un*·ter·tee·tel
Have you seen ...?	Haben Sie ... gesehen? pol *hah*·ben zee ... ge·*zay*·en Hast du ... gesehen? inf hast doo ... ge·*zay*·en
Q **Who's in it?**	Wer spielt da mit? vair shpeelt dah mit
A **It stars ...**	Es ist mit ... es ist mit ...
Are those seats taken?	Sind diese Plätze besetzt? zint *dee*·ze *ple*·tse be·*zetst*
Q **Did you like it?**	Hat es Ihnen/dir gefallen? pol/inf hat es ee·nen/deer ge·fa·len
A **I thought it was excellent.**	Ich fand es ausgezeichnet. ikh fant es ows·ge·*tsaikh*·net
A **I thought it was OK.**	Ich fand es okay. ikh fant es o·*kay*
I thought it was long.	Ich fand es lang. ikh fant es lang

I (don't) like ...	Ich mag ... ikh mahk ...	
action movies	(keine) Actionfilme	(*kai*·ne) *ek*·shen·fil·me
animated films	(keine) Zeichen- trickfilme	(*kai*·ne) *tsai*·khen· trik·fil·me
comedies	(keine) Komödien	(*kai*·ne) ko·*mer*·di·en
documentaries	(keine) Dokumentar -filme	(*kai*·ne) do·ku·men·*tahr*· fil·me
crime/thrillers	(keine) Krimis	(*kai*·ne) *kri*·mis
German cinema	(keine) deutsche(n) Filme	(*kai*·ne) *doyt*·she(n) *fil*·me
horror movies	(keine) Horrorfilme	(*kai*·ne) *ho*·ror·fil·me
sci-fi	(keinen) Sciencefiction	(*kai*·nen) sai·ens·*fik*·shen

VOLUNTEERING

I'd like to volunteer my skills.	Ich möchte meine Mitarbeit als Freiwilliger anbieten. ikh *merkh*·te *mai*·ne *mit*·ar·bait als *frai*·vi·li·ger *an*·bee·ten
Are there any volunteer programmes available in the area?	Gibt es hier in der Region irgendwelche Freiwilligenprogramme? gipt es heer in dair re·*gyawn* *ir*·gent·vel·khe *frai*·vi·li·gen·pro·gra·me

Feelings & Opinions

KEY PHRASES

Are you ...?	Sind Sie ...? pol Bist du ...? inf	zint zee ... bist doo ...
I'm (not) ...	Ich bin (nicht) ...	ikh bin (nikht) ...
What did you think of it?	Wie hat es Ihnen/ dir gefallen? pol/inf	vee hat es *ee*·nen/ deer ge·*fa*·len
It is/was ...	Es ist/war ...	es ist/vahr ...

FEELINGS

Are you ...?
Sind Sie ...? pol
zint zee ...
Bist du ...? inf
bist doo ...

I'm (not) ...
Ich bin (nicht) ...
ikh bin (nikht) ...

annoyed	verärgert	fer·*er*·gert
disappointed	enttäuscht	en·*toysht*
happy	glücklich	*glük*·likh
sad	traurig	*trow*·rikh
tired	müde	*mü*·de

Are you (hungry)?
Haben Sie (Hunger)? pol
hah·ben zee (*hung*·er)
Hast du (Hunger)? inf
hast doo (*hung*·er)

I'm not (thirsty).
Ich habe kein (Durst).
ikh *hah*·be kain (durst)

Q **Are you (hot)?**	Ist Ihnen/dir (heiß)? pol/inf ist *ee*·nen/deer (hais)
A **I'm not (cold).**	Mir ist nicht (kalt). meer ist nikht (kalt).
Q **Are you worried?**	Machen Sie sich Sorgen? pol *ma*·khen zee zikh *zor*·gen Machst du dir Sorgen? inf makhst doo deer *zor*·gen
A **I'm (not) worried.**	Ich mache mir (keine) Sorgen. ikh *ma*·khe meer (*kai*·ne) *zor*·gen
I'm a little (sad).	Ich bin ein bisschen (traurig). ikh bin ain *bis*·khen (*trow*·rikh)
I'm terribly (sorry).	Es tut mir furchtbar (Leid). es toot meer *furkht*·bahr (lait)
I feel very (lucky).	Ich schätze mich sehr (glücklich). ikh *she*·tse mikh zair (*glük*·likh)

If you're not feeling well, see **health** (p152).

OPINIONS

Q **Did you like it?**	Hat es Ihnen/dir gefallen? pol/inf hat es *ee*·nen/deer ge·*fa*·len
Q **What did you think of it?**	Wie hat es Ihnen/dir gefallen? pol/inf vee hat es *ee*·nen/deer ge·*fa*·len
A **It is/was ...**	Es ist/war ... es ist/vahr ...

awful	schrecklich	*shrek*·likh
beautiful	schön	shern
boring	langweilig	*lang*·vai·likh
great	toll	tol
interesting	interessant	in·tre·*sant*
OK	okay	o·*kay*

POLITICS & SOCIAL ISSUES

Q **Who do you vote for?**	Wen wählen Sie? pol vayn *vay*·len zee Wen wählst du? inf vayn vaylst doo
A **I support the labour party.**	Ich unterstütze die Arbeiterpartei. ikh un·ter·*shtü*·tse dee *ar*·bai·ter·par·tai
A **I support the ... party.**	Ich unterstütze die ... Partei. ikh un·ter·*shtü*·tse dee ... par·*tai*

communist	kommunistische	ko·mu·*nis*·ti·she
conservative	konservative	*kon*·zer·va·tee·ve
democratic	demokratische	de·mo·*krah*·tish·e
green	grüne	*grün*·e
liberal	liberale	li·be·*rahl*·e
social democratic	sozial-demokratische	zo·*tsyahl*·de·mo·*krah*·tish·e
socialist	sozialistische	zo·tsya·*lis*·tish·e

Did you hear about ...?	Haben Sie von ... gehört? pol *hah*·ben zee fon ... ge·*hert* Hast du von ... gehört? inf hast doo fon ... ge·*hert*
Are you in favour of ...?	Sind Sie für ...? pol zint zee für ... Bist du für ...? inf bist doo für ...
Are you against ... ?	Sind Sie gegen ...? pol zint zee *gay*·gen ... Bist du gegen ...? inf bist doo *gay*·gen ...

LANGUAGE TIP: GERMAN IDIOMS

If you'd like to underline your opinions with some colourful language and impress your new German-speaking acquaintances, try your hand at these sayings:

Das versteht sich von selbst.	das ver·*shtet* zikh fon zelbst That goes without saying.
Damit können Sie bei mir nicht landen.	*da*·mit *ker*·nen zee bai meer nikht *lan*·den That cuts no ice with me.
Danach kräht kein Hahn.	da·*nakh* krayt kain han Nobody cares two hoots about it.
Bleiben Sie sachlich!	*blai*·ben zee *zakh*·likh Stick to the facts!
Das führt zu nichts.	das fürt tsu nikhts That will get you nowhere.
Das können Sie uns nicht erzählen!	das *kern*·en zee uns nikht er·*tsay*·len Tell us another one!
das letze Wort haben	das *lets*·te vort *hahb*·en to have the final say

Q **Do you agree with it?**	Sind Sie damit einverstanden? pol zint zee dah·*mit ain*·fer·shtan·den Bist du damit einverstanden? inf bist doo dah·*mit ain*·fer·shtan·den
A **I (don't) agree with that.**	Ich bin damit (nicht) einverstanden. ikh bin dah·*mit* (nikht) *ain*·fer·shtan·den

How do people feel about ...?	Was denken die Leute über ...? vas *deng*·ken dee *loy*·te *ü*·ber ...
economy	Wirtschaft f *virt*·shaft
environment	Umwelt f *um*·velt
health care	Gesundheitswesen n ge·*zunt*·haits·vay·zen
immigration	Einwanderung f *ain*·van·de·rung
war in ...	Krieg in ... m kreek in ...

THE ENVIRONMENT

Where can I recycle this?	Wo kann ich das recyceln? vaw kan ikh das ri·*sai*·keln
Is there a ... problem here?	Gibt es hier ein Problem mit ...? gipt es heer ain pro·*blaym* mit ...
What should be done about ...?	Was sollte man gegen ... tun? vas *zol*·te man *gay*·gen ... toon
climate change	Klimawandel m *klee*·ma·wan·del
nuclear energy	Atomenergie f a·*tawm*·e·ner·gee
pollution	Umweltverschmutzung f *um*·velt·fer·shmu·tsung
sustainable energy	nachhaltige Energie f *nahkh*·hal·ti·ge ay·ner·*gee*
Is this a protected forest?	Ist das ein geschützter Wald? ist das ain ge·*shüts*·ter valt
Is this a protected species?	Ist das eine geschützte Art? ist das *ai*·ne ge·*shüts*·te art

Going Out

KEY PHRASES

What's on tonight?	Was ist heute Abend los?	vas ist *hoy*·te *ah*·bent laws
When shall we meet?	Wann sollen wir uns treffen?	van *zo*·len veer uns *tre*·fen
Where shall we meet?	Wo sollen wir uns treffen?	vaw *zo*·len veer uns *tre*·fen

WHERE TO GO

What's there to do in the evenings?	Was kann man abends unternehmen? vas kan man *ah*·bents un·ter·*nay*·men
What's on today?	Was ist heute los? vas ist *hoy*·te laws
What's on tonight?	Was ist heute Abend los? vas ist *hoy*·te *ah*·bent laws
I feel like going out somewhere.	Ich hätte Lust, auszugehen. ikh *he*·te lust *ows*·tsu·gay·en
Where are the ...?	Wo sind die ...? vaw zint dee ...

clubs	Klubs	klups
gay venues	Schwulen- und Lesbenkneipen	*shvoo*·len unt *les*·ben·knai·pen
places to eat	Restaurants	res·to·*rangs*
pubs	Kneipen	*knai*·pen

Is there a local entertainment guide?	Gibt es einen Veranstaltungskalender? gipt es *ai*·nen fer·*an*·shtal·tungks·ka·len·der
Is there a local gay guide?	Gibt es einen Führer für die Schwulen- und Lesbenszene? gipt es *ai*·nen *fü*·rer für dee *shvoo*·len unt *les*·bens·tsay·ne
I feel like going to a/the ...	Ich hätte Lust, ... zu gehen. ikh *he*·te lust ... tsoo *gay*·en

ballet	zum Ballett	tsum ba·*let*
bar/pub	in eine Kneipe	in *ai*·ne *knai*·pe
cafe	in ein Café	in ain ka·*fay*
concert	in ein Konzert	in ain kon·*tsert*
movies	ins Kino	ins *kee*·no
nightclub	in einen Nachtklub	in *ai*·nen *nakht*·klup
opera	in die Oper	in dee *aw*·per
restaurant	in ein Restaurant	in ain res·to·*rang*
theatre	ins Theater	ins te·*ah*·ter

For more on bars, drinks and partying, see **eating out** (p162).

INVITATIONS

What are you doing right now?	Was machst du jetzt gerade? vas makhst doo jetst ge·*rah*·de
What are you doing this evening?	Was machst du heute Abend? vas makhst doo *hoy*·te *ah*·bent
What are you doing this weekend?	Was machst du am Wochenende? vas makhst doo am *vo*·khen·en·de

Would you like to go (for a) ...?	Möchtest du ... gehen? *merkh*·test doo ... *gay*·en

coffee	einen Kaffee trinken	*ai*·nen *ka*·fay *tring*·ken
dancing	tanzen	*tan*·tsen
drink	etwas trinken	*et*·vas *tring*·ken
meal	essen	e·sen

Do you want to come to the ... concert with me?	Möchtest du mit mir zum ...-konzert gehen? *merkh*·test doo mit meer tsum ...·kon·*tsert* *gay*·en
We're having a party.	Wir machen eine Party. veer *ma*·khen *ai*·ne *par*·ti
Would you like to come?	Hättest du Lust zu kommen? *he*·test doo lust tsoo *ko*·men

RESPONDING TO INVITATIONS

Sure!	Klar! klahr
Yes, I'd love to.	Ja, gerne. yah *ger*·ne
That's very kind of you.	Das ist sehr nett von dir/euch. **sg/pl inf** das ist zair net fon deer/oykh
Where shall we go?	Wo sollen wir hingehen? vaw *zo*·len veer *hin*·gay·en
No, I'm afraid I can't.	Nein, es tut mir Leid, aber ich kann nicht. nain es toot meer lait *ah*·ber ikh kan nikht
What about tomorrow?	Wie wäre es mit morgen? vee *vair*·re es mit *mor*·gen

ARRANGING TO MEET

(Q) **When shall we meet?**	Wann sollen wir uns treffen? van *zo*·len veer uns *tre*·fen
(A) **Let's meet at (eight) o'clock.**	Wir treffen uns um (acht) Uhr. veer *tre*·fen uns um (akht) oor
(Q) **Where shall we meet?**	Wo sollen wir uns treffen? vaw *zo*·len veer uns *tre*·fen
(A) **Let's meet at the entrance.**	Wir treffen uns am Eingang. veer *tre*·fen uns am *ain*·gang
I'll see you then.	Bis dann! bis dan
I'll pick you up.	Ich hole dich ab. ikh *haw*·le dikh ap

Wo sollen wir uns treffen?

vaw *zo*·len veer uns *tre*·fen

Where shall we meet?

I'll be coming later. Where will you be?	Ich komme später. Wo wirst du sein? ikh *ko*·me *shpay*·ter vaw virst doo zain
If I'm not there by (nine), don't wait for me.	Wenn ich bis (neun) Uhr nicht da bin, warte nicht auf mich. ven ikh bis (noyn) oor nikht dah bin *var*·te nikht owf mikh
See you later/tomorrow.	Bis später/morgen. bis *shpay*·ter/*mor*·gen
I'm looking forward to it.	Ich freue mich darauf. ikh *froy*·e mikh da·*rowf*
Sorry I'm late.	Es tut mir Leid, dass ich zu spät komme. es toot meer lait das ikh tsoo shpayt *ko*·me
Never mind.	Macht nichts. makht nikhts

DRUGS

I don't take drugs.	Ich nehme keine Drogen. ikh *nay*·me *kai*·ne *draw*·gen
I take ... occasionally.	Ich nehme ab und zu ... ikh *nay*·me ap unt tsoo ...
Do you want to have a smoke?	Wollen wir einen Joint rauchen? *vo*·len veer *ai*·nen dzhoynt *row*·khen
Do you have a light?	Haben Sie Feuer? pol *hah*·ben zee *foy*·er Hast du Feuer? inf hast doo *foy*·er

If the police are talking to you about drugs, see **police** (p150) for useful phrases.

Romance

KEY PHRASES

Would you like to do something tomorrow?	Hättest du Lust, morgen was zu unternehmen?	*he*·test doo lust *mor*·gen vas tsoo un·ter·*nay*·men
I love you.	Ich liebe dich.	ikh *lee*·be dikh
Leave me alone!	Lass mich zufrieden!	las mikh tsu·*free*·den

ASKING SOMEONE OUT

Q **Would you like to do something tomorrow?**	Hättest du Lust, morgen was zu unternehmen? *he*·test doo lust *mor*·gen vas tsoo un·ter·*nay*·men
A **Yes, I'd love to.**	Ja, gerne. yah *ger*·ne
A **Sure, thanks.**	Klar! Das wäre nett. klahr das *vair*·re net
A **I'm busy.**	Ich habe keine Zeit. ikh *hah*·be *kai*·ne tsait
Where would you like to go tonight?	Wo würdest du heute Abend gerne hingehen? vaw *vür*·dest doo *hoy*·te *ah*·bent *ger*·ne *hin*·gay·en
Where would you like to go on the weekend?	Wo würdest du am Wochenende gerne hingehen? vaw *vür*·dest doo am *vo*·khen·en·de *ger*·ne *hin*·gay·en

PICK-UP LINES

Haven't we met before?	Kennen wir uns nicht von irgendwoher? *ke*·nen veer uns nikht fon *ir*·gent·vo·*hair*
Would you like a drink?	Möchtest du etwas trinken? *merkh*·test doo *et*·vas *tring*·ken
Shall we get some fresh air?	Sollen wir ein bisschen an die frische Luft gehen? *zo*·len veer ain *bis*·khen an dee *fri*·she luft *gay*·en
You have a beautiful personality.	Du hast eine wundervolle Persönlichkeit. doo hast *ai*·ne *vun*·der·vo·ler per·*zern*·likh·kait
You have beautiful eyes.	Du hast schöne Augen. doo hast *sher*·ne *ow*·gen
You have a beautiful body.	Du hast einen schönen Körper. doo hast *ai*·nen *sher*·nen *ker*·per

REJECTIONS

I'm here with my boyfriend.	Ich bin mit meinem Freund hier. ikh bin mit *mai*·nem froynt heer
I'm here with my girlfriend.	Ich bin mit meiner Freundin hier. ikh bin mit *mai*·ner *froyn*·din heer

LANGUAGE TIP: M BEFORE F

In this book, masculine forms appear before the feminine forms. If letters have been added to the masculine word to form the feminine word (often *-in*), these will appear in brackets. Where the change involves more than the addition of *-in*, two words are given, separated by a slash. The neuter form – where applicable – is mentioned last. See also **gender** (p18) in the **grammar** chapter.

Excuse me, I have to go now.	Tut mir Leid, ich muss jetzt gehen. toot meer lait ikh mus yetst *gay*·en
No, thank you.	Nein, danke. nain *dang*·ke
I'd rather not.	Lieber nicht. *lee*·ber nikht
Perhaps some other time.	Vielleicht ein andermal. fi·*laikht* ain *an*·der·mahl
I'm not interested.	Ich bin nicht interessiert. ikh bin nikht in·tre·*seert*
Leave me alone!	Lass mich zufrieden! las mikh tsu·*free*·den

GETTING CLOSER

I like you very much.	Ich mag dich sehr. ikh mahk dikh zair
I'm interested in you.	Ich interessiere mich für dich. ikh in·tre·see·re mikh für dikh
Do you like me too?	Magst du mich auch? mahkst doo mikh owkh

Will you take me home?	Kannst du mich nach Hause bringen? kanst doo mikh nahkh *how*·ze *bring*·en
Do you want to come inside for a while?	Möchtest du noch kurz mit reinkommen? *merkh*·test doo nokh kurts mit *rain*·ko·men
You're very nice.	Du bist sehr nett. doo bist zair net
You're great.	Du bist toll. doo bist tol
Can I stay over?	Kann ich hier übernachten? kan ikh heer ü·ber·*nakh*·ten
Can I see you again?	Kann ich dich wiedersehen? kan ikh dikh *vee*·der·zay·en

SEX

Kiss me.	Küss mich. küs mikh
I want to make love to you.	Ich möchte mit dir schlafen. ikh *merkh*·te mit deer *shlah*·fen
Let's go to bed!	Gehen wir ins Bett! *gay*·en veer ins bet
Touch me here.	Berühr mich hier! be·*rür* mikh heer
Q **Do you like this?**	Magst du das? mahkst doo das
A **I (don't) like that.**	Das mag ich (nicht). das mahk ikh (nikht)
Do you have (a condom)?	Hast du (ein Kondom)? hast doo (ain kon·*dawm*)

Let's use (a condom).	Lass uns (ein Kondom) benutzen. las uns (ain kon·*dawm*) be·*nu*·tsen
I won't do it without protection.	Ohne Kondom mache ich es nicht. *aw*·ne kon·*dawm ma*·khe ikh es nikht
Please (don't) stop!	Bitte hör (nicht) auf. *bi*·te her (nikht) owf
I think we should stop now.	Ich denke, wir sollten jetzt aufhören. ikh *deng*·ke veer *zol*·ten yetst *owf*·her·ren
Oh yeah!	Oh ja! aw yah
That's great.	Das ist geil. das ist gail
Easy tiger!	Sachte! *zakh*·te
That was amazing.	Das war fantastisch. das vahr fan·*tas*·tish

LOVE

I think we're good together.	Ich glaube, wir passen gut zueinander. ikh *glow*·be veer *pa*·sen goot tsu·ai·*nan*·der
I love you.	Ich liebe dich. ikh *lee*·be dikh
Will you go out with me?	Willst du mit mir gehen? vilst doo mit meer *gay*·en
Will you marry me?	Willst du mich heiraten? vilst doo mikh *hai*·ra·ten

Beliefs & Culture

KEY PHRASES

What's your religion?	Was ist Ihre/deine Religion? pol/inf	vas ist *ee*·re/ *dai*·ne re·li·*gyawn*
I'm (not) ...	Ich bin (kein/ keine) ... m/f	ikh bin (kain/ *kai*·ne) ...
I'm sorry, it's against my beliefs.	Es tut mir Leid, das ist gegen meine Anschauungen.	es toot meer lait das ist *gay*·gen *mai*·ne *an*·show·ung·en

RELIGION

Ⓠ **What's your religion?**
Was ist Ihre/deine Religion? pol/inf
vas ist *ee*·re/*dai*·ne re·li·*gyawn*

Ⓐ **I'm (not) ...**
Ich bin (kein/keine) ... m/f
ikh bin (kain/*kai*·ne) ...

agnostic	Agnostiker(in) m/f	a·*gnos*·ti·ker/ a·*gnos*·ti·ke·rin
Buddhist	Buddhist(in) m/f	bu·*dist*/bu·*dis*·tin
Catholic	Katholik(in) m/f	ka·to·*leek*/ ka·to·*lee*·kin
Christian	Christ(in) m/f	krist/*kris*·tin
Hindu	Hindu m&f	*hin*·du
Jewish	Jude/Jüdin m/f	*yoo*·de/*yü*·din
Muslim	Moslem/Moslime m/f	*mos*·lem/ mos·*lee*·me

Ⓐ **I'm (not) religious.**	Ich bin (nicht) religiös. ikh bin (nikht) re·li·*gyers*
Ⓐ **I (don't) believe in God.**	Ich glaube (nicht) an Gott. ikh *glow*·be (nikht) an got
Where can I ...?	Wo kann ich ...? vaw kan ikh ...

attend mass	eine Messe besuchen	*ai*·ne *me*·se be·*zoo*·khen
attend a service	einen Gottesdienst besuchen	*ai*·nen *go*·tes·deenst be·*zoo*·khen
pray	beten	*bay*·ten
worship	meine Andacht verrichten	*mai*·ne *an*·dakht fer·*rikh*·ten

CULTURAL DIFFERENCES

Is this a local custom?	Ist das ein örtlicher Brauch? ist das ain *ert*·li·kher browkh
I'm not used to this.	Das ist ganz ungewohnt für mich. das ist gants *un*·ge·vawnt für mikh
I'll try it.	Ich versuche es. ikh fer·*zoo*·khe es
I'm sorry, I didn't mean to do/say anything wrong.	Es tut mir Leid, ich wollte nichts Falsches tun/sagen. es toot meer lait ikh *vol*·te nikhts *fal*·shes toon/*zah*·gen
I'm sorry, it's against my beliefs.	Es tut mir Leid, das ist gegen meine Anschauungen. es toot meer lait das ist *gay*·gen *mai*·ne *an*·show·ung·en

Sports

KEY PHRASES

What sport do you play?	Was für Sport treiben Sie? pol Was für Sport treibst du? inf	vas für shport *trai*·ben zee vas für shport traipst doo
Who's your favourite team?	Was ist Ihre/deine Lieblings-mannschaft? pol/inf	vas ist *ee*·re/*dai*·ne *leep*·lingks·man·shaft
What's the score?	Wie steht es?	vee shtayt es

SPORTING INTERESTS

Q **What sport do you play?**	Was für Sport treiben Sie? pol vas für shport *trai*·ben zee Was für Sport treibst du? inf vas für shport traipst doo
A **I play ...**	Ich spiele ... ikh *shpee*·le ...
A **I follow ...**	Ich interessiere mich für ... ikh in·tre·*see*·re mikh für ...

basketball	Basketball	*bahs*·ket·bal
football/soccer	Fußball	*foos*·bal
ice hockey	Eishockey	*ais*·ho·ki
tennis	Tennis	*te*·nis

For more sports, see the **dictionary** (p197).

Do you like (sport)?	Mögen Sie (Sport)? pol *mer*·gen zee (shport) Magst du (Sport)? inf mahkst doo (shport)
Yes, very much.	Ja, sehr. yah zair
Not really.	Nicht besonders. nikht be·*zon*·ders
I like watching it.	Ich sehe es mir gerne an. ikh *zay*·e es meer *ger*·ne an
Who's your favourite sportsperson?	Wer ist Ihr/dein Lieblingssportler? pol/inf vair ist eer/dain *leep*·lingks·shport·ler
Who's your favourite team?	Was ist Ihre/deine Lieblingsmannschaft? pol/inf vas ist *ee*·re/*dai*·ne *leep*·lingks·man·shaft
Can you play (football/soccer)?	Spielen Sie (Fußball)? pol *shpee*·len zee (*foos*·bal) Spielst du (Fußball)? inf *shpeelst* doo (*foos*·bal)

GOING TO A GAME

Would you like to go to a game?	Möchten Sie zu einem Spiel gehen? pol *merkh*·ten zee tsoo *ai*·nem shpeel *gay*·en Möchtest du zu einem Spiel gehen? inf merkh·test doo tsoo *ai*·nem shpeel *gay*·en

Who are you supporting?	Wen unterstützen Sie? pol vayn un·ter·*shtü*·tsen zee Wen unterstützt du? inf vayn un·ter·*shtütst* doo
Who's playing?	Wer spielt? vair speelt
Who's winning?	Wer gewinnt? vair ge·*vint*
What a ...!	Was für ...! vas für ...

goal	ein Tor	ain tawr
hit	ein Treffer	ain *tre*·fer
kick	ein Schuss	ain shus
pass	ein Pass	ain pas

What's the score?	Wie steht es? vee shtayt es
That was a bad/great game!	Das war ein schlechtes/tolles Spiel! das vahr ain *shlekh*·tes/*to*·les shpeel
What was the final score?	Was war das Endergebnis? vas vahr das *ent*·er·gayp·nis

PLAYING SPORT

Q **Do you want to play?**	Möchten Sie mitspielen? pol *merkh*·ten zee *mit*·shpee·len Möchtest du mitspielen? inf *merkh*·test doo *mit*·shpee·len
A **Yes, that'd be great.**	Ja, das wäre toll. yah das *vair*·re tol

Ⓐ I'm sorry, I can't.	Es tut mir Leid, ich kann nicht. es toot meer lait ikh kan nikht
Ⓐ I have an injury.	Ich habe eine Verletzung. ikh *hah*·be *ai*·ne fer·*le*·tsung
Can I join in?	Kann ich mitspielen? kan ikh *mit*·shpee·len
Your point.	Ihr/Dein Punkt. pol/inf eer/dain pungkt
My point.	Mein Punkt. main pungkt
Kick/Pass it to me!	Hierher! *heer*·hair
Thanks for the game.	Vielen Dank für das Spiel. *fee*·len dangk für das shpeel
Where's the nearest gym?	Wo ist das nächste Fitness-Studio? vaw ist das *naykhs*·te *fit*·nes·shtoo·di·o
Where's the nearest swimming pool?	Wo ist das nächste Schwimmbad? vaw ist das *naykhs*·te *shvim*·baht
Where's the nearest tennis court?	Wo ist der nächste Tennisplatz? vaw ist dair *naykhs*·te *te*·nis·plats
Where's the best place to jog/run around here?	Wo kann man hier am besten joggen/laufen? vaw kan man heer am *bes*·ten *dzho*·gen/*low*·fen
Where are the change rooms?	Wo sind die Umkleideräume? vaw zint dee *um*·klai·de·roy·me

What's the charge per hour/day?	Wie viel kostet es pro Stunde/Tag? vee feel *kos*·tet es praw *shtun*·de/tahk
What's the charge per game/visit?	Wie viel kostet es pro Spiel/Besuch? vee feel *kos*·tet es praw shpeel/be·*zookh*
Can I hire a ...?	Kann ich ...? kan ikh ...

ball	einen Ball leihen	*ai*·nen bal *lai*·en
bicycle	ein Fahrrad leihen	ain *fahr*·raht *lai*·en
court	einen Platz mieten	*ai*·nen plats *mee*·ten
racquet	einen Schläger leihen	*ai*·nen *shlay*·ger *lai*·en

FOOTBALL/SOCCER

Who plays for (Bayern München)?	Wer spielt für (Bayern München)? vair shpeelt für (*bai*·ern *mün*·khen)
Which team is at the top of the league?	Welcher Verein steht an der Tabellenspitze? *vel*·kher fer·*ain* shtayt an dair ta·*be*·len·shpi·tse
What a terrible team!	Was für eine furchtbare Mannschaft! vas für *ai*·ne *furkht*·bah·re *man*·shaft
She's a great player.	Sie ist eine tolle Spielerin. zee ist ain·e *to*·le *shpee*·ler·in

☑ CULTURE TIP: KÖNIG FUSSBALL

The king of German amateur and professional sports is *König Fußball* *ker*·nikh *foos*·bal (king football). Football (or soccer) is played at thousands of amateur clubs known as *Fußballvereine* *foos*·bal·fe·rai·ne. Germans are passionate about the game and professional matches draw around 25,000 fans. One of the longest words in the German language is also from the football sphere. Try getting your tongue around this: *Fußballweltmeisterschaftsqualifikationsspiel* *foos*·bal·*velt*·mais·ter·shafts·kva·li·fi·ka·*tsyawns*·s hpeel (FIFA World Cup qualifying game).

He played brilliantly in the match against (Italy).	Im Spiel gegen (Italien) hat er fantastisch gespielt. im shpeel gay·gen (i·*tah*·li·en) hat air fan·*tas*·tish ge·*shpeelt*
She scored (three) goals.	Sie hat (drei) Tore geschossen. zee hat (drai) *taw*·re ge·*sho*·sen
corner	Ecke f e·ke
free kick	Freistoß m *frai*·shtaws
goalkeeper	Torhüter(in) m/f *tawr*·hü·ter/*tawr*·hü·te·rin
offside	Abseits n *ap*·zaits
penalty	Strafstoß m *shtrahf*·shtaws
3–1	drai tsoo ains drei zu eins

Outdoors

KEY PHRASES

Do we need a guide?	Brauchen wir einen Führer?	*brow*·khen veer *ai*·nen *fü*·rer
I'm lost.	Ich habe mich verlaufen.	ikh *hah*·be mikh fer·*low*·fen
What's the weather like?	Wie ist das Wetter?	vee ist das *ve*·ter

HIKING

Where can I ...?

Wo kann ich ...?
vaw kan ikh ...

buy supplies	Vorräte einkaufen	*fawr*·ray·te *ain*·kow·fen
find out about hiking trails	Informationen über Wanderwege bekommen	in·for·ma·*tsyaw*·nen ü·ber *van*·der·vay·ge be·*ko*·men
find someone who knows this area	jemanden finden, der die Gegend kennt	*yay*·man·den *fin*·den dair dee *gay*·gent kent
get a map	eine Karte bekommen	*ai*·ne *kar*·te be·*ko*·men
hire hiking gear	Wanderausrüstung leihen	*van*·der·ows·rüs·tung *lai*·en

CULTURE TIP: POOLS & SPAS

Aquatic pursuits are popular in Germany and it's hard to find a town that doesn't have a public *Schwimmbad* *shvim*·baht (swimming pool). Often there's a *Hallenbad* *ha*·len·baht (indoor pool) alongside the *Freibad* *frai*·baht (outdoor pool). Spas are popular too, with people seeking to cure a variety of conditions. The most famous spa town in Germany is called Baden Baden *bah*·den *bah*·den. This double-barrelled name represents both the name of the surrounding region and the German word for bathing.

Do we need to take food/water?	Müssen wir Essen/Wasser mitnehmen? *mü*·sen veer *e*·sen/*va*·ser *mit*·nay·men
How long is the trail?	Wie lang ist der Weg? vee lang ist dair vayk
How high is the climb?	Wie hoch führt die Klettertour hinauf? vee hawkh fürt dee *kle*·ter·toor hi·*nowf*
Do we need a guide?	Brauchen wir einen Führer? *brow*·khen veer *ai*·nen *fü*·rer
Are there guided treks?	Gibt es geführte Wanderungen? gipt es ge·*für*·te *van*·de·rung·en
Is it safe?	Ist es ungefährlich? ist es *un*·ge·fair·likh
Is there a hut there?	Gibt es dort eine Hütte? gipt es dort *ai*·ne *hü*·te
When does it get dark?	Wann wird es dunkel? van virt es *dung*·kel
Is the track (well-) marked?	Ist der Weg (gut) markiert? ist dair vayk (goot) mar·*keert*

Is the track open/ scenic?	Ist der Weg offen/schön? ist dair vayk *o*·fen/shern
Which is the easiest route?	Welches ist die einfachste Route? *vel*·khes ist dee *ain*·fakhs·te *roo*·te
Which is the most interesting route?	Welches ist die interessanteste Route? *vel*·khes ist dee in·te·re·*san*·tes·te *roo*·te
Where's the nearest village?	Wo ist das nächste Dorf? vaw ist das *naykhs*·te *dorf*
Where have you come from?	Wo kommen Sie gerade her? pol vaw *ko*·men zee ge·*rah*·de hair Wo kommst du gerade her? inf vaw komst doo ge·*rah*·de hair
How long did it take?	Wie lange hat das gedauert? vee *lang*·e hat das ge·*dow*·ert
Does this path go to ...?	Führt dieser Weg nach ...? fürt *dee*·zer vayk nahkh ...
Can we go through here?	Können wir hier durchgehen? *ker*·nen veer heer *durkh*·gay·en
Is the water OK to drink?	Kann man das Wasser trinken? kan man das *va*·ser *tring*·ken
I'm lost.	Ich habe mich verlaufen. ikh *hah*·be mikh fer·*low*·fen

AT THE BEACH

Where's the best/ nearest beach?	Wo ist der beste/nächste Strand? vaw ist dair *bes*·te/*naykhs*·te shtrant
Do we have to pay?	Müssen wir bezahlen? *mü*·sen veer be·*tsah*·len

LOOK FOR

Schwimmen verboten!	shvi·men fer·*baw*·ten	No Swimming!
Sturmwarnung!	shturm·*var*·nunk	Storm Warning!

Is it safe to dive/swim here?	Kann man hier gefahrlos tauchen/schwimmen? kan man heer ge·*fahr*·laws *tow*·khen/*shvi*·men
What time is high/low tide?	Wann ist Flut/Ebbe? van ist floot/*e*·be
How much for a chair/umbrella?	Was kostet ein Stuhl/Schirm? vas *kos*·tet ain shtool/shirm

WEATHER

Q **What's the weather like?**	Wie ist das Wetter? vee ist das *ve*·ter
A **It's ...**	Es ist ... es ist ...

cloudy	wolkig	*vol*·kikh
cold	kalt	kalt
freezing	eiskalt	*ais*·kalt
hot	heiß	hais
raining	regnerisch	*rayg*·ne·rish
sunny	sonnig	*zo*·nikh
warm	warm	varm
windy	windig	*vin*·dikh

It's snowing.	Es schneit. es shnait
What's the weather forecast?	Wie ist der Wetterbericht? vee ist dair *ve*·ter·be·rikht
Will it be ... tomorrow?	Wird es morgen ... sein? virt es *mor*·gen ... zain
Will it be snowing tomorrow?	Wird es morgen schneien? virt es *mor*·gen *shnai*·en
Where can I buy an umbrella?	Wo kann ich einen Regenschirm kaufen? vaw kan ikh *ai*·nen *ray*·gen·shirm *kow*·fen

FLORA & FAUNA

What ... is that?	Wie heißt ...? vee haist ...

animal	dieses Tier	*dee*·zes teer
bird	dieser Vogel	*dee*·zer *faw*·gel
flower	diese Blume	*dee*·ze *bloo*·me
plant	diese Pflanze	*dee*·ze *pflan*·tse
tree	dieser Baum	*dee*·zer bowm

Is it common?	Ist es weit verbreitet? ist es vait fer·*brai*·tet
Is it dangerous?	Ist es gefährlich? ist es ge·*fair*·likh
Is it protected?	Ist es geschützt? ist es ge·*shütst*
Can you eat it?	Kann man es essen? kan man es *e*·sen

For geographical and agricultural terms and names of animals and plants, see the **dictionary** (p197).

SAFE TRAVEL

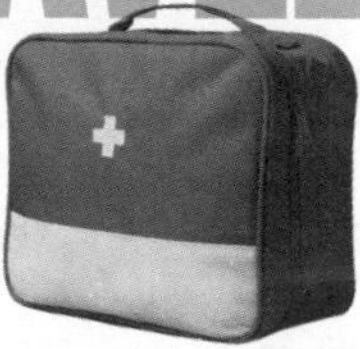

EMERGENCIES 148

POLICE 150

HEALTH 152

Emergencies

KEY PHRASES

Help!	Hilfe!	*hil*·fe
There's been an accident.	Es gab einen Unfall.	es gahp *ai*·nen *un*·fal
It's an emergency!	Es ist ein Notfall!	es ist ain *nawt*·fal

Help!	Hilfe! *hil*·fe
Stop!	Halt! halt
Go away!	Gehen Sie weg! *gay*·en zee vek
Thief!	Dieb! deeb
Fire!	Feuer! *foy*·er
Watch out!	Vorsicht! for·*zikht*
It's an emergency!	Es ist ein Notfall! es ist ain *nawt*·fal
There's been an accident.	Es gab einen Unfall. es gahp *ai*·nen *un*·fal
Do you have a first-aid kit?	Haben Sie einen Erste-Hilfe-Kasten? *hah*·ben zee *ai*·nen ayr·ste·*hil*·fe·ka·sten

LOOK FOR

Polizei	po·li·*tsai*	Police
Polizeirevier	po·li·*tsai*·re·veer	Police Station
Unfallstation	un·fal·sta·*tsyawn*	Casualty

Call the police!	Rufen Sie die Polizei! *roo*·fen zee dee po·li·*tsai*
Call a doctor!	Rufen Sie einen Arzt! *roo*·fen zee *ai*·nen artst
Call an ambulance!	Rufen Sie einen Krankenwagen! *roo*·fen zee *ai*·nen *krang*·ken·vah·gen
Could you please help me/us?	Könnten Sie mir/uns bitte helfen? *kern*·ten zee meer/uns *bi*·te *hel*·fen
Where are the toilets?	Wo ist die Toilette? vo ist dee to·a·*le*·te
I have to use the telephone.	Ich muss das Telefon benutzen. ikh mus das te·le·*fawn* be·*nu*·tsen
I'm lost.	Ich habe mich verirrt. ikh *hah*·be mikh fer·*irt*

Police

KEY PHRASES

Where's the police station?	Wo ist das Polizeirevier?	vaw ist das po·li·*tsai*·re·veer
I want to contact my embassy.	Ich möchte mich mit meiner Botschaft in Verbindung setzen.	ikh *merkh*·te mikh mit *mai*·ner *bawt*·shaft in fer·*bin*·dung *ze*·tsen
My handbag was stolen.	Man hat mir meine Handtasche gestohlen.	man hat meer *mai*·ne *hant*·ta·she ge·*shtaw*·len

Where's the police station?	Wo ist das Polizeirevier? vaw ist das po·li·*tsai*·re·veer
I want to report an offence.	Ich möchte eine Straftat melden. ikh *merkh*·te *ai*·ne *shtrahf*·taht *mel*·den
I've been raped.	Ich bin vergewaltigt worden. ikh bin fer·ge·*val*·tikht *vor*·den
He has been assaulted.	Er ist angegriffen worden. air ist *an*·ge·gri·fen *vor*·den
She has been robbed.	Sie ist bestohlen worden. zee ist be·*shtaw*·len *vor*·den
It was him/her.	Es war er/sie. es vahr air/zee
My ... was/were stolen.	Man hat mir ... gestohlen. man hat meer ... ge·*shtaw*·len

I've lost my... | Ich habe ... verloren.
ikh *hah*·be ... fer·*law*·ren

bags	meine Reisetaschen	*mai*·ne *rai*·ze·ta·shen
handbag	meine Handtasche	*mai*·ne *hant*·ta·she
money	mein Geld	main gelt
passport	meinen Pass	*mai*·nen pas
purse	mein Portemonnaie	main port·mo·*nay*
wallet	meine Brieftasche	*mai*·ne *breef*·ta·she

What am I accused of?
Wessen werde ich beschuldigt?
ve·sen *ver*·de ikh be·*shul*·dikht

I didn't do it.
Das habe ich nicht getan.
das *hah*·be ikh nikht ge·*tahn*

Can I call someone?
Kann ich jemanden anrufen?
kan ikh *yay*·man·den *an*·roo·fen

Can I call a lawyer?
Kann ich einen Rechtsanwalt anrufen?
kan ikh *ai*·nen *rekhts*·an·valt *an*·roo·fen

I want to contact (my consulate/ my embassy).
Ich möchte mich mit (meinem Konsulat/meiner Botschaft) in Verbindung setzen.
ikh *merkh*·te mikh mit (*mai*·nem kon·zu·*laht*/*mai*·ner *bawt*·shaft) in fer·*bin*·dung *ze*·tsen

I have a prescription for this drug.
Ich habe ein Rezept für dieses Medikament.
ikh *hah*·be ain re·*tsept* für *dee*·zes me·di·ka·*ment*

Health

KEY PHRASES

Where's the nearest hospital?	Wo ist das nächste Krankenhaus?	vaw ist das *naykhs*·te *krang*·ken·hows
I'm sick.	Ich bin krank.	ikh bin krangk
I need a doctor.	Ich brauche einen Arzt.	ikh *brow*·khe *ai*·nen artst
I'm allergic to ...	Ich bin allergisch gegen ...	ikh bin a·*lair*·gish *gay*·gen ...

DOCTOR

Where's the nearest ...?
Wo ist der/die/das nächste ...? m/f/n
vaw ist dair/dee/das *naykhs*·te ...

chemist/ pharmacist	Apotheke f	a·po·*tay*·ke
dentist	Zahnarzt m	*tsahn*·artst
doctor	Arzt m	artst
hospital	Krankenhaus n	*krang*·ken·hows
optometrist	Augenoptiker m	*ow*·gen·op·ti·ker

I need a doctor (who speaks English).
Ich brauche einen Arzt (der Englisch spricht).
ikh *brow*·khe *ai*·nen artst (dair *eng*·lish shprikht)

Could I see a female doctor?	Könnte ich von einer Ärztin behandelt werden? *kern*·te ikh fon *ai*·ner *erts*·tin be·*han*·delt *ver*·den
Is there a (night) chemist/pharmacist nearby?	Gibt es in der Nähe eine (Nacht)Apotheke? gipt es in dair *nay*·e *ai*·ne (*nakht*·) a·po·*tay*·ke
I don't want a blood transfusion.	Ich möchte keine Bluttransfusion. ikh *merkh*·te *kai*·ne *bloot*·trans·fu·zyawn
Please use a new syringe.	Bitte benutzen Sie eine neue Spritze. *bi*·te be·*nu*·tsen zee *ai*·ne *noy*·e *shpri*·tse
I have my own syringe.	Ich habe meine eigene Spritze. ikh *hah*·be *mai*·ne *ai*·ge·ne *shpri*·tse
I've been vaccinated for ...	Ich bin gegen ... geimpft worden. ikh bin *gay*·gen ... ge·*impft* *vor*·den
He/She has been vaccinated for ...	Er/Sie ist gegen ... geimpft worden. air/zee ist *gay*·gen ... ge·*impft* *vor*·den

fever	Fieber	*fee*·ber
hepatitis A/B/C	Hepatitis A/B/C	he·pa·*tee*·tis ah/bay/tsay
tetanus	Tätanus	*tay*·ta·nus
typhoid	Typhus	*tü*·fus

I've run out of my medication.	Ich habe keine Medikamente mehr. ikh *hah*·be *kai*·ne me·di·ka·*men*·te mair
My prescription is ...	Mein Rezept ist ... main re·*tsept* ist ...

SYMPTOMS & CONDITIONS

I'm sick.	Ich bin krank. ikh bin krangk
My friend is sick.	Mein Freund/Meine Freundin ist krank. m/f main froynt/*mai*·ne *froyn*·din ist krangk
It hurts here.	Es tut hier weh. es toot heer *vay*
I've been vomiting.	Ich habe mich übergeben. ikh *hah*·be mikh *ü*·ber·*gay*·ben
I can't sleep.	Ich kann nicht schlafen. ikh kan nikht *shlah*·fen
I feel dizzy.	Mir ist schwindelig. meer ist *shvin*·de·likh
I feel hot and cold.	Mir ist abwechselnd heiß und kalt. meer ist *ap*·vek·selnt hais unt kalt
I feel nauseous.	Mir ist übel. meer ist *ü*·bel
I feel shivery.	Mich fröstelt. mikh *frers*·telt
I feel weak.	Ich fühle mich schwach. ikh *fü*·le mikh shvakh
I feel anxious.	Ich habe Ängste. ikh *hah*·be *engs*·te

LISTEN FOR

Was fehlt Ihnen?	*vas faylt ee·nen* What's the problem?
Wo tut es weh?	*vaw toot es vay* Where does it hurt?
Seit wann haben Sie diese Beschwerden?	*zait van hah·ben zee dee·ze be·shver·den* How long have you been like this?
Hatten Sie das schon einmal?	*ha·ten zee das shawn ain·mahl* Have you had this before?
Nehmen Sie irgendwelche Medikamente?	*nay·men zee ir·gent·vel·khe me·di·ka·men·te* Are you on medication?
Sind Sie gegen bestimmte Stoffe allergisch?	*zint zee gay·gen be·shtim·te shto·fe a·lair·gish* Are you allergic to anything?
Trinken Sie?	*tring·ken zee* Do you drink?
Rauchen Sie?	*row·khen zee* Do you smoke?
Nehmen Sie Drogen?	*nay·men zee draw·gen* Do you take drugs?
Hatten Sie ungeschützten Geschlechtsverkehr?	*ha·ten zee un·ge·shüts·ten ge·shlekhts·fer·kair* Have you had unprotected sex?

I feel depressed.	Ich bin deprimiert. *ikh bin de·pri·meert*
I feel better/worse.	Ich fühle mich besser/schlechter. *ikh fü·le mikh be·ser/shlekh·ter*

I have (a) ...	Ich habe ... ikh *hah*·be ...

diarrhoea	Durchfall	*durkh*·fal
fever	Fieber	*fee*·ber
headache	Kopfschmerzen	*kopf*·shmer·tsen
pain	Schmerzen	*shmer*·tsen

I have an infection.	Ich habe eine Infektion. ikh *hah*·be *ai*·ne in·fek·*tsyawn*
I have a rash.	Ich habe einen Ausschlag. ikh *hah*·be *ai*·nen *ows*·shlahk
I've recently had ...	Ich hatte vor kurzem ... ikh *ha*·te fawr *kur*·tsem ...
I'm on medication for ...	Ich nehme Medikamente gegen ... ikh *nay*·me me·di·ka·*men*·te *gay*·gen ...

For more symptoms and conditions, see the **dictionary** (p197).

WOMEN'S HEALTH

(I think) I'm pregnant.	(Ich glaube,) Ich bin schwanger. (ikh *glow*·be) ikh bin *shvang*·er
I'm on the Pill.	Ich nehme die Pille. ikh *nay*·me dee *pi*·le
I haven't had my period for ... weeks.	Ich habe seit ... Wochen meine Periode nicht gehabt. ikh *hah*·be zait ... *vo*·khen *mai*·ne pe·ri·*aw*·de nikht ge·*hahpt*
I have period pain.	Ich habe Regelschmerzen. ikh *hah*·be *ray*·gel·shmer·tsen

LISTEN FOR

Benutzen Sie Verhütungsmittel?	be·*nu*·tsen zee fer·*hü*·tungks·mi·tel Are you using contraception?
Haben Sie Ihre Periode?	*hah*·ben zee ee·re pe·ri·*aw*·de Are you menstruating?
Wann hatten Sie Ihre letzte Periode?	van *ha*·ten zee ee·re *lets*·te pe·ri·*aw*·de When did you last have your period?
Sie sind schwanger.	zee zint *shvang*·er You're pregnant.

pregnancy test	Schwangerschafts-test m *shvang*·er·shafts·test
the morning-after pill	die Pille danach f dee *pi*·le da·*nahkh*
contraception	Verhütungsmittel n fer·*hü*·tungks·mi·tel

ALLERGIES

I have a skin allergy.	Ich habe eine Hautallergie. ikh *hah*·be *ai*·ne *howt*·a·ler·gee
I'm allergic to ...	Ich bin allergisch gegen ... ikh bin a·*lair*·gish *gay*·gen ...

antibiotics	Antibiotika	an·ti·bi·*aw*·ti·ka
anti-inflammatories	entzündungs-hemmende Mittel	en·*tsün*·dungks·he·men·de *mi*·tel
aspirin	Aspirin	as·pi·*reen*
bees	Bienen	*bee*·nen
codeine	Kodein	ko·de·*een*
penicillin	Penizillin	pe·ni·tsi·*leen*
pollen	Pollen	*po*·len

antihistamines	Antihistamine n pl *an*·ti·his·ta·*mee*·ne
inhaler	Inhalator m in·ha·*lah*·tor
injection	Injektion f in·yek·*tsyawn*
sulphur-based drugs	schwefel-basierte Arzneimittel n pl *shvay*·fel·ba·zeer·te arts·*nai*·mi·tel

For food-related allergies, see **special diets & allergies** (p185).

PARTS OF THE BODY

My ... hurts.	Mir tut der/die/das ... weh. m/f/n meer toot dair/dee/das ... vay
I can't move my ...	Ich kann meinen/meine/mein ... nicht bewegen. m/f/n ikh kan *mai*·nen/*mai*·ne/main ... nikht be·*vay*·gen
I have a cramp in my ...	Ich habe einen Krampf in meinem/meiner/meinem ... m/f/n ikh *hah*·be *ai*·nen krampf in *mai*·nem/*mai*·ner/*mai*·nem ...
My ... is swollen.	Mein/Meine/Mein ... ist geschwollen. m/f/n main/*mai*·ne/main ... ist ge·*shvo*·len

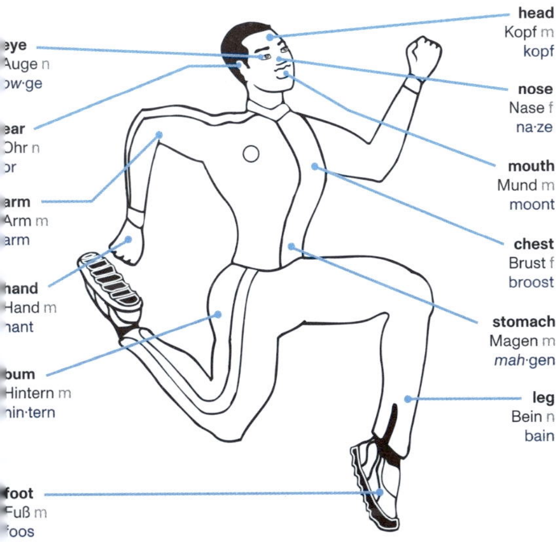

CHEMIST/PHARMACIST

I need something for ...	Ich brauche etwas gegen ... ikh *brow*·khe *et*·vas *gay*·gen ...
Do I need a prescription for ...?	Brauche ich für ... ein Rezept? *brow*·khe ikh für ... ain re·*tsept*
How many times a day?	Wie oft am Tag? vee oft am tahk
Will it make me drowsy?	Macht es müde? makht es *mü*·de

For pharmaceutical items, see the **dictionary** (p197).

LISTEN FOR

Haben Sie das schon einmal eingenommen?	*hah*·ben zee das shawn *ain*·mahl *ain*·ge·no·men Have you taken this before?
Zweimal am Tag (zum Essen).	*tsvai*·mahl am tahk (tsum e·sen) Twice a day (with food).

DENTIST

I have a broken tooth.	Ich habe einen abgebrochenen Zahn. ikh *hah*·be *ai*·nen *ap*·ge·bro·khe·nen tsahn
I have a toothache.	Ich habe Zahnschmerzen. ikh *hah*·be *tsahn*·shmer·tsen
I need an anaesthetic.	Ich brauche eine Betäubung. ikh *brow*·khe *ai*·ne be·*toy*·bung
I need a filling.	Ich brauche eine Füllung. ikh *brow*·khe *ai*·ne *fü*·lung
I've lost a filling.	Ich habe eine Füllung verloren. ikh *hah*·be ai·ne *fü*·lung fer·*law*·ren
My dentures are broken.	Mein Gebiss ist zerbrochen. main ge·*bis* ist tser·*bro*·khen
I don't want it extracted.	Ich will ihn nicht ziehen lassen. ikh vil een nikht *tsee*·en *la*·sen
My gums hurt.	Das Zahnfleisch tut mir weh. das *tsahn*·flaish toot meer vay

FOOD

EATING OUT	162
SELF-CATERING	179
VEGETARIAN & SPECIAL MEALS	184

Eating Out

KEY PHRASES

Can you recommend a restaurant?	Können Sie ein Restaurant empfehlen? pol Kannst du ein Restaurant empfehlen? inf	*ker*·nen zee ain res·to·*rang* emp·*fay*·len kanst doo ain res·to·*rang* emp·*fay*·len
I'd like a table for (two), please.	Ich hätte gern einen Tisch für (zwei) Personen, bitte.	ikh *he*·te gern *ai*·nen tish für (tsvai) per·*zaw*·nen *bi*·te
Can I see the menu, please?	Kann ich die Speisekarte sehen, bitte?	kan ikh dee *shpai*·ze·*kar*·te *zay*·en *bi*·te
I'd like ...	Ich möchte ...	ikh *merkh*·te ...
Please bring the bill.	Bitte bringen Sie die Rechnung.	*bi*·te *bring*·en zee dee *rekh*·nung

BASICS

breakfast	Frühstück n *frü*·shtük
lunch	Mittagessen n *mi*·tahk·e·sen
dinner	Abendessen n *ah*·bent·e·sen
snack	Snack m snek

eat/drink	essen/trinken *e*·sen/*tring*·ken
daily special	Gericht n des Tages ge·*rikht* des *tah*·ges
set menu	Menü n may·*nü*
I'd like ...	Ich möchte ... ikh *merkh*·te ...
Enjoy your meal!	Guten Appetit! *goo*·ten a·pay·*teet*
I'm starving!	Ich bin am Verhungern! ikh bin am fer·*hung*·ern

FINDING A PLACE TO EAT

Can you recommend a bar/pub?	Können Sie eine Kneipe empfehlen? *ker*·nen zee *ai*·ne *knai*·pe emp·*fay*·len
Can you recommend a coffee bar?	Kannst du eine Espressobar empfehlen? inf kanst doo *ai*·ne es·*pre*·so·bahr emp·*fay*·len

LISTEN FOR

Es tut mir Leid, wir haben geschlossen.	es toot meer lait veer *hah*·ben ge·*shlo*·sen Sorry, we're closed.
Wir haben keinen Tisch frei.	veer *hah*·ben *kai*·nen tish frai We have no free tables.
Wir sind voll ausgebucht.	veer zint fol *ows*·ge·bookht We're fully booked.
Wo möchten Sie sitzen?	vaw *merkh*·ten zee *zi*·tsen Where would you like to sit?

Can you recommend a restaurant?	Kannst du ein Restaurant empfehlen? inf kanst doo ain res·to·*rang* emp·*fay*·len
Where would you go for a cheap meal?	Wo kann man hingehen, um etwas Günstiges zu essen? vaw kan man *hin*·gay·en um *et*·vas *gün*·sti·ges tsoo *e*·sen
Where would you go for local specialities?	Wo kann man hingehen, um lokale Spezialitäten zu essen? vaw kan man *hin*·gay·en um lo·*ka*·le shpe·tsya·li·*tay*·ten tsoo *e*·sen
Are you still serving food?	Gibt es noch etwas zu essen? gipt es nokh *et*·vas tsoo *e*·sen
How long is the wait?	Wie lange muss man warten? vee *lang*·e mus man *var*·ten

AT THE RESTAURANT

I'd like to reserve a table for (two) people.	Ich möchte einen Tisch für (zwei) Personen reservieren. ikh *merkh*·te *ai*·nen tish für (tsvai) per·*zaw*·nen re·zer·*vee*·ren
I'd like to reserve a table for (eight) o'clock.	Ich möchte einen Tisch für (acht) Uhr reservieren. ikh *merkh*·te *ai*·nen tish für (akht) oor re·zer·*vee*·ren
I'd like a table for (two), please.	Ich hätte gern einen Tisch für (zwei) Personen, bitte. ikh *he*·te gern *ai*·nen tish für (tsvai) per·*zaw*·nen *bi*·te

For two, please. Für zwei, bitte. für tsvai *bi*·te

LISTEN FOR

Was darf ich Ihnen bringen?	vas darf ikh *ee*·nen *bring*·en What can I get for you?
Ich empfehle Ihnen ...	ikh emp·*fay*·le *ee*·nen ... I suggest the ...
Mögen Sie ...?	*mer*·gen zee ... Do you like ...?
Wie möchten Sie das zubereitet haben?	vee *merkh*·ten zee das *tsoo*·be·rai·tet *hah*·ben How would you like that cooked?
Bitte!	*bi*·te Here you go!

I'd like the nonsmoking section, please.	Ich hätte gern einen Nichtrauchertisch, bitte. ikh *he*·te gern *ai*·nen *nikht*·row·kher·tish *bi*·te
I'd like the smoking section, please.	Ich hätte gern einen Rauchertisch, bitte. ikh *he*·te gern *ai*·nen *row*·kher·tish *bi*·te
Do you have a menu in English?	Haben Sie eine englische Speisekarte? *hah*·ben zee *ai*·ne *eng*·li·she *shpai*·ze·kar·te
Do you have children's meals?	Haben Sie Kinderteller? *hah*·ben zee *kin*·der·te·ler
I'd like the drink list, please.	Ich hätte gern die Getränkekarte, bitte. ikh *he*·te gern dee ge·*treng*·ke·kar·te *bi*·te

LOOK FOR

Beilagen	*bai*·lah·gen	Side Dishes
Hauptgerichte	*howpt*·ge·rikh·te	Main Courses
Nachspeisen	*nahkh*·shpai·zen	Desserts
Salate	za·*lah*·te	Salads
Suppen	*zu*·pen	Soups
Vorspeisen	*fawr*·shpai·zen	Appetisers

I'd like the menu, please.	Ich hätte gern die Speisekarte, bitte. ikh *he*·te gern dee *shpai*·ze·kar·te *bi*·te

Menu, please. Die Karte, bitte. dee *kar*·te *bi*·te

What would you recommend?	Was empfehlen Sie? vas emp·*fay*·len zee
I'll have what they're having.	Ich nehme das gleiche wie sie. ikh *nay*·me das *glai*·khe vee zee
I'd like a local speciality.	Ich möchte etwas Typisches aus der Region. ikh *merkh*·te *et*·vas *tü*·pi·shes ows dair re·*gyawn*
Can you tell me which traditional foods I should try?	Können Sie mir sagen, welche traditionellen Speisen ich probieren sollte? *ker*·nen zee meer *zah*·gen *vel*·khe tra·di·tsyo·*ne*·len *shpai*·zen ikh pro·*bee*·ren *zol*·te
What's in that dish?	Was ist in diesem Gericht? vas ist in *dee*·zem ge·*rikht*
Does it take long to prepare?	Dauert das lange? *dow*·ert das *lang*·e

Eating Out

CAN I SEE THE MENU, PLEASE?
Kann ich die Speisekarte sehen, bitte?
kan ikh dee *shpai*·ze·*kar*·te *zay*·en *bi*·te

WHAT WOULD YOU RECOMMEND FOR ...?
Was würden Sie als ... empfehlen?
vas *vür*·den zee als ... emp·*fay*·len

THE MAIN MEAL
Hauptgericht
howpt·ge·rikht

DESSERT
Dessert
de·*sairt*

DRINKS
Getränk
ge·*trengk*

CAN YOU BRING ME SOME ..., PLEASE?
Bitte bringen Sie ...
bi·te *bring*·en zee ...

I'D LIKE THE BILL, PLEASE.
Ich hätte gern die Rechnung, bitte.
ikh *he*·te gern dee *rekh*·nung *bi*·te

Are these complimentary?	Sind die gratis? zint dee *grah*·tis	
We're just having drinks.	Wir möchten nur etwas trinken. veer *merkh*·ten noor *et*·vas *tring*·ken	
Just drinks.	Nur Getränke.	noor ge·*treng*·ke

REQUESTS

I'd like it ...	Ich hätte es gern ... ikh *he*·te es gern ...
I don't want it ...	Ich möchte es nicht ... ikh *merkh*·te es nikht ...

boiled	gekocht	ge·*kokht*
broiled	gegrillt	ge·*grilt*
deep-fried	frittiert	fri·*teert*
fried	gebraten	ge·*brah*·ten
grilled	gegrillt	ge·*grilt*
mashed	püriert	pü·*reert*
medium	halb durch	halp durkh
rare	blutig	*bloo*·tikh
reheated	aufgewärmt	*owf*·ge·vermt
steamed	gedämpft	ge·*dempft*
well-done	gut durch-gebraten	goot *durkh*·ge·brah·ten
with the dressing on the side	mit dem Dressing daneben	mit daym *dre*·sing da·*nay*·ben
without ...	ohne ...	*aw*·ne ...

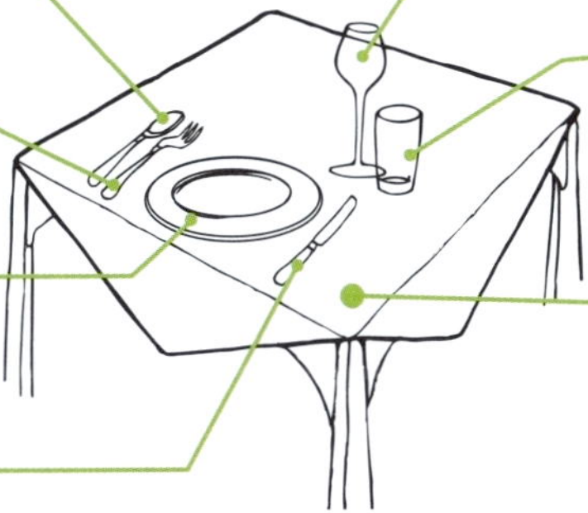

Please bring a cloth.	Bitte bringen Sie eine Tischdecke. *bi*·te *bring*·en zee *ai*·ne *tish*·de·ke
Please bring a (wine) glass.	Bitte bringen Sie ein (Wein) Glas. *bi*·te *bring*·en zee ain (*vain*·) glahs
Is there any ...?	Gibt es ...? gipt es ...

chili sauce	Chilisauce	*chi*·li·zaw·se
ketchup	Ketchup	*ket*·chap
pepper	Pfeffer	*pfe*·fer
salt	Salz	zalts
vinegar	Essig	e·sikh

For other specific requests, see **vegetarian & special meals** (p184).

COMPLIMENTS & COMPLAINTS

I didn't order this.	Das habe ich nicht bestellt. das *hah*·be ikh nikht be·*shtelt*
I love this dish.	Ich mag dieses Gericht. ikh mahk *dee*·zes ge·*rikht*
I love the local cuisine.	Ich mag die regionale Küche. ikh mahk dee re·gyo·*nah*·le *kü*·khe
That was delicious!	Das hat hervorragend geschmeckt! das hat her·*fawr*·rah·gent ge·*shmekt*
This is (too) cold.	Das ist (zu) kalt. das ist (tsoo) kalt
This is spicy.	Das ist scharf. das ist sharf
This is superb.	Das ist exzellent. das ist ek·se·*lent*
My compliments to the chef.	Mein Kompliment an den Koch. main kom·pli·*ment* an dayn kokh
I'm full.	Ich bin satt. ikh bin zat

PAYING THE BILL

Please bring the bill.	Bitte bringen Sie die Rechnung. *bi*·te *bring*·en zee dee *rekh*·nung

Bill, please.	Die Rechnung, bitte.	dee *rekh*·nung *bi*·te

LOOK FOR

One of Germany's favourite and most famous foods is the not-so-humble *Wurst* (sausage). There are over 1500 types. Some of the more common:

Blutwurst f	*bloot*·vurst	blood sausage
Bockwurst f	*bok*·vurst	pork sausage
Bratwurst f	*braht*·vurst	fried pork sausage
Bregenwurst f	*bray*·gen·vurst	brain sausage
Cervelatwurst f	ser·ve·*laht*·vurst	sausage of spicy pork and beef
Katenwurst f	*kah*·ten·vurst	country-style smoked sausage
Knackwurst f	*knak*·vurst	mildly garlic-flavoured sausage
Krakauer f	*krah*·kow·er	thick, paprika-spiced sausage of Polish origin
Landjäger m	*lant*·yay·ger	thin, long, hard spicy sausage
Leberwurst f	*lay*·ber·vurst	liver sausage
Regensburger m	*ray*·gens·bur·ger	highly spiced smoked sausage
Rotwurst f	*rawt*·vurst	black pudding
Thüringer f	*tü*·ring·er	long, thin spicy sausage
Wiener Würstchen n	*vee*·ner *vürst*·khen	frankfurter (small smoked sausage)
Weißwurst f	*vais*·vurst	veal sausage
Würstchen n	*vürst*·khen	small sausage
Zwiebelwurst f	*tsvee*·bel·vurst	liver and onion sausage

Is service included in the bill?	Ist die Bedienung inbegriffen? ist dee be·*dee*·nung *in*·be·gri·fen

NONALCOHOLIC DRINKS

(boiled) water	(heißes) Wasser n (*hai*·ses) *va*·ser
mineral water	Mineralwasser n mi·ne·*rahl*·va·ser
soft drink	Softdrink m *soft*·dringk
coffee	Kaffee m *ka*·fay
tea	Tee m tay
with (milk)	mit (Milch) mit (milkh)
without (sugar)	ohne (Zucker) *aw*·ne (*tsu*·ker)

ALCOHOLIC DRINKS

beer	Bier n beer
light beer	Leichtbier n *laikht*·beer
nonalcoholic beer	alkoholfreies Bier n al·ko·*hawl*·frai·es beer
pilsner/lager	Pils n pils

CULTURE TIP: SOFT DRINKS

In Germany, mineral water is *ein alkoholfreies Getränk* ain al·ko·*hawl*·frai·es ge·*trengk* (a nonalcoholic drink), but not a *Softdrink* *soft*·dringk (soft drink) – this term only designates sweet fizzy drinks, such as lemonade or cola. Keep an eye out for *Schorle* *shaw*·leh: drinks made by diluting juice or wine with mineral water or lemonade.

wheat beer	Weißbier n *vais*·beer
brandy	Weinbrand m *vain*·brant
(French) Champagne	Champagner m sham·*pan*·yer
cocktail	Cocktail m *kok*·tayl
sparkling wine	Sekt m zekt
a shot of (gin)	einen (Gin) *ai*·nen (dzhin)
a beer on tap	ein Bier vom Fass ain beer fom fas
a ... (of) beer	ein ... Bier ain ... beer

glass	Glas	glahs
large	großes	*graw*·ses
pint	halbes	*halb*·es
small	kleines	*klai*·nes

LOOK FOR

Alkoholfreies Bier n	al·ko·*hawl*·frai·es beer nonalcoholic beer
Alster(wasser) n	*als*·ter(·va·ser) mixture of pilsner and orange lemonade
Alt(bier) n	*alt*(·beer) amber-coloured speciality beer from Düsseldorf, with a strong taste of hops
Altbierbowle f	*alt*·beer·baw·le Altbier with strawberries or other fruit
Alt-Schuss n	alt·*shus* Altbier with a shot of syrup or Malzbier
Berliner Weiße f	ber·*lee*·ner *vai*·se slightly fizzy and cloudy, often served with a shot of raspberry *(rot)* or woodruff *(grün)* syrup
Bockbier n	*bok*·beer light or dark beer with a high alcohol content
Eisbock m	*ais*·bok Bockbier from which water has been extracted by freezing, thus increasing its alcoholic potency
Export n	eks·*port* lager
Gose f	*gaw*·ze wheat beer from Leipzig
Hefeweizen n	*hay*·fe·vai·tsen cloudy wheat beer – comes in light *(hell)* or dark *(dunkel)* varieties
Helles n	*he*·les lager (Bavaria)

Kölsch n	kerlsh yellow-golden coloured beer from Cologne
Kräusen n	*kroy*·zen unfiltered beer, gold-coloured or dark
Krefelder n	*kray*·fel·der Altbier mixed with cola
Kristallweizen n	kris·*tal*·vai·tsen clear light *(hell)* or dark *(dunkel)* wheat beer
Leichtbier n	*laikht*·beer beer with half the alcohol content of normal beer
Maibock m	*mai*·bok special Bockbier brewed in May
Malzbier n	*malts*·beer nonalcoholic malt beer
Märzen n	*mer*·tsen special Bavarian beer brewed at the end of winter
Pils/ Pils(e)ner n	pils/*pil*·z(e·)ner pilsner, similar to lager
Radler n	*raht*·ler mixture of pilsner or lager and sweet lemonade
Rauchbier n	*rowkh*·beer smoky-flavoured beer from Bamberg
Schwarzbier n	*shvarts*·beer stout (lit: black beer)
Weizenbier/ Weißbier n	*vai*·tsen·beer/*vais*·beer wheat beer

a bottle of ... wine	eine Flasche ... *ai*·ne *fla*·she ...
a glass of ... wine	ein Glas ... ain glahs ...

dessert	Dessertwein	de·*sair*·vain
mulled	Glühwein	*glü*·vain
red	Rotwein	*rawt*·vain
rose	Rosé	ro·*zay*
sparkling	Sekt	zekt
white	Weißwein	*vais*·vain

IN THE BAR

Excuse me!	Entschuldigung! ent·*shul*·di·gung
I'm next.	Ich bin dran. ikh bin dran
Q **What would you like?**	Was möchten Sie? pol vas *merkh*·ten zee Was möchtest du? inf vas *merkh*·test doo
A **I'll have ...**	Ich hätte gern ... ikh *he*·te gern ...
A **Same again, please.**	Dasselbe nochmal, bitte. das·*zel*·be nokh·*mahl* *bi*·te
I don't drink alcohol.	Ich trinke keinen Alkohol. ikh *tring*·ke *kai*·nen *al*·ko·hawl
No thanks, I'm driving.	Nein danke, ich fahre. nain *dang*·ke ikh *fah*·re
No ice, thanks.	Kein Eis, bitte. kain ais *bi*·te

CULTURE TIP: GRAPE VARIETIES

Germany is famous for its wines. There are three basic wine categories – *trocken* *tro*·ken (dry), *halbtrocken* *halp*·tro·ken (medium-dry) and *lieblich* *leep*·likh (sweet).

I'll buy you a drink.	Ich gebe Ihnen/dir einen aus. pol/inf ikh *gay*·be *ee*·nen/deer *ai*·nen ows
It's my round.	Diese Runde geht auf mich. *dee*·ze *run*·de gayt owf mikh
Do you serve meals here?	Gibt es hier auch etwas zu essen? gipt es heer owkh *et*·vas tsoo *e*·sen

DRINKING UP

Cheers!	Prost! prawst
This is hitting the spot.	Das kommt jetzt echt gut. das komt yetst ekht goot
I'm feeling drunk.	Ich glaube, ich bin betrunken. ikh *glow*·be ikh bin be·*trung*·ken
I feel fantastic!	Ich fühle mich fantastisch! ikh *fü*·le mikh fan·*tas*·tish
I'm tired, I'd better go home.	Ich bin müde, ich sollte besser nach Hause gehen. ikh bin *mü*·de ikh *zol*·te *be*·ser nahkh *how*·ze *gay*·en

☑ CULTURE TIP: DINING ETIQUETTE

The main meal of the day in German-speaking countries is *das Mittagsessen* das *mi*·tahk·e·sen or lunch.

It's good manners to say *Guten Appetit goo*·ten a·pay·*teet* or *Mahlzeit mahl*·tsait (Enjoy your meal) to your fellow diners. Observing German table etiquette is easy – there are no particularly elaborate rules. It's customary, however, to keep your hands on the table at all times.

If you've really enjoyed your meal, say *Das hat geschmeckt* das hat gesh·*mekt*. To get the attention of a waiter, call out *say Entschuldigung* ent·*schul*·di·gung. To indicate that you want to pay your bill, say *Die Rechnung bitte!* dee *rekh*·nung *bi*·te.

Germans are fond of toasts. If they break out the drink, wait until everyone is served. Then raise your glasses in unison, look your fellow toasters in the eye and give a hearty *Prost!* prawst or *Zum Wohl!* tsum vawl.

I think I've had one too many.	Ich glaube, ich habe ein bisschen zu viel getrunken. ikh *glow*·be ikh *hah*·be ain *bis*·khen tsoo feel ge·*trung*·ken
Can you call a taxi for me?	Können Sie mir ein Taxi rufen? pol *ker*·nen zee meer ain *tak*·si *roo*·fen Kannst du mir ein Taxi rufen? inf kanst doo meer ain *tak*·si *roo*·fen

Self-Catering

KEY PHRASES

What's the local speciality?	Was ist eine lokale Spezialität?	vas ist *ai*·ne lo·*ka*·le· shpe·tsya·li·*tayt*
Where can I find the ... section?	Wo kann ich die ... finden?	vaw kan ikh dee ... *fin*·den
I'd like some ...	Ich möchte etwas ...	ikh *merkh*·te *et*·vas ...

BUYING FOOD

Where can I find the ... section?
Wo kann ich die ... finden?
vaw kan ikh dee ... *fin*·den

dairy	Abteilung für Milchprodukte	ap·*tai*·lung für *milkh*·pro·duk·te
frozen goods	Abteilung für Tiefkühlprodukte	ap·*tai*·lung für *teef*·kül·pro·duk·te
fruit and vegetable	Obst- und Gemüseabteilung	awpst· unt ge·*mü*·ze· ap·tai·lung
meat	Fleischabteilung	*flaish*·ap·tai·lung

Where's the health-food section?
Wo ist die Nahrungsmittel- und Drogerie-Abteilung?
vaw ist dee *nah*·rungs·mi·tel· unt draw·ge·*ree*·ap·tai·lung

LISTEN FOR

Kann ich Ihnen helfen?	kan ikh *ee*·nen *hel*·fen Can I help you?
Was möchten Sie?	vas *merkh*·ten zee? What would you like?
Das ist aus.	das ist ows There's none left.
Möchten Sie noch etwas?	*merkh*·ten zee nokh *et*·vas Would you like anything else?

What's the local speciality?	Was ist eine lokale Spezialität? vas ist *ai*·ne lo·*ka*·le shpe·tsya·li·*tayt*
Do you sell locally produced food?	Verkaufen Sie lokal produzierte Lebensmittel? fer·*kow*·fen zee lo·*kal* pro·du·*tseer*·te *lay*·bens·mi·tel
Do you sell organic produce?	Verkaufen Sie Bioprodukte? fer·*kow*·fen zee *bee*·o·pro·duk·te
What's that?	Was ist das? vas ist das
Can I taste it?	Kann ich das probieren? kan ikh das pro·*bee*·ren
How much is (a kilo of cheese)?	Was kostet (ein Kilo Käse)? vas *kos*·tet (ain *kee*·lo *kay*·ze)
Do you have anything cheaper?	Haben Sie etwas Günstigeres? *hah*·ben zee *et*·vas *gün*·sti·ge·res
Do you have other kinds?	Haben Sie andere Sorten? *hah*·ben zee *an*·de·re *zor*·ten

How much?	Wie viel? vee feel
I'd like ...	Ich möchte ... ikh *merkh*·te ...

(200) grams	(200) Gramm	(*tsvai*·hun·dert) gram
(two) kilos	(zwei) Kilo	(tsvai) *kee*·lo
(three) pieces	(drei) Stück	(drai) shtük
(six) slices	(sechs) Scheiben	(zeks) *shai*·ben
some ...	etwas ...	*et*·vas ...

For other useful amounts, see **numbers & amounts** (p30).

Was ist eine lokale Spezialität?

vas ist *ai*·ne lo·*ka*·le shpe·tsya·li·*tayt*

What's the local speciality?

A piece.	Ein Stück. ain shtük
A slice.	Eine Scheibe. *ai*·ne *shai*·be
That one.	Dieses da. *dee*·zes dah
This.	Dieses. *dee*·zes
A bit more.	Ein bisschen mehr. ain *bis*·khen mair
Less.	Weniger. *vay*·ni·ger
Enough.	Genug. ge·*nook*
Can I have a bag, please?	Könnte ich bitte eine Tüte haben? *kern*·te ikh *bi*·te *ai*·ne *tü*·te *hah*·ben

For food items see the **menu decoder** (p187), and **dictionary** (p197).

COOKING

Could I please borrow a ...?	Könnte ich bitte ... ausleihen? *kern*·te ikh *bi*·te ... *ows*·lai·en

bottle opener	einen Flaschenöffner	*ai*·nen *fla*·shen·erf·ner
chopping board	ein Schneidebrett	ain *shnai*·de·bret
frying pan	eine Bratpfanne	*ai*·ne *braht*·pfa·ne
knife	ein Messer	ain *me*·ser
saucepan	einen Kochtopf	*ai*·nen *kokh*·topf

☑ LANGUAGE TIP: TONGUE TWISTERS

If you're feeling comfortable with the language and want to impress the locals, try these tongue twisters:

Blaukraut bleibt Blaukraut und Brautkleid bleibt Brautkleid.
blow·krowt blaipt *blow*·krowt unt *browt*·klait blaipt *browt*·klait
Red cabbage remains red cabbage and a wedding dress remains a wedding dress.

Der Potsdamer Postkutscher putzt den Potsdamer Postkutschkasten.
dair *pots*·dah·mer *post*·ku·cher putst dayn *pots*·dah·mer *post*·kuch·kah·sten
The Potsdam mailcoach driver cleans the Potsdam mailcoach postboxes.

Der Dachdecker deckt dein Dach, drum dank dem Dachdecker, der dein Dach deckt.
dair *dakh*·de·ker dekt dain dakh drum dank daym *dakh*·de·ker dair dain dakh dekt
The roofer roofs your roof, for that thank the roofer, who roofs your roof.

cooked	gekocht ge·*kokht*
dried	getrocknet ge·*trok*·net
fresh	frisch frish
frozen	eingefroren *ain*·ge·fraw·ren
raw	roh raw
smoked	geräuchert ge·*roy*·khert

For more cooking terminology, see the **dictionary** (p197).

Vegetarian & Special Meals

KEY PHRASES

Do you have vegetarian food?	Haben Sie vegetarisches Essen?	*hah*·ben zee ve·ge·*tah*·ri·shes e·sen
Could you prepare a meal without ...?	Können Sie ein Gericht ohne ... zubereiten?	*ker*·nen zee ain ge·*rikht aw*·ne ... *tsoo*·be·rai·ten
I'm allergic to ...	Ich bin allergisch gegen ...	ikh bin a·*lair*·gish *gay*·gen ...

SPECIAL DIETS & ALLERGIES

Is there a (vegetarian) restaurant near here?	Gibt es ein (vegetarisches) Restaurant hier in der Nähe? gipt es ain vege·*tar*·ish·shes res·to·*rang* heer in dair *nay*·e
Do you have halal food?	Haben Sie Halal-Essen? *hah*·ben zee ha·*lal*·e·sen
Do you have kosher food?	Haben Sie koscheres Essen? *hah*·ben zee *kaw*·she·res *e*·sen
Do you have vegetarian food?	Haben Sie vegetarisches Essen? *hah*·ben zee ve·ge·*tah*·ri·shes *e*·sen
I'm vegan.	Ich bin Veganer(in). m/f ikh bin ve·*gah*·ner/ve·*gah*·ne·rin

I'm vegetarian.	Ich bin Vegetarier(in). m/f ikh bin ve·ge·*tah*·ri·er/ ve·ge·*tah*·ri·e·rin
I'm on a special diet.	Ich bin auf einer Spezialdiät. ikh bin owf *ai*·ner shpe·*tsyahl*·di·et
I'm allergic to ...	Ich bin allergisch gegen ... ikh bin a·*lair*·gish *gay*·gen ...
I don't eat ...	Ich esse kein ... ikh *e*·se kain ...

dairy produce	Milchprodukte	*milkh*·pro·duk·te
eggs	Eier	*ai*·er
fish	Fisch	fish
gelatine	Gelatine	zhe·la·*tee*·ne
gluten	Gluten	*gloo*·ten
honey	Honig	*haw*·nikh
meat	Fleisch	flaish
MSG	Natriumglutamat	*nah*·tri·um·glu·ta·maht
nuts	Nüsse	*nü*·se
pork	Schweinefleisch	*shwai*·ne·flaish
seafood	Meeresfrüchte	*meer*·es·frükh·te
shellfish	Schaltiere	*shahl*·tee·re

ORDERING

Is it cooked with butter?	Ist es mit Butter zubereitet? ist es mit *bu*·ter *tsoo*·be·rai·tet
Is it cooked with eggs?	Ist es mit Eiern zubereitet? ist es mit *ai*·ern *tsoo*·be·rai·tet

LISTEN FOR

Da ist überall (Fleisch) drin.	dah ist ü·ber·*al* (flaish) drin It all has (meat) in it.
Ich frage mal in der Küche.	ikh *frah*·ge mahl in dair *kü*·khe I'll check with the chef.
Können Sie ... essen?	*ker*·nen zee ... *e*·sen Can you eat ...?

Is it cooked in meat stock?	Ist es in Fleischbrühe zubereitet? ist es in *flaish*·brü·e *tsoo*·be·rai·tet
Does this dish have ... in it?	Enthält dieses Gericht ...? ent·*helt dee*·zes ge·*rikht* ...
Could you prepare a meal without ...?	Können Sie ein Gericht ohne ... zubereiten? *ker*·nen zee ain ge·*rikht aw*·ne ... *tsoo*·be·rai·ten
Is this ...?	Ist das ...? ist das ...

free of animal produce	ohne tierische Produkte	*aw*·ne *tee*·ri·she pro·*duk*·te
free-range	von freilaufenden Tieren	fon *frai*·low·fen·den *tee*·ren
genetically modified	gentechnisch verändert	*gayn*·tek·nish fer·*an*·dert
gluten-free	glutenfrei	*gloo*·ten·frai
low in sugar	zuckerarm	*tsu*·ker·arm
low-fat	fettarm	*fet*·arm
organic	organisch	or·*gah*·nish
salt-free	ohne Salz	*aw*·ne zalts

MENU Decoder

KULINARISCHES WÖRTERVERZEICHNIS

This miniguide to German cuisine is designed to help you navigate menus. German nouns, and adjectives affected by gender, have their gender indicated by ⓕ, ⓜ or ⓝ. If it's a plural noun, you'll also see pl. Where relevant, we've noted in brackets the region/country a particular item is associated with.

A

Aachener Printen pl *ah*·khe·ner *prin*·ten cakes with chocolate, nuts, fruit peel, honey & spices
Aal ⓜ ahl eel
—suppe ⓕ *ahl*·zu·pe eel soup
geräucherter Aal ⓜ ge·*roy*·kher·ter ahl smoked eel
Alpzirler ⓜ *alp*·tsir·ler cow's milk cheese from Austria
Apfel ⓜ *ap*·fel apple
—strudel ⓜ *ap*·fel·shtroo·del apple strudel
Apfelsine ⓕ ap·fel·*zee*·ne orange
Aprikose ⓕ a·pri·*kaw*·ze apricot
—nmarmelade ⓕ a·pri·*kaw*·zen·mar·me·lah·de apricot jam
Artischocke ⓕ ar·ti·*sho*·ke artichoke
Auflauf ⓜ *owf*·lowf souffle · casserole
Auster ⓕ *ows*·ter oyster

B

Bäckerofen ⓜ *be*·ker·aw·fen 'baker's oven' – pork & lamb bake (Saarland)
Backhähnchen ⓝ *bak*·hayn·khen fried chicken
Backobst ⓝ *bak*·awpst dried fruit
Backpflaume ⓕ *bak*·pflow·me prune
Banane ⓕ ba·*nah*·ne banana
Barsch ⓜ barsh perch
Bauern
—brot ⓝ *bow*·ern·brawt 'farmer's bread' – rye or wholemeal bread
—frühstück ⓝ *bow*·ern·frü·shtük 'farmer's breakfast' – scrambled eggs, bacon, diced potatoes, onions & tomatoes
—schmaus ⓜ *bow*·ern·shmows 'farmer's feast' – sauerkraut garnished with bacon, smoked pork, sausages & dumpling or potatoes
—suppe ⓕ *bow*·ern·zu·pe 'farmer's soup' made of cabbage & sausage
Bayrisch Kraut ⓝ *bai*·rish krowt shredded cabbage cooked with sliced apples, wine & sugar
Beefsteak ⓝ *beef*·stayk hamburger patty
Berliner ⓜ ber·*lee*·ner jam doughnut

Beuschel ⓝ *boy*·shel heart, liver & kidney of a calf or lamb in a slightly sour sauce
Bienenstich ⓜ *bee*·nen·shtikh cake, baked on a tray with a coating of almonds & sugar
Birne ⓕ *bir*·ne pear
Bischofsbrot ⓝ *bi*·shofs·brawt fruit & nut cake
Blaubeere ⓕ *blow*·bey·re bilberry • blueberry
Blaukraut ⓝ *blow*·krowt red cabbage
Blumenkohl ⓜ *bloo*·men·kawl cauliflower
Blutwurst ⓕ *bloot*·vurst blood pudding • blood sausage
Bockwurst ⓕ *bok*·vurst pork sausage
Bohnen ⓕ pl *baw*·nen beans
Brat
—huhn ⓝ *braht*·hoon roast chicken
—kartoffeln ⓕ pl *braht*·kar·to·feln fried potatoes
—wurst ⓕ *braht*·vurst fried pork sausage
Bregenwurst ⓕ *bray*·gen·vurst brain sausage, found mainly in Lower Saxony & Western Saxony-Anhalt
Brezel ⓕ *bray*·tsel pretzel
Brokkoli ⓜ pl *bro*·ko·li broccoli
Brombeere ⓕ *brom*·bey·re blackberry
Brot ⓝ brawt bread
belegtes Brot ⓝ be·*layk*·tes brawt open sandwich
Brötchen ⓝ *brert*·khen roll
Brühwürfel ⓜ *brü*·vür·fel stock cube
Bulette ⓕ bu·*le*·te meatball (Berlin)
Butter ⓕ *bu*·ter butter

C

Cervelatwurst ⓕ ser·ve·*laht*·vurst spicy pork & beef sausage
Christstollen ⓜ *krist*·shto·len spiced loaf with candied peel, traditionally eaten at Christmas
Cremespeise ⓕ *kraym*·shpai·ze mousse

D

Damenkäse ⓜ *dah*·men·kay·ze soft, buttery cheese
Dampfnudeln ⓕ pl *dampf*·noo·deln hot yeast dumplings with vanilla sauce
Dattel ⓕ *da*·tel date
Dorsch ⓜ dorsh cod
Dotterkäse ⓜ *do*·ter·kay·ze cheese made from skimmed milk & egg yolk

E

Ei ⓝ ai egg
Eierkuchen ⓜ *ai*·er·koo·khen pancake
Eierschwammerln ⓜ pl *ai*·er·shva·merln chanterelle mushrooms (Austria)
Eierspeispfandl ⓝ *ai*·er·shpais·pfandl special Viennese omelette (Austria)
Eintopf ⓜ *ain*·topf stew
Eis ⓝ ais ice cream
Eisbein ⓝ *ais*·bain pickled pork knuckles
Emmentaler ⓜ e·men·tah·ler Swiss Emmental, whole-milk hard cheese
Ennstaler ⓜ *ens*·tah·ler blue cheese produced from mixed milk
Ente ⓕ *en*·te duck
Erbse ⓕ *erp*·se pea
Erbsensuppe ⓕ *erp*·sen·zu·pe pea soup
Erdäpfel ⓜ pl *ert*·ep·fel potatoes
—gulasch ⓝ *ert*·ep·fel·goo·lash spicy sausage & potato stew
—knödel ⓜ pl *ert*·ep·fel·kner·del potato & semolina dumplings
—nudeln ⓕ pl *ert*·ep·fel·noo·deln boiled potato balls fried & tossed in fried breadcrumbs
Erdbeere ⓕ *ert*·bey·re strawberry

Erdbeermarmelade ⓕ *ert*·bair·mar·me·lah·de strawberry jam
Erdnuss ⓕ *ert*·nus peanut
Essig ⓜ *e*·sikh vinegar

F

Falscher Hase ⓜ *fal*·sher *hah*·ze 'false hare' – baked mince meatloaf
Fasan ⓜ fa·*zahn* pheasant
Feige ⓕ *fai*·ge fig
Filet ⓝ fi·*lay* fillet
Fisch ⓜ fish fish
Fladen ⓜ *flah*·den flat dough cake
Flädle ⓜ pl *flayt*·le thin strips of pancake, added to soup
Fledermaus ⓕ *flay*·der·mows 'bat' – boiled beef in horseradish cream
Fleisch ⓝ flaish meat
—brühe ⓕ *flaish*·brü·e bouillon
—pflanzerl ⓝ *flaish*·pflan·tserl meat-balls, a Bavarian speciality
—sülze ⓕ *flaish*·zül·tse aspic
Fondue ⓝ fon·*dü* melted cheese with wine served with bread for dipping
Forelle ⓕ fo·*re*·le trout
— blau fo·*re*·le blow steamed trout with potatoes & vegetables
— Müllerin fo·*re*·le *mü*·le·rin trout fried in batter with almonds
Frankfurter Kranz ⓜ *frank*·fur·ter krants sponge cake with rum, butter, cream & cherries (Frankfurt)
Frikadelle ⓕ fri·ka·*de*·le meatball
Frischling ⓜ *frish*·ling young wild boar
Frucht ⓕ frukht fruit
Frühlingssuppe ⓕ *frü*·lingks·zu·pe vegetable soup
Frühstücksspeck ⓜ *frü*·shtüks·shpek bacon

G

Gans ⓕ gans goose
Garnele ⓕ gar·*nay*·le prawn • shrimp
Gebäck ⓝ ge·*bek* pastries
Geflügel ⓝ ge·*flü*·gel poultry
gekocht ge·*kokht* boiled • cooked
gekochte Eier ⓝ pl ge·*kokh*·te *ai*·er boiled eggs
gekochter Schinken ⓜ ge·*kokh*·ter *shing*·ken cooked ham
Gemüse ⓝ ge·*mü*·ze vegetables
—suppe ⓕ ge·*mü*·ze·zu·pe vegetable soup
geräuchert ge·*roy*·khert smoked
geräucherte Forelle ⓕ ge·*roy*·kher·te fo·*re*·le smoked trout
geräucherter Lachs ⓜ ge·*roy*·kher·ter laks smoked salmon
geräucherter Schinken ⓜ ge·*roy*·kher·ter *shing*·ken gammon
Geschnetzeltes ⓝ ge·*shne*·tsel·tes small slices of meat
Gitziprägel ⓝ *gi*·tsi·pray·gel baked rabbit in batter (Switzerland)
Graf Görz ⓜ grahf gerts Austrian soft cheese
Granat ⓜ gra·*naht* shrimp
Granatapfel ⓜ gra·*naht*·ap·fel pomegranate
Gratin ⓜ gra·*teng* a dish topped with cheese & baked in the oven
Graupensuppe ⓕ *grow*·pen·zu·pe barley soup
Greyerzer ⓜ *grai*·er·tser Gruyère, a smooth, rich cheese
Grießklößchensuppe ⓕ *grees*·klers·khen·zu·pe soup with semolina dumplings
Gröstl ⓝ gerstl grated fried potatoes with meat (Tyrol)
grüner Salat ⓜ *grü*·ner za·*laht* green salad
Grünkohl ⓜ **mit Pinkel** *grün*·kawl mit *ping*·kel cabbage with sausages (Bremen)
Güggeli ⓝ *gü*·ge·lee spring chicken (Switzerland)
Gurke ⓕ *gur*·ke cucumber • gherkin

H

Hack
—braten ⓜ *hak*·brah·ten meatloaf
—fleisch ⓝ *hak*·flaish minced meat
Haferbrei ⓜ *hah*·fer·brai porridge
Hähnchen ⓝ *hayn*·khen chicken
Hämchen ⓝ *hem*·khen pork or hock shank, served with sauerkraut & potatoes (Cologne)
Handkäs ⓜ **mit Musik** *hant*·kays mit mu·*zeek* spicy cheese, marinated in vinegar & white wine
Hartkäse ⓜ *hart*·kay·ze hard cheese
Hase ⓜ *hah*·ze hare
—nläufe ⓜ pl **in Jägerrahmsauce** *hah*·zen·loy·fe in *yay*·ger·rahm·zaw·se hare in dark cream sauce of mushroom, shallots, white wine & parsley
—npfeffer ⓜ *hah*·zen·pfe·fer hare stew with mushrooms & onions
Haselnuß ⓕ *hah*·zel·nus hazelnut
Haxe ⓕ *hak*·se knuckle
Hecht ⓜ hekht pike
Heidelbeere ⓕ *hai*·del·bey·re bilberry • blueberry
Heidelbeermarmelade ⓕ *hai*·del·bair·mar·me·lah·de blueberry/bilberry jam
Heilbutt ⓜ *hail*·but halibut
Hering ⓜ *hay*·ring herring
—sschmaus ⓜ *hay*·ringks·shmows herring in creamy sauce
—ssalat ⓜ *hay*·ringks·za·laht salad with herring & beetroot
Himbeere ⓕ *him*·bey·re raspberry
Himmel und Erde *hi*·mel unt *er*·de 'Heaven & Earth' – mashed potatoes & apple sauce, sometimes served with slices of black pudding
Hirsch ⓜ hirsh male deer
Holsteiner Schnitzel ⓝ *hol*·shtai·ner *shni*·tsel veal schnitzel with fried egg, accompanied by seafood
Honig ⓜ *haw*·nikh honey
Hörnchen ⓝ *hern*·khen croissant
Hühnerbrust ⓕ *hü*·ner·brust chicken breast
Hühnersuppe ⓕ *hü*·ner·zu·pe chicken soup
Hummer ⓜ *hu*·mer lobster
Husarenfleisch ⓝ hu·*zah*·ren·flaish braised beef, veal & pork fillets with sweet peppers, onions & sour cream
Hutzelbrot ⓝ *hu*·tsel·brawt bread made of prunes & other dried fruit

I

Ingwer ⓜ *ing*·ver ginger
italienischer Salat ⓜ i·tal·*yay*·ni·sher za·*laht* finely sliced veal, salami, anchovies, tomatoes, cucumber & celery in mayonnaise

J

Joghurt ⓜ *yaw*·gurt yoghurt

K

Kabeljau ⓜ *kah*·bel·yow cod
Kaiserschmarren ⓜ *kai*·zer·shmar·ren 'emperor's pancakes' – fluffy pancakes with raisins, served with fruit compote or chocolate sauce
Kaisersemmeln ⓕ pl *kai*·zer·ze·meln 'emperor's rolls' – Austrian bread rolls
Kalbfleisch ⓝ *kalp*·flaish veal
Kalbsnierenbraten ⓜ *kalps*·nee·ren·brah·ten roast veal stuffed with kidneys
Kaninchen ⓝ ka·*neen*·khen rabbit
Kapern ⓕ pl *kah*·pern capers
Karotte ⓕ ka·*ro*·te carrot
Karpfen ⓜ *karp*·fen carp
Kartoffel ⓕ kar·*to*·fel potato
—auflauf ⓜ kar·*to*·fel·owf·lowf potato casserole
—brei ⓜ kar·*to*·fel·brai mashed potatoes

—püree Ⓝ kar·*to*·fel·pü·ray mashed potatoes
—salat Ⓜ kar·*to*·fel·za·laht potato salad
Käse Ⓜ *kay*·ze cheese
—fondue Ⓝ *kay*·ze·fon·dü melted cheese with wine & *Kirschwasser,* into which bread is dipped
Kasseler Ⓝ *kas*·ler smoked pork
— Rippe mit Sauerkraut Ⓕ *kas*·ler *ri*·pe mit *zow*·er·krowt smoked pork rib with sauerkraut
Katenwurst Ⓕ *kah*·ten·vurst country-style smoked sausage
Katzenjammer Ⓜ *ka*·tsen·ya·mer cold slices of beef in mayonnaise with cucumbers or gherkin
Keule Ⓕ *koy*·le leg • haunch
Kieler Sprotten Ⓕ pl *kee*·ler *shpro*·ten small smoked herring
Kirsche Ⓕ *kir*·she cherry
Kirschwasser Ⓝ *kirsh*·va·ser clear, non-sweet cherry brandy
Kirtagssuppe Ⓕ *kir*·tahks·zu·pe soup with caraway seed, thickened with potato
Klöße Ⓜ pl *kler*·se dumplings
Knackwurst Ⓕ *knak*·vurst sausage lightly flavoured with garlic
Knoblauch Ⓜ *knawp*·lowkh garlic
Knödel Ⓜ *kner*·del dumpling
—beignets Ⓜ pl *kner*·del·ben·yays fruit dumplings
Kohl Ⓜ kawl cabbage
—rabi Ⓜ kawl·*rah*·bi kohlrabi
—roulade Ⓕ *kawl*·ru·lah·de cabbage leaves stuffed with minced meat
Kompott Ⓝ kom·*pot* stewed fruit
Königinsuppe Ⓕ *ker*·ni·gin·zu·pe creamy chicken soup
Königsberger Klopse Ⓜ pl *ker*·niks·ber·ger *klop*·se meatballs in a sour cream & caper sauce
Königstorte Ⓕ *ker*·niks·tor·te rum-flavoured fruit cake
Kopfsalat Ⓜ *kopf*·za·laht lettuce
Kotelett Ⓝ kot·*let* chop
Krabbe Ⓕ *kra*·be crab
Krakauer Ⓕ *krah*·kow·er thick, paprika-spiced sausage of Polish origin
Kraut Ⓝ krowt cabbage
—salat Ⓜ *krowt*·za·laht coleslaw
Kräuter Ⓝ pl *kroy*·ter herbs
Krebs Ⓜ krayps crab • crayfish
Kren Ⓜ krayn horseradish (Bavaria & Austria)
Krokette Ⓕ kro·*ke*·te croquette
Kuchen Ⓜ *koo*·khen cake
Kümmel Ⓜ *kü*·mel caraway (seeds)
Kürbis Ⓜ *kür*·bis pumpkin
Kutteln Ⓕ pl *ku*·teln tripe

L

Labskaus Ⓜ *laps*·kows thick meat & potato stew
Lachs Ⓜ laks salmon
Lamm
—fleisch Ⓝ *lam*·flaish lamb
—keule Ⓕ *lam*·koy·le leg of lamb
Landjäger Ⓜ *lant*·yay·ger thin, long, hard, spicy sausage
Languste Ⓕ lan·*gus*·te crayfish
Lappenpickert Ⓜ *la*·pen·pi·kert pan-sized potato pancake usually served with jam or salted fish (Westphalia)
Lauch Ⓜ lowkh leek
Leber Ⓕ *lay*·ber liver
—käse Ⓜ *lay*·ber·kay·ze seasoned meatloaf made of minced liver, pork & bacon
—knödel Ⓜ *lay*·ber·kner·del liver dumpling
—knödelsuppe Ⓕ *lay*·ber·kner·del·zu·pe hot broth with liver dumplings
—wurst Ⓕ *lay*·ber·vurst liver sausage
Lebkuchen Ⓜ *layp*·koo·khen gingerbread
Leckerli Ⓝ *le*·ker·lee honey-flavoured ginger biscuit

Leipziger Allerlei ⓝ *laip*·tsi·ger a·ler·lai mixed vegetable stew (Leipzig)
Lende ⓕ *len*·de loin
Limburger ⓜ *lim*·bur·ger strong cheese flavoured with herbs
Linsen ⓕ pl *lin*·zen lentils
— mit Spätzle mit *shpets*·le lentil stew with noodles & sausages
—suppe ⓕ *lin*·zen·zu·pe lentil soup
Linzer Torte ⓕ *lin*·tser *tor*·te latticed tart with jam topping
Lorbeerblätter ⓝ pl *lor*·bayr·ble·ter bay leaves
Lübecker Marzipan ⓝ *lü*·be·ker *mar*·tsi·pahn marzipan (Lübeck)
Lucullus-Eier ⓝ pl lu·*ku*·lus·ai·er poached, boiled or scrambled eggs with goose liver, truffle & other garnishes, served with a sauce

M

Mais ⓜ mais sweet corn
Majonnaise ⓕ ma·yo·*nay*·ze mayonnaise
Makrele ⓕ ma·*kray*·le mackerel
Mandarine ⓕ man·da·*ree*·ne mandarin • tangerine
Mandel ⓕ *man*·del almond
Marmelade ⓕ mar·me·*lah*·de jam
Matjes ⓜ *mat*·yes young herring
Maultasche ⓕ *mowl*·ta·she filled pasta (Swabia)
Meeresfrüchte ⓕ pl *meer*·res·frükh·te seafood
Meerrettich ⓜ *meer*·re·tikh horseradish
Mehl ⓝ mayl flour
Mett ⓝ met lean minced pork
Mettenden ⓝ *met*·ent·en semidried sausage
Milch ⓕ milkh milk
—rahmstrudel ⓜ *milkh*·rahm·shtroo·del strudel filled with egg custard & soft cheese
Mohnbrötchen ⓝ *mawn*·brert·khen bread roll with poppy seeds
Möhre ⓕ *mer*·re carrot
Muschel ⓕ *mu*·shel clam • mussel
Muskat ⓜ mus·*kaht* nutmeg
Müesli/ Müsli ⓝ *mü*·es·li muesli

N

Nelken ⓕ pl *nel*·ken cloves
Niere ⓕ *nee*·re kidney
Nockerl ⓝ *no*·kerl small dumpling (Austria)
Nudeln ⓕ pl *noo*·deln noodles • pasta
Nudelauflauf ⓜ *noo*·del·owf·lowf pasta casserole
Nürnberger Lebkuchen ⓜ *nürn*·ber·ger *layp*·koo·khen cakes with chocolate, nuts, fruit peel, honey & spices

O

Obatzter ⓜ *aw*·bats·ter Bavarian soft cheese mousse
Obst ⓝ awpst fruit
—salat ⓜ *awpst*·za·laht fruit salad
Ochsenschwanz ⓜ *ok*·sen·shvants oxtail
—suppe ⓕ *ok*·sen·shvants·zu·pe oxtail soup
Öl ⓝ erl oil
Orangenmarmelade ⓕ o·*rahng*·zhen·mar·me·lah·de marmalade

P

Palatschinken ⓜ *pa*·lat·shing·ken pancake, usually filled with jam or cheese, sometimes served with a hot chocolate & nut topping
Pampelmuse ⓕ pam·pel·*moo*·ze grapefruit
Paprika ⓕ *pap*·ri·kah sweet pepper

Pastetchen ⓝ *pas·tayt·khen* filled puff-pastry case
Pastete ⓕ *pas·tay·te* pastry • pie
Pellkartoffeln ⓕ pl *pel·kar·to·feln* small baked potatoes served in their skins, often with quark
Petersilie ⓕ *pay·ter·zee·li·e* parsley
Pfälzer Saumagen ⓜ *pfel·tser zow·mah·gen* stuffed stomach of pork
Pfannkuchen ⓜ *pfan·koo·khen* pancake
Pfeffer ⓜ *pfe·fer* pepper
Pfifferling ⓜ *pfi·fer·ling* chanterelle mushroom
Pfirsich ⓜ *pfir·zikh* peach
Pflaume ⓕ *pflow·me* plum
Pilz ⓜ *pilts* mushroom
Pichelsteiner ⓜ *pi·khel·shtai·ner* meat & vegetable stew
Pökelfleisch ⓝ *per·kel·flaish* marinated meat
Pomeranzensoße ⓕ *po·me·ran·tsen·zaw·se* sauce made of bitter oranges, wine & brandy, usually served with duck
Pommes Frites pl *pom frit* chips • French fries
Porree ⓜ *por·ray* leek
Preiselbeere ⓕ *prai·zel·bey·re* cranberry
Printe ⓕ *prin·te* honey-flavoured biscuit
Pumpernickel ⓜ *pum·per·ni·kel* very dark bread made with coarse wholemeal rye flour
Putenbrust ⓕ *poo·ten·brust* turkey breast
Puter ⓜ *poo·ter* turkey

Q

Quargel ⓜ *kvar·gel* small, round, salty & slightly acidic cheese
Quark ⓜ *kvark* quark (curd cheese)
Quitte ⓕ *kvi·te* quince

R

Radieschen ⓝ *ra·dees·khen* radish
Ragout ⓝ *ra·goo* stew
Rahm ⓜ *rahm* cream
Rebhuhn ⓝ *rayp·hoon* partridge
Regensburger ⓜ *ray·gens·bur·ger* highly spiced smoked sausage
Reh ⓝ *ray* venison
—pfeffer ⓜ *ray·pfe·fer* jugged venison, fried & braised in its marinade, served with sour cream
—rücken ⓜ *ray·rü·ken* saddle of venison
Reibekuchen ⓜ *rai·be·koo·khen* potato cake
Reis ⓜ *rais* rice
Remouladensauce ⓕ *re·mu·lah·den·zaw·se* mayonnaise sauce with mustard, anchovies, capers, gherkins, tarragon & chervil
Rettich ⓜ *re·tikh* radish
Rhabarber ⓜ *ra·bar·ber* rhubarb
Rheinischer Sauerbraten ⓜ **mit Kartoffelklößen** *rai·ni·sher zow·er·brah·ten mit kar·to·fel·kler·sen* roasted marinated meat, slightly sour, often served with potato dumpling
Rindfleisch ⓝ *rint·flaish* beef
Rippenspeer ⓜ *ri·pen·shpair* spare ribs
Rogen ⓜ *raw·gen* roe
Roggenbrot ⓝ *ro·gen·brawt* rye bread
Rohkost ⓕ *raw·kost* uncooked vegetables • vegetarian food
Rollmops ⓜ *rol·mops* pickled herring fillet rolled around chopped onions or gherkins
Rosenkohl ⓜ *raw·zen·kawl* Brussels sprouts
Rosinen ⓕ pl *ro·zee·nen* raisins
Rosmarin ⓜ *raws·ma·reen* rosemary
Rost
—braten ⓜ *rost·brah·ten* roast

—brätl ⓝ *rost*·braytl grilled meat
—hähnchen ⓝ *rost*·hayn·khen roast chicken
Rösti pl *rers*·tee grated, fried potatoes (Switzerland)
rot rawt red
—e Beete ⓕ *raw*·te *bay*·te beetroot • beet
—e Grütze ⓕ *raw*·te *grü*·tse fruit pudding of cooked & sweetened berries, thickened & put in moulds
—e Johannisbeere ⓕ *raw*·te yo·*ha*·nis·bey·re redcurrant
—kohl ⓜ *rawt*·kawl red cabbage
—e Rüben ⓕ pl *raw*·te *rü*·ben beetroot • beet
—wurst ⓕ *rawt*·vurst black pudding
Roulade ⓕ ru·*lah*·de collared beef – thin slices of beef stuffed with onion, bacon and dill pickles then rolled & braised
Rühreier ⓝ pl *rür*·ai·er scrambled eggs
Russische Eier ⓝ pl *ru*·si·she *ai*·er 'Russian eggs' – eggs with mayonnaise

S

Sahne ⓕ *zah*·ne cream
Salat ⓜ za·*laht* salad
Salbei ⓜ *zal*·bai sage
Salz ⓝ zalts salt
Salzburger Nockerln ⓝ pl *zalts*·bur·ger *no*·kerln Austrian dessert of sweet dumplings poached in milk & served with warm vanilla sauce
Salzkartoffeln ⓕ pl *zalts*·kar·to·feln boiled potatoes
Sauerbraten ⓜ *zow*·er·brah·ten marinated roasted beef served with a sour cream sauce
Sauerkraut ⓝ *zow*·er·krowt pickled cabbage
Schafskäse ⓜ *shahfs*·kay·ze feta-style sheep's milk cheese
Schellfisch ⓜ *shel*·fish haddock
Schinken ⓜ *shing*·ken ham
Schlachtplatte ⓕ *shlakht*·pla·te selection of pork & sausage
Schmalzbrot ⓝ *shmalts*·brawt slice of bread with dripping
Schmorbraten ⓜ *shmawr*·brah·ten beef pot roast
Schnitte ⓕ *shni*·te slice of bread • small square piece of cake
Schnittlauch ⓜ *shnit*·lowkh chives
Schnitzel ⓝ *shni*·tsel pork, veal or chicken breast pounded flat, covered in breadcrumbs & pan-fried
Scholle ⓕ *sho*·le plaice
schwarze Johannisbeere ⓕ *shvar*·tse yo·*ha*·nis·bey·re blackcurrant
Schwarzwälder Kirschtorte ⓕ *shvarts*·vel·der *kirsh*·tor·te Black Forest cake (chocolate layer cake filled with cream & cherries)
Schwein ⓝ *shvain* pork
—ebraten ⓜ *shvai*·ne·brah·ten roast pork
—efleisch ⓝ *shvai*·ne·flaish pork
—shaxe ⓕ *shvains*·hak·se crispy leg of pork served with dumplings
Seezunge ⓕ *zay*·tsung·e sole
Seidfleisch ⓝ *zait*·flaish boiled meat
Sekt ⓜ zekt German sparkling wine
Selchfleisch ⓝ *zelkh*·flaish smoked pork
Sellerie ⓜ *ze*·le·ree celery
Semmel ⓕ *ze*·mel bread roll (Austria & Bavaria)
—knödel ⓜ pl *ze*·mel·kner·del dumplings made of dry rolls dunked in milk (Bavaria)
Senf ⓜ zenf mustard
Sonnenblumenkerne ⓜ pl *zo*·nen·bloo·men·ker·ne sunflower seeds
Soße ⓕ *zaw*·se sauce • gravy
spanische Soße ⓕ *shpah*·ni·she *zaw*·se brown sauce with herbs

Spanferkel (n) *shpahn*·fer·kel suckling pig
Spargel (m) *shpar*·gel asparagus
Spätzle pl *shpets*·le thick noodles
Speck (m) shpek bacon
Spekulatius (m) shpe·ku·*lah*·tsi·us almond biscuits
Spiegelei (n) *shpee*·gel·ai fried egg
Spinat (m) shpi·*naht* spinach
Sprossenkohl (m) *shpro*·sen·kawl Brussels sprouts
Sprotten (f) pl *shpro*·ten sprats (small herring-like fish)
Steckrübe (f) *shtek*·rü·be turnip
Steinbuscher (m) *shtain*·bu·sher semi-hard, creamy cheese with a strong, slightly bitter flavour
Steinbutt (m) *shtain*·but turbot (flatfish)
Stelze (f) *shtel*·tse knuckle of pork
Sterz (m) shterts Austrian polenta
Stollen (m) *shto*·len spiced loaf with candied peel, traditionally eaten at Christmas
Strammer Max (m) *shtra*·mer maks sandwich with ham (or sausage or spiced minced pork), served with fried eggs & sometimes onions
Streichkäse (m) *shtraikh*·kay·ze any kind of soft cheese spread
Streuselkuchen (m) *shtroy*·zel·koo·khen coffee cake topped with a mixture of butter, sugar, flour & cinnamon
Strudel (m) *shtroo*·del loaf-shaped pastry filled with something sweet or savoury
Suppe (f) *zu*·pe soup

T

Tascherl (n) *ta*·sherl pastry turnover with meat, cheese or jam filling
Tatarenbrot (n) ta·*tah*·ren·brawt open sandwich topped with raw spiced minced beef
Teigwaren pl *taik*·vah·ren pasta
Thunfisch (m) *toon*·fish tuna
Thüringer (f) *tü*·ring·er long, thin, spiced sausage
Thymian (m) *tü*·mi·ahn thyme
Toast (m) tawst toast
Tomate (f) to·*mah*·te tomato
—nketchup (m) to·*mah*·ten·ket·chap tomato sauce
—nsuppe (f) to·*mah*·ten·zu·pe tomato soup
Topfen (m) *top*·fen curd cheese (Austria)
Törtchen (n) *tert*·khen small tart or cake
Torte (f) *tor*·te layer cake
Truthahn (m) *troot*·hahn turkey
Tunke (f) *tung*·ke sauce • gravy

V

Vollkornbrot (n) *fol*·korn·brawt wholemeal bread
Voressen (n) *fawr*·e·sen meat stew

W

Wachtel (f) *vakh*·tel quail
Walnuss (f) *val*·nus walnut
Wecke (f) *ve*·ke bread roll (Austria & southern Germany)
Weichkäse (m) *vaikh*·kay·ze soft cheese
Weinbergschnecken (f) pl *vain*·berk·shne·ken snails
Weinkraut (n) *vain*·krowt white cabbage, braised with apples & simmered in wine
Weintraube (f) *vain*·trow·be grape
Weißbrot (n) *vais*·brawt white bread
Weißwurst (f) *vais*·vurst veal sausage, found mainly in southern Germany
Westfälischer Schinken (m) vest·*fay*·li·sher *shing*·ken variety of cured & smoked ham

Wiener *vee*·ner in the Viennese style
— Würstchen ⓝ *vee*·ner *vürst*·khen frankfurter (sausage)
— Schnitzel ⓝ *vee*·ner *shni*·tsel crumbed veal
Wiezenbrot ⓝ *vai*·tsen·brawt wheat bread
Wild ⓝ *vilt* game
—braten ⓜ *vilt*·brah·ten roast venison
—ente ⓕ *vilt*·en·te wild duck
—schwein ⓝ *vilt*·shvain wild boar
Wilstermarschkäse ⓜ *vils*·ter·marsh·kay·ze semi-hard cheese
Wurst ⓕ vurst sausage
Würstchen ⓝ *vürst*·khen small sausage
Wurstplatte ⓕ *vurst*·pla·te cold cuts

Z

Ziege ⓕ *tsee*·ge goat
Zimt ⓜ tsimt cinnamon
Zitrone ⓕ tsi·*traw*·ne lemon
Zucker ⓜ *tsu*·ker sugar
Zunge ⓕ *tsung*·e tongue
Züricher Geschnetzeltes ⓝ *tsü*·ri·kher ge·*shne*·tsel·tes sliced veal with mushrooms & onions cooked in a white wine & cream sauce
Zwetschge ⓕ *tsvetsh*·ge plum
—ndatschi ⓜ *tsvetsh*·gen·dat·shi damson plum tart
Zwieback ⓜ *tsvee*·bak rusk
Zwiebel ⓕ *tsvee*·bel onion
—fleisch ⓝ *tsvee*·bel·flaish beef sauteed with onion
—kuchen ⓜ *tsvee*·bel·koo·khen onion quiche, often served with *Federweißer* (new wine)
—suppe ⓕ *tsvee*·bel·zu·pe onion soup
—wurst ⓕ *tsvee*·bel·vurst liver & onion sausage
Zwischenrippenstück ⓝ *tsvi*·shen·ri·pen·shtük rib eye steak

DICTIONARY

English to German

ENGLISCH-DEUTSCH

Nouns in the dictionary, and adjectives affected by gender, have their gender indicated by ⓕ, ⓜ or ⓝ. If it's a plural noun, you'll also see pl. Where a word that could be either a noun or a verb has no gender indicated, it's a verb.

A

(to be) able können *ker*·nen
aboard an Bord an bort
abortion Abtreibung ⓕ *ap*·trai·bung
about über *ü*·ber
above über *ü*·ber
abroad im Ausland im *ows*·lant
accident Unfall ⓜ *un*·fal
accommodation Unterkunft ⓕ *un*·ter·kunft
accountant Buchhalter(in) ⓜ/ⓕ *bookh*·hal·ter/*bookh*·hal·te·rin
across (from) gegenüber gay·gen·*ü*·ber
across (to) hinüber hi·*nü*·ber
activist Aktivist(in) ⓜ/ⓕ ak·ti·*vist*/ ak·ti·*vis*·tin
actor Schauspieler(in) ⓜ/ⓕ *show*·shpee·ler/*show*·shpee·le·rin
acupuncture Akupunktur ⓕ a·ku·pungk·*toor*
adaptor Adapter ⓜ a·*dap*·ter
addicted abhängig *ap*·heng·ikh
address Adresse ⓕ a·*dre*·se
administration Verwaltung ⓕ fer·*val*·tung
admire bewundern be·*vun*·dern
admission price Eintrittspreis ⓜ *ain*·trits·prais
admit (allow to enter) einlassen *ain*·la·sen
admit (accept as true) zugeben *tsoo*·gay·ben
adult Erwachsene ⓜ&ⓕ er·*vak*·se·ne
advertisement Anzeige ⓕ *an*·tsai·ge
advice Rat ⓜ raht
advise raten *rah*·ten
aerobics Aerobics pl e·*ro*·biks
aeroplane Flugzeug ⓝ *flook*·tsoyk
(to be) afraid Angst (haben) angkst (*hah*·ben)
Africa Afrika ⓝ *a*·fri·kah
after nach nahkh
(this) afternoon (heute) Nachmittag ⓜ (*hoy*·te) *nahkh*·mi·tahk
aftershave Aftershave ⓝ *ahf*·ter·shayf
again wieder *vee*·der
against gegen *gay*·gen
age Alter ⓝ *al*·ter
(three days) ago vor (drei Tagen) fawr (drai *tah*·gen)
agree zustimmen *tsoo*·shti·men

agriculture Landwirtschaft Ⓕ *lant*·virt·shaft
ahead vor uns fawr uns
AIDS AIDS Ⓝ aydz
air Luft Ⓕ luft
airmail Luftpost Ⓕ *luft*·post
air pollution Luftverschmutzung Ⓕ *luft*·fer·shmu·tsung
air-conditioned mit Klimaanlage Ⓕ mit *klee*·ma·an·lah·ge
airline Fluglinie Ⓕ *flook*·lee·ni·e
airplane Flugzeug Ⓝ *flook*·tsoyk
airport Flughafen Ⓜ *flook*·hah·fen
airport tax Flughafengebühr Ⓕ *flook*·hah·fen·ge·bür
airsickness Luftkrankheit Ⓕ *luft*·krangk·hait
aisle Gang Ⓜ gang
aisle seat Platz am Gang Ⓜ plats am gang
alarm clock Wecker Ⓜ *ve*·ker
alcohol Alkohol Ⓜ *al*·ko·hawl
alcoholic Alkoholiker(in) Ⓜ/Ⓕ al·ko·*haw*·li·ker/al·ko·*haw*·li·ke·rin
alcoholic alkoholisch al·ko·*haw*·lish
all alle a·le
allergy Allergie Ⓕ a·lair·*gee*
allow erlauben er·*low*·ben
almond Mandel Ⓕ *man*·del
almost fast fast
alone allein a·*lain*
already schon shawn
also auch owkh
altar Altar Ⓜ al·*tahr*
altitude Höhe Ⓕ *her*·e
always immer *i*·mer
amateur Amateur(in) Ⓜ/Ⓕ a·ma·*ter*/a·ma·*ter*·rin
amazing erstaunlich er·*shtown*·likh
ambassador Botschafter(in) Ⓜ/Ⓕ *bawt*·shaf·ter/*bawt*·shaf·te·rin
ambulance Krankenwagen Ⓜ *krang*·ken·vah·gen
among unter *un*·ter
amount Betrag Ⓜ be·*trahk*
anaesthetic Betäubung Ⓕ be·*toy*·bung
anarchist Anarchist(in) Ⓜ/Ⓕ a·nar·*khist*/a·nar·*khis*·tin
ancient alt alt
and und unt
angry wütend *vü*·tent
animal Tier Ⓝ teer
ankle Knöchel Ⓜ *kner*·khel
answer Antwort Ⓕ *ant*·vort
answer antworten *ant*·vor·ten
ant Ameise Ⓕ *ah*·mai·ze
antibiotics Antibiotika Ⓝ pl an·ti·bi·*aw*·ti·ka
antinuclear Anti-Atom- an·ti·a·*tawm*·
antique Antiquität Ⓕ an·ti·kvi·*tayt*
antiseptic Antiseptikum Ⓝ an·ti·*zep*·ti·kum
any irgendein ir·gent·*ain*
anything (irgend)etwas (*ir*·gent·)*et*·vas
anywhere irgendwo ir·gent·*vaw*
apart from (besides) außer *ow*·ser
apartment Wohnung Ⓕ *vaw*·nung
appendix Blinddarm Ⓜ *blint*·darm
apple Apfel Ⓜ *ap*·fel
appointment Termin Ⓜ ter·*meen*
apprentice Auszubildende Ⓜ&Ⓕ *ows*·tsu·bil·den·de
approximately ungefähr un·ge·*fair*
apricot Aprikose Ⓕ a·pri·*kaw*·ze
archaeological archäologisch ar·khe·o·*law*·gish
architecture Architektur Ⓕ ar·khi·tek·*toor*
area code Vorwahl Ⓕ *fawr*·vahl
argue streiten *shtrai*·ten
arm Arm Ⓜ arm
aromatherapy Aromatheraphie Ⓕ a·*raw*·ma·tay·ra·*pee*
arrest Verhaftung Ⓕ fer·*haf*·tung
arrivals Ankunft Ⓕ *an*·kunft
arrive ankommen *an*·ko·men
art Kunst Ⓕ kunst
art collection Kunstsammlung Ⓕ *kunst*·zam·lung

art gallery Kunstgalerie ⓕ *kunst*·ga·le·ree
artist Künstler(in) ⓜ/ⓕ *künst*·ler/*künst*·le·rin
arts & crafts Kunstgewerbe ⓝ *kunst*·ge·ver·be
as far as bis zu bis tsoo
ashtray Aschenbecher ⓜ a·shen·be·kher
Asia Asien ⓝ *ah*·zi·en
ask a question eine Frage stellen ai·ne *frah*·ge *shte*·len
ask (for something) um etwas bitten um *et*·vas *bi*·ten
asleep schlafen *shlah*·fen
asparagus Spargel ⓜ *shpar*·gel
aspirin Aspirin ⓝ as·pi·*reen*
asthma Asthma ⓝ *ast*·ma
asylum seeker Asylant(in) ⓜ/ⓕ a·zü·*lant*/a·zü·*lan*·tin
at in • an • auf • bei • zu in • an • owf • bai • tsoo
athletics Leichtathletik ⓕ *laikht*·at·lay·tik
atmosphere Atmosphäre ⓕ at·mos·*fair*·re
attic Dachboden ⓜ *dakh*·baw·den
aubergine Aubergine ⓕ aw·ber·*zhee*·ne
aunt Tante ⓕ *tan*·te
Australia Australien ⓝ ows·*trah*·li·en
Austria Österreich ⓝ *ers*·ter·raikh
author Autor(in) ⓜ/ⓕ *ow*·tor/ow·*taw*·rin
automatic automatisch ow·to·*mah*·tish
automatic teller machine (ATM) Geldautomat ⓜ *gelt*·ow·to·maht
autumn Herbst ⓜ herpst
avalanche Lawine ⓕ la·*vee*·ne
avenue Allee ⓕ a·*lay*
avocado Avokado ⓕ a·vo·*kah*·do
axe Axt ⓕ akst

B

baby Baby ⓝ *bay*·bi
baby food Babynahrung ⓕ *bay*·bi·nah·rung
baby powder Babypuder ⓝ *bay*·bi·poo·der
babysitter Babysitter ⓜ *bay*·bi·si·ter
back (body) Rücken ⓜ *rü*·ken
back (return) zurück tsu·*rük*
backpack Rucksack ⓜ *ruk*·zak
bacon Frühstücksspeck ⓜ *frü*·shtüks·shpek
bad schlecht shlekht
badger Dachs ⓜ daks
bag Tasche ⓕ *ta*·she
baggage Gepäck ⓝ ge·*pek*
baggage allowance Freigepäck ⓝ *frai*·ge·pek
baggage claim Gepäckausgabe ⓕ ge·*pek*·ows·gah·be
bait Köder ⓜ *ker*·der
bakery Bäckerei ⓕ be·ke·*rai*
balance (account) Kontostand ⓜ *kon*·to·shtant
balcony Balkon ⓜ bal·*kawn*
ball Ball ⓜ bal
ballet Ballett ⓝ ba·*let*
banana Banane ⓕ ba·*nah*·ne
band (music) Band ⓕ bent
bandage Verband ⓜ fer·*bant*
Band-Aids Pflaster ⓝ *pflas*·ter
bank Bank ⓕ bangk
bank account Bankkonto ⓝ *bangk*·kon·to
bankdraft Bankauszug ⓜ *bangk*·ows·tsook
banknote Geldschein ⓜ *gelt*·shain
baptism Taufe ⓕ *tow*·fe
bar Lokal ⓝ lo·*kahl*
baseball Baseball ⓜ *bays*·bawl
basket Korb ⓜ korp
bath Bad ⓝ baht
bath towel Badetuch ⓝ *bah*·de·tookh
bathing suit Badeanzug ⓜ *bah*·de·an·tsook

bathroom Badezimmer ⓝ *bah*·de·tsi·mer
battery Batterie ⓕ ba·te·*ree*
bay Bucht ⓕ bukht
be sein zain
beach Strand ⓜ shtrant
bean Bohne ⓕ *baw*·ne
bear Bär ⓜ bayr
beautiful schön shern
beauty salon Schönheitssalon ⓜ *shern*·haits·za·long
because weil vail
because of wegen *vay*·gen
bed Bett ⓝ bet
bed & breakfast Pension ⓕ pahng·*zyawn*
bedding Bettzeug ⓝ *bet*·tsoyk
bedroom Schlafzimmer ⓝ *shlahf*·tsi·mer
bee Biene ⓕ *bee*·ne
beef Rindfleisch ⓝ *rint*·flaish
beer Bier ⓝ beer
beetroot/beet rote Beete ⓕ *raw*·te *bay*·te
before vor fawr
beggar Bettler(in) ⓜ/ⓕ *bet*·ler/ *bet*·le·rin
begin beginnen be·*gi*·nen
behind hinter *hin*·ter
Belgium Belgien ⓝ *bel*·gi·en
below unter *un*·ter
belt Gürtel ⓜ *gür*·tel
beside neben *nay*·ben
best beste *bes*·te
bet Wette ⓕ *ve*·te
better besser *be*·ser
between zwischen *tsvi*·shen
bible Bibel ⓕ *bee*·bel
bicycle Fahrrad ⓝ *fahr*·raht
big groß graws
bike Fahrrad ⓕ *fahr*·raht
bike chain Fahrradkette ⓕ *fahr*·raht·ke·te
bike path Radweg ⓜ *raht*·vayk
bill (account) Rechnung ⓕ *rekh*·nung
bin (rubbish) Mülleimer ⓝ *mül*·ai·mer
binoculars Fernglas ⓝ *fern*·glahs
bird Vogel ⓜ *faw*·gel
birth certificate Geburtsurkunde ⓕ ge·*burts*·oor·kun·de
birthday Geburtstag ⓜ ge·*burts*·tahk
biscuit Keks ⓜ kayks
bite (dog) Biss ⓜ bis
bite (insect) Stich ⓜ shtikh
bitter bitter *bi*·ter
black schwarz shvarts
B&W (film) schwarzweiß shvarts·*vais*
blanket Decke ⓕ *de*·ke
bless segnen *zayg*·nen
blind blind blint
blister Blase ⓕ *blah*·ze
blocked blockiert blo·*keert*
blood Blut ⓝ bloot
blood group Blutgruppe ⓕ *bloot*·gru·pe
blood pressure Blutdruck ⓜ *bloot*·druk
blood test Bluttest ⓜ *bloot*·test
blue blau blow
boar Wildschwein ⓝ *vilt*·shvain
board Brett ⓝ bret
board (plane, ship) besteigen be·*shtai*·gen
boarding house Pension ⓕ pahng·*zyawn*
boarding pass Bordkarte ⓕ *bort*·kar·te
boat Boot ⓝ bawt
body Körper ⓜ *ker*·per
bone Knochen ⓜ *kno*·khen
book Buch ⓝ bookh
book (reserve) buchen *boo*·khen
booked out ausgebucht *ows*·ge·bookht
bookshop Buchhandlung ⓕ *bookh*·hand·lung
boot (trunk) Kofferraum ⓜ *ko*·fer·rowm
boot (footwear) Stiefel ⓜ *shtee*·fel
border Grenze ⓕ *gren*·tse
bored gelangweilt ge·*lang*·vailt
boring langweilig *lang*·vai·likh

borrow (aus)leihen *(ows·)lai·en*
boss Chef(in) ⓜ/ⓕ shef/*she*·fin
botanic garden
Botanischer Garten ⓜ bo·*tah*·ni·sher *gar*·ten
both beide *bai*·de
bottle Flasche ⓕ *fla*·she
bottle opener Flaschenöffner ⓜ *fla*·shen·erf·ner
bottom (at the) unten *un*·ten
bouncer (doorman) Türsteher ⓜ *tür*·shtay·er
bowl Schüssel ⓕ *shü*·sel
box Karton ⓜ kar·*tong*
boxer shorts Shorts pl shorts
boxing Boxen ⓝ *bok*·sen
boy Junge ⓜ *yung*·e
boyfriend Freund ⓜ froynt
bra BH ⓜ bay·*hah*
Braille Blindenschrift ⓕ *blin*·den·shrift
brake fluid Bremsflüssigkeit ⓕ *brems*·flü·sikh·kait
brakes Bremsen ⓕ pl *brem*·zen
brandy Weinbrand ⓜ *vain*·brant
brave mutig *moo*·tikh
bread Brot ⓝ brawt
bread roll Brötchen ⓝ *brert*·khen
break (zer)brechen (tser·)*bre*·khen
break down eine Panne haben *ai*·ne *pa*·ne *hah*·ben
breakdown service Abschleppdienst ⓜ *ap*·shlep·deenst
breakfast Frühstück ⓝ *frü*·shtük
breast Brust ⓕ brust
breathe atmen *aht*·men
brewery Brauerei ⓕ brow·e·*rai*
bribe bestechen be·*shte*·khen
bricklayer Maurer(in) ⓜ/ⓕ *mow*·rer/ *mow*·re·rin
bridge Brücke ⓕ *brü*·ke
bridle path Reitweg ⓜ *rait*·vayk
briefcase Aktentasche ⓕ *ak*·ten·ta·she
brilliant brillant bril·*yant*
bring bringen *bring*·en
broccoli Brokkoli ⓜ pl *bro*·ko·li

brochure Broschüre ⓕ bro·*shü*·re
broken kaputt ka·*put*
bronchitis Bronchitis ⓕ bron·*khee*·tis
brother Bruder ⓜ *broo*·der
brown braun brown
bruise Bluterguss ⓜ *bloot*·er·oos
Brussels sprouts Rosenkohl ⓜ *raw*·zen·kawl
bucket Eimer ⓜ *ai*·mer
Buddhist Buddhist(in) ⓜ/ⓕ bu·*dist*/ bu·*dis*·tin
buffet Buffet ⓝ bü·*fay*
bug (insect) Insekt ⓝ in·*zekt*
build bauen *bow*·en
building Gebäude ⓝ ge·*boy*·de
bumbag Hüfttasche ⓕ *hüft*·ta·she
burn (ver)brennen (fer·)*bre*·nen
bus (city) Bus ⓜ bus
bus (intercity) Fernbus ⓜ *fern*·bus
bus station Busbahnhof ⓜ *bus*·bahn·hawf
bus stop Bushaltestelle ⓕ *bus*·hal·te·shte·le
business Geschäft ⓝ ge·*sheft*
business class Business Class ⓕ *bi*·zi·nes klahs
business person Geschäftsmann/ Geschäftsfrau ⓜ/ⓕ ge·*shefts*·man/ ge·*shefts*·frow
business trip Geschäftsreise ⓕ ge·*shefts*·rai·ze
busker Straßenmusiker(in) ⓜ/ⓕ *shtrah*·sen·moo·zi·ker/ *shtrah*·sen·moo·zi·ke·rin
busy (person) beschäftigt be·*shef*·tikht
busy (phone) besetzt be·*zetst*
but aber *ah*·ber
butcher's shop Metzgerei ⓕ mets·ge·*rai*
butter Butter ⓕ *bu*·ter
butterfly Schmetterling ⓜ *shme*·ter·ling
button Knopf ⓜ knopf
buy kaufen *kow*·fen

C

cabbage Kohl ⓜ *kawl*
cable Kabel ⓝ *kah·bel*
cable car Seilbahn ⓕ *zail·bahn*
cafe Café ⓝ *ka·fay*
cake Kuchen ⓜ *koo·khen*
cake shop Konditorei ⓕ *kon·dee·to·rai*
calculator Taschenrechner ⓜ *ta·shen·rekh·ner*
calendar Kalender ⓜ *ka·len·der*
camera Kamera ⓕ *kah·me·ra*
camp zelten *tsel·ten*
camping ground Campingplatz ⓜ *kem·ping·plats*
camping stove Kocher ⓜ *ko·kher*
camp site Zeltplatz ⓜ *tselt·plats*
can (be able) können *ker·nen*
can (have permission) können *ker·nen*
can (tin) Dose ⓕ *daw·ze*
can opener Dosenöffner ⓜ *daw·zen·erf·ner*
Canada Kanada ⓝ *ka·na·dah*
canary Kanarienvogel ⓜ *ka·nah·ri·en·faw·gel*
cancel stornieren *shtor·nee·ren*
cancer Krebs ⓜ *krayps*
candle Kerze ⓕ *ker·tse*
candy Bonbon ⓜ *bong·bong*
cantaloupe Beutelmelone ⓕ *boy·tel·me·law·ne*
canteen Kantine ⓕ *kan·tee·ne*
cape (offshore) Kap ⓝ *kap*
capitalism Kapitalismus ⓜ *ka·pi·ta·lis·mus*
capsicum Paprika ⓕ *pap·ri·kah*
car Auto ⓝ *ow·to*
car hire Autoverleih ⓜ *ow·to·fer·lai*
car owner's title (document) Fahrzeugpapiere ⓝ pl *fahr·tsoyk·pa·pee·re*
car park Parkplatz ⓜ *park·plats*
car registration Fahrzeugzulassung ⓕ *fahr·tsoyk·tsoo·la·sung*
caravan Wohnwagen ⓜ *vawn·vah·gen*
carburettor Vergaser ⓜ *fer·gah·zer*
cards Karten ⓕ pl *kar·ten*
care (for someone) sich kümmern um *zikh kü·mern um*
careful vorsichtig *fawr·zikh·tikh*
caring liebevoll *lee·be·fol*
carpenter Schreiner(in) ⓜ/ⓕ *shrai·ner/shrai·ne·rin*
carriage (train) Wagen ⓜ *vah·gen*
carrot Möhre ⓕ *mer·re*
carry tragen *trah·gen*
carton Karton ⓜ *kar·tong*
carton (milk) Tüte ⓕ *tü·te*
cash Bargeld ⓝ *bahr·gelt*
cash (a cheque) (einen Scheck) einlösen *(ai·nen shek) ain·ler·zen*
cash register Kasse ⓕ *ka·se*
cashew Cashewnuss ⓕ *kesh·yoo·nus*
cashier Kassierer(in) ⓜ/ⓕ *ka·see·rer/ka·see·re·rin*
casino Kasino ⓝ *ka·zee·no*
castle Burg ⓕ *burk*
casual work Gelegenheitsarbeit ⓕ *ge·lay·gen·haits·ar·bait*
cat Katze ⓕ *ka·tse*
cathedral Dom ⓜ *dawm*
Catholic Katholik(in) ⓜ/ⓕ *ka·to·leek/ka·to·lee·kin*
cauliflower Blumenkohl ⓜ *bloo·men·kawl*
cave Höhle ⓕ *her·le*
caviar Kaviar ⓜ *kah·vi·ahr*
CD CD ⓕ *tsay·day*
celebration Feier ⓕ *fai·er*
cellar Keller ⓜ *ke·ler*
cemetery Friedhof ⓜ *freet·hawf*
cent Cent ⓜ *sent*
centigrade Celsius ⓜ *tsel·zi·us*
centimetre Zentimeter ⓜ *tsen·ti·may·ter*
central heating Zentralheizung ⓕ *tsen·trahl·hai·tsung*
centre Zentrum ⓝ *tsen·trum*

ceramic Keramik (f) ke·*rah*·mik
cereal Frühstücksflocke (f) *frü*·shtüks·flo·ke
certificate Zertifikat (n) tser·ti·fi·*kaht*
chain Kette (f) *ke*·te
chair Stuhl (m) shtool
chairlift (skiing) Sessellift (m) *ze*·se·lift
championships Meisterschaften (f) pl *mais*·ter·shaf·ten
chance Zufall (m) *tsoo*·fal
change (coins) Wechselgeld (n) *vek*·sel·gelt
change (money) wechseln *vek*·seln
change (trains) umsteigen *um*·shtai·gen
changing room Umkleideraum (m) *um*·klai·de·rowm
chapel Kapelle (f) ka·*pe*·le
charming charmant shar·*mant*
chat up anbaggern *an*·ba·gern
cheap billig *bi*·likh
cheat Betrüger(in) (m)/(f) be·*trü*·ger/be·*trü*·ge·rin
check (banking) Scheck (m) shek
check (bill) Rechnung (f) *rekh*·nung
check prüfen *prü*·fen
check-in (desk) Abfertigungsschalter (m) *ap*·fer·ti·gungks·shal·ter
checkpoint Kontrollstelle (f) kon·*trol*·shte·le
cheese Käse (m) *kay*·ze
chef Koch/Köchin (m)/(f) kokh/*ker*·khin
chemist Apotheke (f) a·po·*tay*·ke
cheque (banking) Scheck (m) shek
chess Schach (n) shakh
chest Brustkorb (m) *brust*·korp
chewing gum Kaugummi (n) *kow*·gu·mi
chicken Huhn (n) hoon
chicken breast Hühnerbrust (f) *hü*·ner·brust
chicken drumstick Hähnchenschenkel (m) *hayn*·khen·sheng·kel
chickpea Kichererbse (f) *ki*·kher·erp·se
child Kind (n) kint
child seat Kindersitz (m) *kin*·der·zits
childminding Kinderbetreuung (f) *kin*·der·be·troy·ung
children Kinder (n) pl *kin*·der
chiropractor Chiropraktiker (m) khee·ro·*prak*·ti·ker
chocolate Schokolade (f) sho·ko·*lah*·de
choose (aus)wählen (*ows*·)*vay*·len
christening Taufe (f) *tow*·fe
Christian Christ(in) (m)/(f) krist/*kris*·tin
Christian name Vorname (m) *fawr*·nah·me
Christmas Weihnachten (n) *vai*·nakh·ten
Christmas Day (erster) Weihnachtsfeiertag (m) (*ers*·ter) *vai*·nakhts·fai·er·tahk
Christmas Eve Heiligabend (m) hai·likh·*ah*·bent
Christmas tree Weihnachtsbaum (m) *vai*·nakhts·bowm
church Kirche (f) *kir*·khe
cider Apfelmost (m) *ap*·fel·most
cigar Zigarre (f) tsi·*ga*·re
cigarette Zigarette (f) tsi·ga·*re*·te
cigarette lighter Feuerzeug (n) *foy*·er·tsoyk
cinema Kino (n) *kee*·no
circus Zirkus (m) *tsir*·kus
citizenship Staatsbürgerschaft (f) *shtahts*·bür·ger·shaft
city Stadt (f) shtat
city centre Innenstadt (f) *i*·nen·shtat
civil rights Bürgerrechte (n) pl *bür*·ger·rekh·te
civil servant Beamte/Beamtin (m)/(f) be·*am*·te/be·*am*·tin
class Klasse (f) *kla*·se
classical klassisch *kla*·sish
clean sauber *zow*·ber
cleaning Reinigung (f) *rai*·ni·gung

client Kunde/Kundin ⓜ/ⓕ kun·de/kun·din
cliff Klippe ⓕ kli·pe
climate Klima ⓝ klee·ma
climb klettern kle·tern
cloak Mantel ⓜ man·tel
cloakroom Garderobe ⓕ gar·draw·be
clock Uhr ⓕ oor
close (shut) schließen shlee·sen
close (nearby) nahe nah·e
closed geschlossen ge·shlo·sen
clothesline Wäscheleine ⓕ ve·she·lai·ne
clothing Kleidung ⓕ klai·dung
clothing store Bekleidungsgeschäft ⓝ be·klai·dungks·ge·sheft
cloud Wolke ⓕ vol·ke
cloudy wolkig vol·kikh
clove (spice) Gewürznelke ⓕ ge·vürts·nel·ke
clove (of garlic) Zehe ⓕ tsay·e
clutch (car) Kupplung ⓕ kup·lung
coach (bus) Bus ⓜ bus
coach (sport) Trainer(in) ⓜ/ⓕ tray·ner/tray·ne·rin
coast Küste ⓕ küs·te
coat Mantel ⓜ man·tel
cocaine Kokain ⓝ ko·ka·een
cockroach Kakerlake ⓕ kah·ker·lah·ke
cocoa Kakao ⓜ ka·kow
coffee Kaffee ⓜ ka·fay
coins Münzen ⓕ pl mün·tsen
cold kalt kalt
cold (have a) erkältet sein er·kel·tet zain
colleague Kollege/Kollegin ⓜ/ⓕ ko·lay·ge/ko·lay·gin
collect call R-Gespräch ⓝ air·ge·shpraykh
college College ⓝ ko·lidzh
colour Farbe ⓕ far·be
comb Kamm ⓜ kam
come kommen ko·men
comedy Komödie ⓕ ko·mer·di·e
comfortable bequem be·kvaym
communion Kommunion ⓕ ko·mun·yawn
companion Begleiter(in) ⓜ/ⓕ be·glai·ter/be·glai·te·rin
company Firma ⓕ fir·ma
compass Kompass ⓜ kom·pas
complain sich beschweren zikh be·shvair·ren
computer Computer ⓜ kom·pyoo·ter
computer game Computerspiel ⓝ kom·pyoo·ter·shpeel
concert Konzert ⓝ kon·tsert
concert hall Konzerthalle ⓕ kon·tsert·ha·le
conditioner Spülung ⓕ shpü·lung
condom Kondom ⓝ kon·dawm
conductor Schaffner(in) ⓜ/ⓕ shaf·ner/shaf·ne·rin
confession (religious) Beichte ⓕ baikh·te
confirm (a booking) bestätigen be·shtay·ti·gen
connection Verbindung ⓕ fer·bin·dung
conservative konservativ kon·zer·va·teef
constipation Verstopfung ⓕ fer·shtop·fung
consulate Konsulat ⓝ kon·zu·laht
contact lenses Kontaktlinsen ⓕ pl kon·takt·lin·zen
contraceptives Verhütungsmittel ⓝ fer·hü·tungks·mi·tel
contract Vertrag ⓜ fer·trahk
convenience store Kiosk ⓜ kee·osk
convent Kloster ⓝ klaws·ter
cook Koch/Köchin ⓜ/ⓕ kokh/ker·khin
cook kochen ko·khen
cookie Keks ⓜ kayks
corner Ecke ⓕ e·ke
cornflakes Cornflakes pl korn·flayks
corrupt korrupt ko·rupt
cost kosten kos·ten
cottage cheese Hüttenkäse ⓜ hü·ten·kay·ze

cotton Baumwolle ⓕ *bowm*·vo·le
cotton balls Watte-Pads pl
va·te·pedz
cough husten *hoos*·ten
cough medicine Hustensaft ⓜ
hoos·ten·zaft
count zählen *tsay*·len
counter (at bar) Theke ⓕ *tay*·ke
country Land ⓝ lant
countryside Land ⓝ lant
coupon Coupon ⓜ ku·*pong*
courgette Zucchini ⓕ tsu·*kee*·ni
court (legal) Gericht ⓝ ge·*rikht*
court (tennis) Platz ⓜ plats
couscous Couscous ⓜ *kus*·kus
cousin Cousin(e) ⓜ/ⓕ ku·*zen*/
ku·*zee*·ne
cover charge Eintrittsgeld ⓝ
ain·trits·gelt
cow Kuh ⓕ koo
cracker Cracker ⓜ *kre*·ker
crafts Handwerk ⓝ *hant*·verk
cramp Krampf ⓜ krampf
crash Zusammenstoß ⓜ
tsu·*za*·men·staws
crazy verrückt fe·*rükt*
cream Sahne ⓕ *zah*·ne
cream cheese Frischkäse ⓜ
frish·kay·ze
creche Kinderkrippe ⓕ *kin*·der·kri·pe
credit card Kreditkarte ⓕ
kre·*deet*·kar·te
cricket Cricket ⓝ *kri*·ket
crop Feldfrucht ⓕ *felt*·frukht
cross (religious) Kreuz ⓝ kroyts
cross (angry) wütend *vü*·tent
crowded überfüllt ü·ber·*fült*
cuckoo clock Kuckucksuhr ⓕ
ku·kuks·oor
cucumber Gurke ⓕ *gur*·ke
cup Tasse ⓕ *ta*·se
cupboard Schrank ⓜ shrangk
currency Währung ⓕ *vair*·rung
currency exchange
Geldwechsel ⓜ *gelt*·vek·sel
current (electricity) Strom ⓜ
shtrawm
current affairs Aktuelles ⓝ ak·tu·*e*·les
curry (powder) Curry(pulver) ⓝ
ker·ri(·pul·ver)
customs Zoll ⓜ tsol
cut schneiden *shnai*·den
cutlery Besteck ⓝ be·*shtek*
CV Lebenslauf ⓜ *lay*·bens·lowf
cycle radfahren *raht*·fah·ren
cycling Radsport ⓜ *raht*·shport
cyclist Radfahrer(in) ⓜ/ⓕ *raht*·fah·rer/
raht·fah·re·rin
cystitis Blasenentzündung ⓕ
blah·zen·en·tsün·dung

D

dad Papa ⓜ *pa*·pa
daily täglich *tayk*·likh
dairy products Milchprodukte ⓝ pl
milkh·pro·duk·te
damp feucht foykht
dance tanzen *tan*·tsen
dangerous gefährlich ge·*fair*·likh
dark dunkel *dung*·kel
date (a person) mit jemandem
ausgehen mit *yay*·man·dem
ows·gay·en
date (appointment) Verabredung ⓕ
fer·*ap*·ray·dung
date (day) Datum ⓝ *dah*·tum
date of birth Geburtsdatum ⓝ
ge·*burts*·dah·tum
daughter Tochter ⓕ *tokh*·ter
daughter-in-law
Schwiegertochter ⓕ
shvee·ger·tokh·ter
dawn Dämmerung ⓕ *de*·me·rung
day Tag ⓜ tahk
day after tomorrow übermorgen
ü·ber·mor·gen
day before yesterday vorgestern
fawr·ges·tern
dead tot tawt
deaf taub towp

deal (cards) austeilen *ows*·tai·len
decide entscheiden ent·*shai*·den
deep tief teef
deforestation Abholzung ⓕ *ap*·hol·tsung
degree Grad ⓜ graht
delay Verspätung ⓕ fer·*shpay*·tung
delicatessen Feinkostgeschäft ⓝ *fain*·kost·ge·sheft
delicious köstlich *kerst*·likh
deliver (aus)liefern (*ows*·)*lee*·fern
demand Forderung ⓕ *for*·de·rung
democracy Demokratie ⓕ de·mo·kra·*tee*
demonstration Demonstration ⓕ de·mons·tra·*tsyawn*
Denmark Dänemark ⓝ *dair*·ne·mark
dental floss Zahnseide ⓕ *tsahn*·zai·de
dentist Zahnarzt/Zahnärztin ⓜ/ⓕ *tsahn*·artst/*tsahn*·erts·tin
deodorant Deo ⓝ *day*·o
depart (leave) abfahren *ap*·fah·ren
department store Warenhaus ⓝ *vah*·ren·hows
departure Abfahrt ⓕ *ap*·fahrt
deposit Anzahlung ⓕ *an*·tsah·lung
descendant Nachkomme ⓜ *nahkh*·ko·me
desert Wüste ⓕ *vüs*·te
design entwerfen ent·*ver*·fen
destination (Reise)Ziel ⓝ (*rai*·ze·)tseel
detail Detail ⓝ de·*tai*
diabetes Diabetis ⓕ di·a·*bay*·tis
dial tone Wählton ⓜ *vayl*·tawn
diaper Windel ⓕ *vin*·del
diaphragm (body) Zwerchfell ⓝ *tsverkh*·fel
diarrhoea Durchfall ⓜ *durkh*·fal
diary (for appointments) Terminkalender ⓜ ter·*meen*·ka·len·der
diary (record of events) Tagebuch ⓝ *tah*·ge·bookh
dice (die) Würfel ⓜ *vür*·fel
dictionary Wörterbuch ⓝ *ver*·ter·bookh
die sterben *shter*·ben
diet Diät ⓕ di·*ayt*
different andere *an*·de·re
difficult schwierig *shvee*·rikh
dining car Speisewagen ⓜ *shpai*·ze·vah·gen
dinner Abendessen ⓝ *ah*·bent·e·sen
direct direkt di·*rekt*
direct-dial Durchwahl ⓕ *durkh*·vahl
director Regisseur(in) ⓜ/ⓕ re·zhi·*ser*/re·zhi·*ser*·rin
directory enquiries Telefonauskunft ⓕ te·le·*fawn*·ows·kunft
dirty schmutzig *shmu*·tsikh
disability Behinderung be·*hin*·der·ung
disco Disko(thek) ⓕ *dis*·ko(·*tayk*)
discount Rabatt ⓜ ra·*bat*
discrimination Diskriminierung ⓕ dis·kri·mi·*nee*·rung
disease Krankheit ⓕ *krangk*·hait
diving Tauchen ⓝ *tow*·khen
dizzy schwindelig *shvin*·de·likh
do tun toon
doctor (medical) Arzt/Ärztin ⓜ/ⓕ artst/*erts*·tin
doctor (title) Doktor(in) ⓜ/ⓕ *dok*·tor/dok·*taw*·rin
documentary Dokumentation ⓕ do·ku·men·ta·*tsyawn*
dog Hund ⓜ hunt
dole (unemployment benefit) Arbeitslosengeld ⓝ *ar*·baits·law·zen·gelt
doll Puppe ⓕ *pu*·pe
dollar Dollar ⓜ *do*·lahr
door Tür ⓕ tür
dope (drugs) Dope ⓝ dawp/dohp
double doppelt *do*·pelt
double bed Doppelbett ⓝ *do*·pel·bet
down (nach) unten (nahkh) *un*·ten
downhill abwärts *ap*·verts
dozen Dutzend ⓝ *du*·tsent
drama Schauspiel ⓝ *show*·shpeel
dream träumen *troy*·men
dress Kleid ⓝ klait

dried fruit Trockenobst ⓝ *tro·ken·awpst*
drink Getränk ⓝ *ge·trengk*
drink trinken *tring·ken*
drive fahren *fah·ren*
driving licence Führerschein ⓜ *fü·rer·shain*
drug Droge ⓕ *draw·ge*
drug addiction Drogenabhängigkeit ⓕ *draw·gen·ap·heng·ikh·kait*
drug dealer Drogenhändler ⓜ *draw·gen·hen·dler*
drunk betrunken *be·trung·ken*
dry (clothes) trocknen *trok·nen*
dry (wine) trocken *tro·ken*
dry-cleaner chemische Reinigung ⓕ *khay·mi·she rai·ni·gung*
duck Ente ⓕ *en·te*
dummy (pacifier) Schnuller ⓜ *shnu·ler*
during während *vair·rent*
dusk Dämmerung ⓕ *de·me·rung*

E

each jeder/jede/jedes ⓜ/ⓕ/ⓝ *yay·der/yay·de/yay·des*
ear Ohr ⓝ *awr*
early früh *frü*
earn verdienen *fer·dee·nen*
earplugs Ohrenstöpsel ⓜ *aw·ren·shterp·sel*
earrings Ohrringe ⓜ pl *awr·ring·e*
Earth Erde ⓕ *er·de*
earthquake Erdbeben ⓝ *ert·bay·ben*
east Osten ⓜ *os·ten*
Easter Ostern ⓝ *aws·tern*
easy leicht *laikht*
eat essen *e·sen*
economy class Touristenklasse ⓕ *tu·ris·ten·kla·se*
eczema Ekzem ⓝ *ek·tsaym*
editor Herausgeber(in) ⓜ/ⓕ *he·rows·gay·ber/he·rows·gay·be·rin*
education Erziehung ⓕ *er·tsee·ung*
egg Ei ⓝ *ai*
eggplant Aubergine ⓕ *aw·ber·zhee·ne*
elections Wahlen ⓕ pl *vah·len*
electrical store Elektrogeschäft ⓝ *e·lek·tro·ge·sheft*
electrician Elektriker(in) ⓜ/ⓕ *e·lek·tri·ker/e·lek·tri·ke·rin*
electricity Elektrizität ⓕ *e·lek·tri·tsi·tayt*
elevator Lift ⓜ *lift*
embarrassed verlegen *fer·lay·gen*
embassy Botschaft ⓕ *bawt·shaft*
embroidery Stickerei ⓕ *shti·ke·rai*
emergency Notfall ⓜ *nawt·fal*
emotional emotional *e·mo·tsyo·nahl*
employee Angestellte ⓜ&ⓕ *an·ge·shtel·te*
employer Arbeitgeber ⓜ *ar·bait·gay·ber*
empty leer *lair*
end Ende ⓝ *en·de*
end beenden *be·en·den*
endangered (species) bedrohte (Art) ⓕ *be·draw·te art*
energy Energie ⓕ *e·ner·gee*
engagement (marriage) Verlobung ⓕ *fer·law·bung*
engine Motor ⓜ *maw·tor/mo·tawr*
engineer Ingenieuer(in) ⓜ/ⓕ *in·zhe·nyer/in·zhe·nyer·rin*
engineering Ingenieurwesen ⓝ *in·zhe·nyer·vay·zen*
England England ⓝ *eng·lant*
English Englisch ⓝ *eng·lish*
enjoy (oneself) sich amüsieren *zikh a·mü·zee·ren*
enough genug *ge·nook*
enter eintreten *ain·tray·ten*
entertainment guide Veranstaltungskalender ⓜ *fer·an·shtal·tungks·ka·len·der*
envelope Briefumschlag ⓜ *breef·um·shlahk*
environment Umwelt ⓕ *um·velt*
epilepsy Epilepsie ⓕ *e·pi·lep·see*

equal opportunity Chancengleichheit ⓕ *shahng*·sen·glaikh·hait
equality Gleichheit ⓕ *glaikh*·hait
equipment Ausrüstung ⓕ *ows*·rüs·tung
escalator Rolltreppe ⓕ *rol*·tre·pe
euro Euro ⓜ *oy*·ro
Europe Europa ⓝ oy·*raw*·pa
euthanasia Euthanasie ⓕ oy·ta·na·*zee*
evening Abend ⓜ *ah*·bent
every jeder/jede/jedes ⓜ/ⓕ/ⓝ *yay*·der/*yay*·de/*yay*·des
every day alltäglich al·*tayk*·likh
everyone jeder *yay*·der
everything alles *a*·les
example Beispiel ⓝ *bai*·shpeel
for example zum Beispiel tsum *bai*·shpeel
excellent ausgezeichnet ows·ge·*tsaikh*·net
excess baggage Übergepäck ⓝ *ü*·ber·ge·pek
exchange Umtausch ⓜ *um*·towsh
exchange wechseln *vek*·seln
exchange rate Wechselkurs ⓜ *vek*·sel·kurs
excluded ausgeschlossen *ows*·ge·shlo·sen
exhaust (car) Auspuff ⓜ *ows*·puf
exhibition Ausstellung ⓕ *ows*·shte·lung
exit Ausgang ⓜ *ows*·gang
expensive teuer *toy*·er
experience Erfahrung ⓕ er·*fah*·rung
exploitation Ausbeutung ⓕ *ows*·boy·tung
express Express- eks·*pres*·
express mail Expresspost ⓕ eks·*pres*·post
extension (visa) Verlängerung ⓕ fer·*leng*·e·rung
eye Auge ⓝ *ow*·ge
eye drops Augentropfen ⓜ pl *ow*·gen·trop·fen

F

fabric Gewebe ⓝ ge·*vay*·be
face Gesicht ⓝ ge·*zikht*
face cloth Waschlappen ⓜ *vash*·la·pen
factory Fabrik ⓕ fa·*breek*
factory worker Fabrik-arbeiter(in) ⓜ/ⓕ fa·*breek*·ar·bai·ter/ fa·*breek*·ar·bai·te·rin
fair (trade) Messe ⓕ *me*·se
fall (autumn) Herbst ⓜ herpst
false falsch falsh
family Familie ⓕ fa·*mee*·li·e
family name Familienname ⓜ fa·*mee*·li·en·nah·me
famous berühmt be·*rümt*
fan (sports) Fan ⓜ fen
fan (machine) Ventilator ⓜ ven·ti·*lah*·tor
fanbelt Keilriemen ⓜ *kail*·ree·men
far weit vait
farm Bauernhof ⓜ *bow*·ern·hawf
farmer Bauer/Bäuerin ⓜ/ⓕ *bow*·er/ *boy*·e·rin
fast schnell shnel
fat dick dik
father Vater ⓜ *fah*·ter
father-in-law Schwiegervater ⓜ *shvee*·ger·fah·ter
faucet Wasserhahn ⓜ *va*·ser·hahn
fault (someone's) Schuld ⓕ shult
faulty fehlerhaft *fay*·ler·haft
fax Fax ⓝ faks
feed füttern *fü*·tern
feel fühlen *fü*·len
feelings Gefühle ⓝ pl ge·*fü*·le
fence Zaun ⓜ tsown
fencing (sport) Fechten ⓝ *fekh*·ten
ferry Fähre ⓕ *fair*·re
festival Fest ⓝ fest
fever Fieber ⓝ *fee*·ber
few wenige *vay*·ni·ge
a few ein paar ain pahr

fiancé/fiancée Verlobte ⓜ&ⓕ *fer·lawp·te*
fiction Prosa ⓕ *praw·za*
field Feld ⓝ felt
fig Feige ⓕ *fai·ge*
fight Kampf ⓜ kampf
fill füllen *fü·len*
fillet Filet ⓝ fi·*lay*
film (cinema) Film ⓜ film
film (camera) Film ⓜ film
filtered gefiltert ge·*fil*·tert
find finden *fin*·den
fine (payment) Geldbuße ⓕ *gelt*·boo·se
finger Finger ⓜ *fing*·er
finish beenden be·*en*·den
fire Feuer ⓝ *foy*·er
firewood Brennholz ⓝ *bren*·holts
first erste *ers*·te
first class erste Klasse ⓕ *ers*·te *kla*·se
first-aid kit Verbandskasten ⓜ fer·*bants*·kas·ten
fish Fisch ⓜ fish
fish shop Fischgeschäft ⓝ *fish*·ge·sheft
fishing Fischen ⓝ *fi*·shen
fishing rod Angel ⓕ *ang*·el
flag Flagge ⓕ *fla*·ge
flash Blitz ⓜ blits
flashlight Taschenlampe ⓕ *ta*·shen·lam·pe
flat flach flakh
flea Floh ⓜ flaw
flea market Flohmarkt ⓜ *flaw*·markt
flight Flug ⓜ flook
flooding Überschwemmung ⓕ ü·ber·*shve*·mung
floor Boden ⓜ *baw*·den
floor (storey) Stock ⓜ shtok
florist Blumenhändler ⓜ *bloo*·men·hen·dler
flour Mehl ⓝ mayl
flower Blume ⓕ *bloo*·me
fly Fliege ⓕ *flee*·ge
fly fliegen *flee*·gen
foggy neblig *nay*·blikh
follow folgen *fol*·gen
food Essen ⓝ *e*·sen
food poisoning Lebensmittelvergiftung ⓕ *lay*·bens·mi·tel·fer·*gif*·tung
foot Fuß ⓜ foos
football (soccer) Fußball ⓜ *foos*·bal
footpath Gehweg ⓜ *gay*·vayk
for für für
foreign ausländisch *ows*·len·dish
forest Wald ⓜ valt
forever immer *i*·mer
forget vergessen fer·*ge*·sen
forgive verzeihen fer·*tsai*·en
fork Gabel ⓕ *gah*·bel
formal formell for·*mel*
fortnight vierzehn Tage ⓜ pl *feer*·tsayn *tah*·ge
foul Foul ⓝ fowl
fountain Brunnen ⓜ *bru*·nen
foyer Foyer ⓝ fo·a·*yay*
fragile zerbrechlich tser·*brekh*·likh
frame Rahmen ⓜ *rah*·men
France Frankreich ⓝ *frangk*·raikh
free (gratis) gratis *grah*·tis
free (not bound) frei frai
freeze gefrieren ge·*free*·ren
fresh (not stale) frisch frish
Friday Freitag ⓜ *frai*·tahk
friend Freund(in) ⓜ/ⓕ froynt/*froyn*·din
friendly freundlich *froynt*·likh
frog Frosch ⓜ frosh
from aus • von ows • fon
in front of vor fawr
frost Frost ⓜ frost
fruit Frucht ⓕ frukht
fruit picking Obsternte ⓕ *awpst*·ern·te
fry braten *brah*·ten
frying pan Bratpfanne ⓕ *braht*·pfa·ne
fuel Brennstoff ⓜ *bren*·shtof

full voll *fol*
full-time Vollzeit ⓕ *fol·tsait*
fun Spaß ⓜ *shpahs*
funeral Begräbnis ⓝ *be·grayp·nis*
funny lustig *lus·tikh*
furniture Möbel ⓝ pl *mer·bel*
fuse Sicherung ⓕ *zi·khe·rung*
future Zukunft ⓕ *tsoo·kunft*

G

game (sport) Spiel ⓝ *shpeel*
garage (car repair) Werkstatt ⓕ *verk·shtat*
garage (car shelter) Garage ⓕ *ga·rah·zhe*
garbage Abfall ⓜ *ap·fal*
garden Garten ⓜ *gar·ten*
garlic Knoblauch ⓜ *knawp·lowkh*
gas (cooking) Gas ⓝ *gahs*
gas (petrol) Benzin ⓝ *ben·tseen*
gas cartridge Gaskartusche ⓕ *gahs·kar·tu·she*
gas cylinder Gasflasche ⓕ *gahs·fla·she*
gastroenteritis Magen-Darm-Katarrh ⓜ *mah·gen·darm·ka·tar*
gate Tor ⓝ *tawr*
gay schwul *shvool*
gears Gänge ⓝ pl *geng·e*
general allgemein *al·ge·main*
German Deutsch ⓝ *doytsh*
Germany Deutschland ⓝ *doytsh·lant*
gift Geschenk ⓝ *ge·shengk*
gig Auftritt ⓜ *owf·trit*
gin Gin ⓜ *dzhin*
ginger Ingwer ⓜ *ing·ver*
girl Mädchen ⓝ *mayt·khen*
girlfriend Freundin ⓕ *froyn·din*
give geben *gay·ben*
glacier Gletscher ⓜ *glet·sher*
glandular fever Drüsenfieber ⓝ *drü·zen·fee·ber*
glass Glas ⓝ *glahs*
glasses (spectacles) Brille ⓕ *bri·le*
glove Handschuh ⓜ *hant·shoo*
go (on foot) gehen *gay·en*
go (by vehicle) fahren *fah·ren*
go out with ausgehen mit *ows·gay·en mit*
go shopping einkaufen gehen *ain·kow·fen gay·en*
goal Tor ⓝ *tawr*
goalkeeper Torwart/Torhüterin ⓜ/ⓕ *tawr·vart/tawr·hü·te·rin*
goat Ziege ⓕ *tsee·ge*
god Gott ⓜ *got*
goggles (skiing) Skibrille ⓕ *shee·bri·le*
gold Gold ⓝ *golt*
golf ball Golfball ⓜ *golf·bal*
golf course Golfplatz ⓜ *golf·plats*
good gut *goot*
gorge Schlucht ⓕ *shlukht*
government Regierung ⓕ *re·gee·rung*
gram Gramm ⓝ *gram*
grandchild Enkelkind ⓝ *eng·kel·kint*
grandfather Großvater • Opa ⓜ *graws·fah·ter • aw·pa*
grandmother Großmutter • Oma ⓕ *graws·mu·ter • aw·ma*
grandparents Großeltern ⓝ pl *graws·el·tern*
grapefruit Pampelmuse ⓕ *pam·pel·moo·ze*
grapes Weintrauben ⓕ pl *vain·trow·ben*
graphic art grafische Kunst ⓕ *grah·fi·she kunst*
grass Gras ⓝ *grahs*
grave Grab ⓝ *grahp*
gray grau *grow*
great (large) groß *graws*
green grün *grün*
greengrocer Lebensmittelhändler ⓜ *lay·bens·mi·tel·hen·dler*
grey grau *grow*
grocery store Lebensmittelladen ⓜ *lay·bens·mi·tel·lah·den*
groundnut Erdnuss ⓕ *ert·nus*
grow wachsen *vak·sen*
guess raten *rah·ten*

guide (audio) Führer ⓜ *fü*·rer
guide (person) Führer ⓜ *fü*·rer
guide dog Blindenhund ⓜ *blin*·den·hunt
guidebook Reiseführer ⓜ *rai*·ze·fü·rer
guided tour Führung ⓕ *fü*·rung
guilty schuldig *shul*·dikh
guitar Gitarre ⓕ gi·*ta*·re
gum (mouth) Zahnfleisch ⓝ *tsahn*·flaish
gym Fitness-Studio ⓝ *fit*·nes·shtoo·di·o
gymnastics Gymnastik ⓕ güm·*nas*·tik
gynaecologist Gynäkologe/Gynäkologin ⓜ/ⓕ gü·ne·ko·*law*·ge/gü·ne·ko·*law*·gin

H

hair Haar ⓝ hahr
hairbrush Haarbürste ⓕ *hahr*·bürs·te
hairdresser Friseur(in) ⓜ/ⓕ fri·*zer*/fri·*zer*·rin
Halal Halal- ha·*lal*·
half Hälfte ⓕ *helf*·te
half a litre ein halber Liter ⓜ ain *hal*·ber *lee*·ter
hallucinate halluzinieren ha·lu·tsi·*nee*·ren
ham Schinken ⓜ *shing*·ken
hammer Hammer ⓜ *ha*·mer
hammock Hängematte ⓕ *heng*·e·ma·te
hamster Hamster ⓜ *hams*·ter
hand Hand ⓕ hant
handbag Handtasche ⓕ *hant*·ta·she
handicrafts Kunsthandwerk ⓝ *kunst*·hant·verk
handlebar Lenker ⓜ *leng*·ker
handmade handgemacht *hant*·ge·makht
handsome gutaussehend *goot*·ows·zay·ent
hang-gliding Drachenfliegen ⓝ *dra*·khen·flee·gen
happy glücklich *glük*·likh
harassment Belästigung ⓕ be·*les*·ti·gung
harbour Hafen ⓜ *hah*·fen
hard (difficult) schwer shvair
hard (not soft) hart hart
hardware store Eisenwarengeschäft ⓝ *ai*·zen·vah·ren·ge·sheft
hash Haschee ⓝ ha·*shay*
hat Hut ⓜ hoot
hate hassen *ha*·sen
have haben *hah*·ben
hay fever Heuschnupfen ⓜ *hoy*·shnup·fen
he er air
head Kopf ⓜ kopf
headache Kopfschmerzen ⓜ pl *kopf*·shmer·tsen
headlights Scheinwerfer ⓜ pl *shain*·ver·fer
health Gesundheit ⓕ ge·*zunt*·hait
hear hören *her*·ren
hearing aid Hörgerät ⓝ *her*·ge·rayt
heart Herz ⓝ herts
heart condition Herzleiden ⓝ *herts*·lai·den
heat Hitze ⓕ *hi*·tse
heater Heizgerät ⓝ *haits*·ge·rayt
heavy schwer shvair
hello hallo *ha*·lo
helmet Helm ⓜ helm
help helfen *hel*·fen
hepatitis Hepatitis ⓕ he·pa·*tee*·tis
her ihr eer
herbalist Naturheilkundige ⓜ&ⓕ na·*toor*·hail·kun·di·ge
herbs Kräuter ⓝ pl *kroy*·ter
here hier heer
heroin Heroin ⓝ he·ro·*een*
herring Hering ⓜ *hay*·ring
high hoch hawkh
high school Sekundarschule ⓕ ze·kun·*dahr*·shoo·le

hike wandern *van*·dern
hiking Wandern ⓝ *van*·dern
hiking boots Wanderstiefel ⓜ pl *van*·der·shtee·fel
hiking route Wanderweg ⓜ *van*·der·vayk
hill Hügel ⓜ *hü*·gel
Hindu Hindu ⓜ&ⓕ *hin*·du
hire mieten *mee*·ten
his sein zain
historical historisch his·*taw*·rish
hitchhike trampen *trem*·pen
HIV positive HIV-positiv *hah*·ee·fow·*paw*·zi·teef
hockey Hockey ⓝ *ho*·ki
holiday Urlaub ⓜ *oor*·lowp
holidays Ferien pl *fair*·ri·en
holy heilig *hai*·likh
Holy Week Karwoche ⓕ *kahr*·vo·khe
home Heim ⓝ haim
(at) home zu Hause tsoo *how*·ze
(go) home nach Hause nahkh *how*·ze
homeless obdachlos *op*·dakh·laws
homemaker Hausmann/Hausfrau ⓜ/ⓕ *hows*·man/*hows*·frow
to be homesick Heimweh haben *haim*·vay *hah*·ben
homeopathic medicine homöopathisches Mittel ⓝ haw·mer·o·*pah*·ti·shes *mi*·tel
homosexual homosexuell haw·mo·zek·su·*el*
honest ehrlich *air*·likh
honey Honig ⓜ *haw*·nikh
honeymoon Flitterwochen ⓕ pl *fli*·ter·vo·khen
horoscope Horoskop ⓝ ho·ros·*kawp*
horse Pferd ⓝ pfert
horse riding Reiten ⓝ *rai*·ten
horseradish Meerrettich ⓜ *mair*·re·tikh
hospital Krankenhaus ⓝ *krang*·ken·hows
hospitality Gastfreundschaft ⓕ *gast*·froynt·shaft
hot heiß hais
hot water warmes Wasser ⓝ *var*·mes *va*·ser
hotel Hotel ⓝ ho·*tel*
house Haus ⓝ hows
housework Hausarbeit ⓕ *hows*·ar·bait
how wie vee
hug umarmen um·*ar*·men
huge riesig *ree*·zikh
human menschlich *mensh*·likh
human rights Menschenrechte ⓝ pl *men*·shen·rekh·te
humanities Geisteswissenschaften ⓕ pl *gais*·tes·vi·sen·shaf·ten
hundred hundert *hun*·dert
hungry hungrig *hung*·rikh
hunting Jagd ⓕ yahkt
in a hurry in Eile in *ai*·le
hurt verletzen fer·*le*·tsen
hurt (yourself) sich weh tun zikh vay toon
husband Ehemann ⓜ *ay*·e·man
hut Hütte ⓕ *hü*·te

I

I ich ikh
ice Eis ⓝ ais
ice axe Eispickel ⓜ *ais*·pi·kel
ice cream Eiscreme ⓕ *ais*·kraym
ice cream parlour Eisdiele ⓕ *ais*·dee·le
ice hockey Eishockey ⓝ *ais*·ho·ki
ice skating Eislaufen ⓝ *ais*·low·fen
idea Idee ⓕ i·*day*
identification Ausweis ⓜ *ows*·vais
identification card Personalausweis ⓜ per·zo·*nahl*·ows·vais
idiot Idiot ⓜ i·di·*awt*
if wenn ven
ignition Zündung ⓕ *tsün*·dung
ill krank krangk
illegal illegal *i*·le·gahl
imagination Phantasie ⓕ fan·ta·*zee*

immediately sofort zo·fort
immigration Immigration ⓕ i·mi·gra·tsyawn
important wichtig vikh·tikh
impossible unmöglich un·merk·likh
in in in
in front of vor fawr
included inbegriffen in·be·gri·fen
income tax Einkommensteuer ⓕ ain·ko·men·shtoy·er
India Indien ⓝ in·di·en
indicator Blinker ⓜ bling·ker
indigestion Magenverstimmung ⓕ mah·gen·fer·shti·mung
industry Industrie ⓕ in·dus·tree
inequality Ungleichheit ⓕ un·glaikh·hait
infection Entzündung ⓕ en·tsün·dung
inflammation Entzündung ⓕ en·tsün·dung
influenza Grippe ⓕ gri·pe
information Auskunft ⓕ ows·kunft
ingredient Zutat ⓕ tsoo·taht
inject spritzen shprit·zen
injection (car) Einspritzung ⓕ ain·shpri·tsung
injection (medical) Injektion ⓕ in·yek·tsyawn
injury Verletzung ⓕ fer·le·tsung
in-line skating Rollschuhfahren ⓝ rol·shoo·fah·ren
innocent unschuldig un·shul·dikh
insect repellent Insektenschutzmittel ⓝ in·zek·ten·shuts·mi·tel
inside innen i·nen
instead of (an)statt (an·)shtat
instructor Lehrer(in) ⓜ/ⓕ lair·rer/lair·re·rin
insurance Versicherung ⓕ fer·zi·khe·rung
interesting interessant in·tre·sant
intermission Pause ⓕ pow·ze
international international in·ter·na·tsyo·nahl
internet Internet ⓝ in·ter·net
interpreter Dolmetscher(in) ⓜ/ⓕ dol·met·sher/dol·met·she·rin
interview Interview ⓝ in·ter·vyoo
invite einladen ain·lah·den
Ireland Irland ⓝ ir·lant
iron (clothes) bügeln bü·geln
island Insel ⓕ in·zel
IT Informationstechnologie ⓕ in·for·ma·tsyawns·tekh·no·lo·gee
Italy Italien ⓝ ee·tah·li·en
itch Juckreiz ⓜ yuk·raits
itemised einzeln aufgeführt ain·tseln owf·ge·fürt
itinerary Reiseroute ⓕ rai·ze·roo·te

J

jacket Jacke ⓕ ya·ke
jail Gefängnis ⓝ ge·feng·nis
jam Marmelade ⓕ mar·me·lah·de
Japan Japan ⓝ yah·pahn
jar Glas ⓝ glahs
jaw Kiefer ⓜ kee·fer
jealous eifersüchtig ai·fer·zükh·tikh
jeans Jeans ⓕ pl dzheens
jeep Jeep ⓜ dzheep
jet lag Jetlag ⓜ dzhet·leg
jewellery Schmuck ⓜ shmuk
Jewish jüdisch yü·dish
job Arbeitsstelle ⓕ ar·baits·shte·le
jockey Jockey ⓜ dzho·ki
jogging Joggen ⓝ dzho·gen
joke Witz ⓜ vits
journalist Journalist(in) ⓜ/ⓕ zhur·na·list/zhur·na·lis·tin
journey Reise ⓕ rai·ze
judge Richter(in) ⓜ/ⓕ rikh·ter/rikh·te·rin
juice Saft ⓜ zaft
jump springen shpring·en
jumper (sweater) Pullover ⓜ pu·law·ver
jumper leads Überbrückungskabel ⓝ ü·ber·brü·kungks·kah·bel
justice Gerechtigkeit ⓕ ge·rekh·tikh·kait

K

ketchup Ketchup ⓜ *ket*·chap
kettle Kessel ⓜ *ke*·sel
key Schlüssel ⓜ *shlü*·sel
keyboard Tastatur ⓕ tas·ta·*toor*
kick treten *tray*·ten
kill töten *ter*·ten
kilogram Kilogramm ⓝ *kee*·lo·gram
kilometre Kilometer ⓜ ki·lo·*may*·ter
kind nett net
kindergarten Kindergarten ⓜ *kin*·der·gar·ten
king König ⓜ *ker*·nikh
kiss Kuss ⓜ kus
kiss küssen *kü*·sen
kitchen Küche ⓕ *kü*·khe
kitten Kätzchen ⓝ *kets*·khen
kiwi fruit Kiwifrucht ⓕ *kee*·vi·frukht
knapsack Rucksack ⓜ *ruk*·zak
knee Knie ⓝ knee
knife Messer ⓝ *me*·ser
know (a person) kennen *ke*·nen
know (something) wissen *vi*·sen
kosher koscher *kaw*·sher

L

labourer Arbeiter(in) ⓜ/ⓕ *ar*·bai·ter/*ar*·bai·te·rin
lace Spitze ⓕ *shpi*·tse
lager Lager ⓝ *lah*·ger
lake See ⓜ zay
lamb Lamm ⓝ lam
land Land ⓝ lant
landlady Vermieterin ⓕ fer·*mee*·te·rin
landlord Vermieter ⓜ fer·*mee*·ter
language Sprache ⓕ *shprah*·khe
laptop Laptop ⓜ *lep*·top
lard Schmalz ⓝ shmalts
large groß graws
last (week) letzte (Woche) *lets*·te (*vo*·khe)
late spät shpayt
laugh lachen *la*·khen
laundrette Wäscherei ⓕ ve·she·*rai*
laundry (room) Waschküche ⓕ *vash*·kü·khe
law (subject) Jura ⓝ *yoo*·ra
law (rules) Gesetz ⓝ ge·*zets*
lawyer Rechtsanwalt/Rechtsanwältin ⓜ/ⓕ *rekhts*·an·valt/*rekhts*·an·vel·tin
laxatives Abführmittel ⓝ *ap*·für·mi·tel
lazy faul fowl
leader Anführer ⓜ *an*·fü·rer
leaf Blatt ⓝ blat
learn lernen *ler*·nen
lease Mietvertrag ⓜ *meet*·fer·trahk
leather Leder ⓝ *lay*·der
leave (depart) abfahren *ap*·fah·ren
lecturer Dozent(in) ⓜ/ⓕ do·*tsent*/do·*tsen*·tin
leek Lauch ⓜ lowkh
left (direction) links lingks
left luggage Gepäckaufbewahrung ⓕ ge·*pek*·owf·be·vah·rung
left-wing links(gerichtet) *lingks*(·ge·rikh·tet)
leg (body) Bein ⓝ bain
legal legal le·*gahl*
legislation Gesetzgebung ⓕ ge·*zets*·gay·bung
legume Hülsenfrucht ⓕ *hül*·zen·frukht
lemon Zitrone ⓕ tsi·*traw*·ne
lemonade Limonade ⓕ li·mo·*nah*·de
lens (camera) Objektiv ⓝ op·yek·*teef*
Lent Fastenzeit ⓕ *fas*·ten·tsait
lentil Linse ⓕ *lin*·ze
lesbian Lesbierin ⓕ *les*·bi·e·rin
less weniger *vay*·ni·ger
letter Brief ⓜ breef
lettuce Kopfsalat ⓜ *kopf*·za·laht
liar Lügner(in) ⓜ/ⓕ *lüg*·ner/*lüg*·ne·rin
library Bibliothek ⓕ bi·bli·o·*tayk*
lice Läuse ⓕ pl *loy*·ze
licence plate number Autokennzeichen ⓝ *ow*·to·ken·tsai·khen
lie (not stand) liegen *lee*·gen
life Leben ⓝ *lay*·ben

life jacket Schwimmweste ⓕ shvim·ves·te
lift (elevator) Lift ⓜ lift
light Licht ⓝ likht
light hell hel
light bulb Glühbirne ⓕ glü·bir·ne
light meter Belichtungsmesser ⓜ be·likh·tungks·me·ser
lighter (cigarette) Feuerzeug ⓝ foy·er·tsoyk
lightning Blitz ⓜ blits
lights (on car) Scheinwerfer ⓜ pl shain·ver·fer
like mögen mer·gen
lime Limone ⓕ li·maw·ne
line Linie ⓕ lee·ni·e
linen (bed) Bettwäsche ⓕ bet·ve·she
linen (fabric) Leinen ⓝ lai·nen
lip balm Lippenbalsam ⓜ li·pen·bal·zahm
lips Lippen ⓕ pl li·pen
lipstick Lippenstift ⓜ li·pen·shtift
liquor store Getränkehandel ⓜ ge·treng·ke·han·del
listen hören her·ren
little klein klain
little (not much) wenig vay·nikh
a little ein bisschen ain bis·khen
live leben lay·ben
live (reside) wohnen vaw·nen
liver Leber ⓕ lay·ber
lizard Echse ⓕ ek·se
local örtlich ert·likh
lock Schloss ⓝ shlos
locked abgeschlossen ap·ge·shlo·sen
lollies Süßigkeiten ⓕ pl zü·sikh·kai·ten
lonely einsam ain·zahm
long lang lang
long-sleeved langärmelig lang·er·me·likh
look (an)sehen (an·)zay·en
look after sich kümmern um zikh kü·mern um
look for suchen nach zoo·khen nahkh
lookout Aussichtspunkt ⓜ ows·zikhts·pungkt
loose change Kleingeld ⓝ klain·gelt
lose verlieren fer·lee·ren
lost verloren fer·law·ren
lost property office Fundbüro ⓝ funt·bü·raw
a lot (of) viel feel
loud laut lowt
love lieben lee·ben
lover Liebhaber(in) ⓜ/ⓕ leep·hah·ber/leep·hah·be·rin
low niedrig nee·drikh
lubricant Schmiermittel ⓝ shmeer·mi·tel
luck Glück ⓝ glük
lucky glücklich glük·likh
luggage Gepäck ⓝ ge·pek
luggage lockers Schließfächer ⓝ pl shlees·fe·kher
luggage tag Adressanhänger ⓜ a·dres·an·heng·er
lump (health) Knoten ⓜ knaw·ten
lunch Mittagessen ⓝ mi·tahk·e·sen
lungs Lungen ⓕ pl lung·en
luxury luxuriös luk·su·ri·ers

M

machine Maschine ⓕ ma·shee·ne
made of (cotton) aus (Baumwolle) ows (bowm·vo·le)
magazine Zeitschrift ⓕ tsait·shrift
magician Zauberer(in) ⓜ/ⓕ tsow·be·rer/tsow·be·re·rin
mail Post ⓕ post
mailbox Briefkasten ⓜ breef·kas·ten
main Haupt- howpt·
main square Hauptplatz ⓜ howpt·plats
make machen ma·khen
make-up Schminke ⓕ shming·ke
mammogram Mammogramm ⓝ ma·mo·gram
man Mann ⓜ man

man (human being) Mensch ⓜ *mensh*
manager Manager(in) ⓜ/ⓕ *me·ne·dzher/me·ne·dzhe·rin*
mandarin Mandarine ⓕ *man·da·ree·ne*
mango Mango ⓕ *mang·go*
manual worker Arbeiter(in) ⓜ/ⓕ *ar·bai·ter/ar·bai·te·rin*
many viele *fee·le*
map Karte ⓕ *kar·te*
margarine Margarine ⓕ *mar·ga·ree·ne*
marijuana Marihuana ⓝ *ma·ri·hu·ah·na*
marital status Familienstand ⓜ *fa·mee·li·en·shtant*
market Markt ⓜ *markt*
market square Marktplatz ⓜ *markt·plats*
marmalade Orangenmarmelade ⓕ *o·rahng·zhen·mar·me·lah·de*
marriage Ehe ⓕ *ay·e*
marry heiraten *hai·rah·ten*
martial arts Kampfsport ⓜ *kampf·shport*
mass (Catholic) Messe ⓕ *me·se*
massage Massage ⓕ *ma·sah·zhe*
masseur Masseur ⓜ *ma·ser*
masseuse Masseurin ⓕ *ma·ser·rin*
mat Matte ⓕ *ma·te*
match (sport) Spiel ⓝ *shpeel*
matches Streichhölzer ⓝ pl *shtraikh·herl·tser*
material Material ⓝ *ma·te·ri·ahl*
mattress Matratze ⓕ *ma·tra·tse*
maybe vielleicht *fi·laikht*
mayonnaise Majonnaise ⓕ *ma·yo·nay·ze*
mayor Bürgermeister(in) ⓜ/ⓕ *bür·ger·mais·ter/bür·ger·mais·te·rin*
measles Masern pl *mah·zern*
meat Fleisch ⓝ *flaish*
mechanic Mechaniker(in) ⓜ/ⓕ *me·khah·ni·ker/me·khah·ni·ke·rin*
media Medien pl *may·di·en*
medicine Medizin ⓕ *me·di·tseen*
meditation Meditation ⓕ *me·di·ta·tsyawn*
meet treffen *tre·fen*
melon Melone ⓕ *me·law·ne*
member Mitglied ⓝ *mit·gleet*
member of parliament Abgeordnete ⓜ&ⓕ *ap·ge·ord·ne·te*
menstruation Menstruation ⓕ *mens·tru·a·tsyawn*
menu Speisekarte ⓕ *shpai·ze·kar·te*
message Mitteilung ⓕ *mi·tai·lung*
metal Metall ⓝ *me·tal*
metre Meter ⓜ *may·ter*
metro station U-Bahnhof ⓜ *oo·bahn·hawf*
microwave Mikrowelle ⓕ *mee·kro·ve·le*
Middle East Nahe Osten ⓜ *nah·e os·ten*
midnight Mitternacht ⓕ *mi·ter·nakht*
migraine Migräne ⓕ *mi·gray·ne*
military Militär ⓝ *mi·li·tair*
military service Wehrdienst ⓜ *vair·deenst*
milk Milch ⓕ *milkh*
millimetre Millimeter ⓜ *mi·li·may·ter*
million Million ⓕ *mi·lyawn*
mince Gehacktes ⓝ *ge·hak·tes*
mind (look after) aufpassen *owf·pa·sen*
mineral water Mineralwasser ⓝ *mi·ne·rahl·va·ser*
mints Pfefferminzbonbons ⓝ pl *pfe·fer·mints·bong·bongs*
minute Minute ⓕ *mi·noo·te*
mirror Spiegel ⓜ *shpee·gel*
miscarriage Fehlgeburt ⓕ *fayl·ge·burt*
miss (feel absence of) vermissen *fer·mi·sen*
miss (the bus) verpassen *fer·pa·sen*
mistake Fehler ⓜ *fay·ler*
mix mischen *mi·shen*

mobile phone Handy ⓝ *hen*·di
modem Modem ⓝ *maw*·dem
moisturiser Feuchtigkeitscreme ⓕ *foykh*·tikh·kaits·kraym
monastery Kloster ⓝ *klaws*·ter
Monday Montag ⓜ *mawn*·tahk
money Geld ⓝ gelt
month Monat ⓜ *maw*·nat
monument Denkmal ⓝ *dengk*·mahl
(full) moon (Voll) Mond ⓜ (*fol*·)mawnt
more mehr mair
morning (6am–10am) Morgen ⓜ *mor*·gen
morning (10am–12pm) Vormittag ⓜ *fawr*·mi·tahk
morning sickness (Schwangerschafts-)Erbrechen ⓝ (*shvang*·er·shafts·)er·*bre*·khen
mosque Moschee ⓕ mo·*shay*
mosquito Stechmücke ⓕ *shtekh*·mü·ke
mosquito coil Moskitospirale ⓕ mos·*kee*·to·shpi·rah·le
mother Mutter ⓕ *mu*·ter
mother-in-law Schwiegermutter ⓕ *shvee*·ger·mu·ter
motorboat Motorboot ⓝ *maw*·tor·bawt
motorcycle Motorrad ⓝ *maw*·tor·raht
motorway (tollway) Autobahn ⓕ *ow*·to·bahn
mountain Berg ⓜ berk
mountain bike Mountainbike ⓝ *mown*·ten·baik
mountain hut Berghütte ⓕ *berk*·hü·te
mountain path Bergweg ⓜ *berk*·vayk
mountain range Gebirgszug ⓜ ge·*birks*·tsook
mountaineering Bergsteigen ⓝ *berk*·shtai·gen
mouse Maus ⓕ mows
mouth Mund ⓜ munt
movie Film ⓜ film
mud Schlamm ⓜ shlam
muesli Müsli ⓝ *müs*·li
muggy schwül shvül
mum Mama ⓕ *ma*·ma
muscle Muskel ⓜ *mus*·kel
museum Museum ⓝ mu·*zay*·um
mushroom Pilz ⓜ pilts
music Musik ⓕ mu·*zeek*
musician Musiker(in) ⓜ/ⓕ *moo*·zi·ker/*moo*·zi·ke·rin
Muslim Moslem/Moslime ⓜ/ⓕ *mos*·lem/mos·*lee*·me
mussel Muschel ⓕ *mu*·shel
mustard Senf ⓜ zenf
mute stumm shtum
my mein/meine/mein ⓜ/ⓕ/ⓝ main/*mai*·ne/main

N

nail clippers Nagelknipser ⓜ pl *nah*·gel·knip·ser
name Name ⓜ *nah*·me
napkin Serviette ⓕ zer·*vye*·te
nappy Windel ⓕ *vin*·del
nappy rash Windeldermatitis ⓕ *vin*·del·der·ma·tee·tis
national park Nationalpark ⓜ na·tsyo·*nahl*·park
nationality Staatsangehörigkeit ⓕ *shtahts*·an·ge·her·rikh·kait
nature Natur ⓕ na·*toor*
nature reserve Naturreservat ⓝ na·*toor*·re·zer·vaht
nausea Übelkeit ⓕ *ü*·bel·kait
near nahe *nah*·e
nearby in der Nähe in dair *nay*·e
nearest nächste *naykhs*·te
necessary notwendig *nawt*·ven·dikh
necklace Halskette ⓕ *hals*·ke·te
need brauchen *brow*·khen
needle (sewing) Nadel ⓕ *nah*·del
needle (syringe) Nadel ⓕ *nah*·del
nephew Neffe ⓜ *ne*·fe

net Netz ⓝ nets
Netherlands Niederlande pl *nee*·der·lan·de
never nie nee
new neu noy
New Year's Day Neujahrstag ⓜ *noy*·yahrs·tahk
New Year's Eve Silvester ⓝ zil·*ves*·ter
New Zealand Neuseeland ⓝ noy·*zay*·lant
news Nachrichten ⓕ pl *nahkh*·rikh·ten
newsagency Zeitungshändler ⓜ *tsai*·tungks·hen·dler
newspaper Zeitung ⓕ *tsai*·tung
newsstand Zeitungskiosk ⓜ *tsai*·tungks·kee·osk
next nächste *naykhs*·te
next to neben *nay*·ben
nice nett net
nickname Spitzname ⓜ *shpits*·nah·me
niece Nichte ⓕ *nikh*·te
night Nacht ⓕ nakht
no nein nain
noisy laut lowt
none keine *kai*·ne
nonsmoking Nichtraucher *nikht*·row·kher·
noodles Nudeln ⓕ pl *noo*·deln
noon Mittag ⓜ *mi*·tahk
north Norden ⓜ *nor*·den
nose Nase ⓕ *nah*·ze
not nicht nikht
notebook Notizbuch ⓝ no·*teets*·bookh
nothing nichts nikhts
now jetzt yetst
nuclear energy Atomenergie ⓕ a·*tawm*·e·ner·gee
nuclear testing Atomtest ⓜ a·*tawm*·test
nuclear waste Atommüll ⓜ a·*tawm*·mül
number (numeral) Zahl ⓕ tsahl
number (telephone) Nummer ⓕ *nu*·mer
nun Nonne ⓕ *no*·ne
nurse Krankenpfleger/Krankenschwester ⓜ/ⓕ *krang*·ken·pflay·ger/ *krang*·ken·shves·ter
nut Nuss ⓕ nus

O

oats Hafer(flocken) ⓜ pl *hah*·fer(·flo·ken)
obvious offensichtlich o·fen·*zikht*·likh
occupation Beruf ⓜ be·*roof*
ocean Ozean ⓜ *aw*·tse·ahn
off (food) schlecht shlekht
office Büro ⓝ bü·*raw*
office worker Büroangestellte ⓜ&ⓕ bü·*raw*·an·ge·shtel·te
offside abseits *ap*·zaits
often oft oft
oil Öl ⓝ erl
OK okay o·*kay*
old alt alt
olive Olive ⓕ o·*lee*·ve
olive oil Olivenöl ⓝ o·*lee*·ven·erl
Olympic Games Olympische Spiele ⓝ pl o·*lüm*·pi·she *shpee*·le
on auf owf
once einmal *ain*·mahl
one ein(s) ain(s)
onion Zwiebel ⓕ *tsvee*·bel
only nur noor
open offen *o*·fen
open (unlock) öffnen *erf*·nen
opening hours Öffnungszeiten ⓕ pl *erf*·nungks·tsai·ten
opera Oper ⓕ *aw*·per
opera house Opernhaus ⓝ *aw*·pern·hows
operation Operation ⓕ o·pe·ra·*tsyawn*
operator Vermittlung ⓕ fer·*mit*·lung
opinion Meinung ⓕ *mai*·nung

opposite gegenüber gay·gen·ü·ber
optician Optiker(in) ⓜ/ⓕ op·ti·ker/op·ti·ke·rin
or oder aw·der
orange (fruit) Orange ⓕ o·rahng·zhe
orange (colour) orange o·rahngzh
orange juice Orangensaft ⓜ o·rahng·zhen·zaft
orchestra Orchester ⓝ or·kes·ter
order (restaurant) Bestellung ⓕ be·shte·lung
order bestellen be·shte·len
ordinary normal nor·mahl
organ (church) Orgel ⓕ or·gel
organise organisieren or·ga·ni·zee·ren
orgasm Orgasmus ⓜ or·gas·mus
original (not copied) Original- o·ri·gi·nahl·
other andere an·de·re
our unser un·zer
out aus ows
outside draußen drow·sen
ovarian cyst Eierstockzyste ⓕ ai·er·shtok·tsüs·te
oven Ofen ⓜ aw·fen
over über ü·ber
overcoat Mantel ⓜ man·tel
overdose Überdosis ⓕ ü·ber·daw·zis
overnight über Nacht ü·ber nakht
owe schulden shul·den
owner Besitzer(in) ⓜ/ⓕ be·zi·tser/be·zi·tse·rin
oxygen Sauerstoff ⓜ zow·er·shtof
oyster Auster ⓕ ows·ter
ozone layer Ozonschicht ⓕ o·tsawn·shikht

P

pacemaker (heart) Herzschrittmacher ⓜ herts·shrit·ma·kher
pacifier (dummy) Schnuller ⓜ shnu·ler
package Paket ⓝ pa·kayt
packet (general) Packung ⓕ pa·kung
padlock Vorhängeschloss ⓝ fawr·heng·e·shlos
page Seite ⓕ zai·te
pain Schmerz ⓜ shmerts
painful schmerzhaft shmerts·haft
painkillers Schmerzmittel ⓝ shmerts·mi·tel
painter Maler(in) ⓜ/ⓕ mah·ler/mah·le·rin
painting (the art) Malerei ⓕ mah·le·rai
paints Farben ⓕ pl far·ben
pair (couple) Paar ⓝ pahr
palace Schloss ⓝ shlos
pan Pfanne ⓕ pfa·ne
pants (trousers) Hose ⓕ haw·ze
panty liner Slipeinlage ⓕ slip·ain·lah·ge
pantyhose Strumpfhose ⓕ shtrumpf·haw·ze
pap smear Abstrich ⓜ ap·shtrikh
paper Papier ⓝ pa·peer
paperback Taschenbuch ⓝ ta·shen·bookh
paperwork Schreibarbeit ⓕ shraip·ar·bait
parachuting Fallschirmspringen ⓝ fal·shirm·shpring·en
paragliding Gleitschirmfliegen ⓝ glait·shirm·flee·gen
paraplegic Querschnittsgelähmte ⓜ&ⓕ kvair·shnits·ge·laym·te
parcel Paket ⓝ pa·kayt
parents Eltern ⓝ pl el·tern
park Park ⓜ park
park (car) Parkplatz ⓜ park·plats
parliament Parlament ⓝ par·la·ment
parrot Papagei ⓜ pa·pa·gai
parsley Petersilie ⓕ pay·ter·zee·li·e
part Teil ⓝ tail
participate sich beteiligen zikh be·tai·li·gen
part-time Teilzeit- ⓕ tail·tsait·

party (fiesta/ball) Fest ⓝ fest
party (politics) Partei ⓕ par·*tai*
pass Pass ⓜ pas
passenger (bus/taxi) Fahrgast ⓜ *fahr*·gast
passenger (plane) Fluggast ⓜ *flook*·gast
passenger (train) Reisende(r) ⓜ/ⓕ *rai*·zen·de
passport (Reise)Pass ⓜ (*rai*·ze·)pas
passport number Passnummer ⓕ *pas*·nu·mer
past Vergangenheit ⓕ fer·*gang*·en·hait
pasta Nudeln ⓕ pl *noo*·deln
path Pfad ⓜ pfaht
patio Terrasse ⓕ ter·*ra*·se
pay bezahlen be·*tsah*·len
pay phone Münztelefon ⓝ *münts*·te·le·fawn
payment Zahlung ⓕ *tsah*·lung
pea Erbse ⓕ *erp*·se
peace Frieden ⓜ *free*·den
peach Pfirsich ⓜ *pfir*·zikh
peak Gipfel ⓜ *gip*·fel
peanuts Erdnüsse ⓕ pl *ert*·nü·se
pear Birne ⓕ *bir*·ne
pedal Pedal ⓝ pe·*dahl*
pedestrian Fußgänger(in) ⓜ/ⓕ *foos*·geng·er/*foos*·geng·e·rin
pen (ballpoint) Kugelschreiber ⓜ *koo*·gel·shrai·ber
pencil Bleistift ⓜ *blai*·shtift
penis Penis ⓜ *pay*·nis
penknife Taschenmesser ⓝ *ta*·shen·me·ser
pensioner Rentner(in) ⓜ/ⓕ *rent*·ner/*rent*·ne·rin
people Menschen ⓜ pl *men*·shen
pepper Pfeffer ⓜ *pfe*·fer
pepper (bell) Paprika ⓕ *pap*·ri·kah
per pro praw
percent Prozent ⓝ pro·*tsent*
performance Aufführung ⓕ *owf*·fü·rung
perfume Parfüm ⓝ par·*füm*
period pain Menstruationsbeschwerden ⓕ pl mens·tru·a·*tsyawns*·be·shver·den
permission Erlaubnis ⓕ er·*lowp*·nis
permit Genehmigung ⓕ ge·*nay*·mi·gung
person Person ⓕ per·*zawn*
personal persönlich per·*zern*·likh
petition Petition ⓕ pe·ti·*tsyawn*
petrol Benzin ⓝ ben·*tseen*
petrol can Benzinkanister ⓜ ben·*tseen*·ka·nis·ter
pharmacy Apotheke ⓕ a·po·*tay*·ke
phone book Telefonbuch ⓝ te·le·*fawn*·bookh
phone box Telefonzelle ⓕ te·le·*fawn*·tse·le
phonecard Telefonkarte ⓕ te·le·*fawn*·kar·te
photo Foto ⓝ *faw*·to
photograph Fotografie ⓕ fo·to·gra·*fee*
photograph fotografieren fo·to·gra·*fee*·ren
photographer Fotograf(in) ⓜ/ⓕ fo·to·*grahf*/fo·to·*grah*·fin
photography Fotografie ⓕ fo·to·gra·*fee*
phrasebook Sprachführer ⓜ *shprahkh*·fü·rer
physics Physik ⓕ fü·*zeek*
piano Klavier ⓝ kla·*veer*
pick pflücken *pflü*·ken
pick up aufheben *owf*·hay·ben
pickaxe Spitzhacke ⓕ *shpits*·ha·ke
picnic Picknick ⓝ *pik*·nik
pie Pastete ⓕ pas·*tay*·te
piece Stück ⓝ shtük
pig Schwein ⓝ shvain
pilgrimage Pilgerfahrt ⓕ *pil*·ger·fahrt
pill Pille ⓕ *pi*·le
the Pill die Pille ⓕ dee *pi*·le
pillow Kissen ⓝ *ki*·sen
pillowcase Kissenbezug ⓜ

ki·sen·be·tsook
pineapple Ananas ⓕ a·na·nas
pink rosa raw·za
pipe Pfeife ⓕ pfai·fe
pistachio Pistazie ⓕ pis·tah·tsi·e
place Platz ⓜ plats
place of birth Geburtsort ⓜ ge·burts·ort
plain Ebene ⓕ ay·be·ne
plane Flugzeug ⓝ flook·tsoyk
planet Planet ⓜ pla·nayt
plant Pflanze ⓕ pflan·tse
plastic Plastik ⓝ plas·tik
plate Teller ⓜ te·ler
plateau Hochebene ⓕ hawkh·ay·be·ne
platform Bahnsteig ⓜ bahn·shtaik
play (theatre) Schauspiel ⓝ show·shpeel
play (game) spielen shpee·len
play (instrument) spielen shpee·len
please bitte bi·te
plenty viel feel
plug (bath) Stöpsel ⓜ shterp·sel
plug (electricity) Stecker ⓜ shte·ker
plum Pflaume ⓕ pflow·me
plumber Installateur(in) ⓜ/ⓕ in·sta·la·ter/in·sta·la·ter(·rin)
pocket Tasche ⓕ ta·she
poetry Dichtung ⓕ dikh·tung
point Punkt ⓜ pungkt
point zeigen tsai·gen
poisonous giftig gif·tikh
poker (game) Poker ⓝ paw·ker
police Polizei ⓕ po·li·tsai
police station Polizeirevier ⓝ po·li·tsai·re·veer
policy Politik ⓕ po·li·teek
politician Politiker(in) ⓜ/ⓕ po·lee·ti·ker/po·lee·ti·ke·rin
politics Politik ⓕ po·li·teek
pollen Pollen ⓜ po·len
polls Umfrage ⓕ um·frah·ge
pollution Umweltverschmutzung ⓕ um·velt·fer·shmu·tsung
pony Pony ⓝ po·ni
pool (game) Billard ⓝ bil·yart
pool (swimming, indoors) Hallenbad ⓝ ha·len·baht
pool (swimming, outdoors) Freibad ⓝ frai·baht
poor arm arm
popular beliebt be·leept
pork Schweinefleisch ⓝ shvai·ne·flaish
port Hafen ⓜ hah·fen
possible möglich merk·likh
post office Postamt ⓝ post·amt
postage Porto ⓝ por·to
postcard Postkarte ⓕ post·kar·te
postcode Postleitzahl ⓕ post·lai·tsahl
poste restante postlagernd post·lah·gernt
poster Plakat ⓝ pla·kaht
pot (ceramics) Topf ⓜ topf
pot (dope) Gras ⓝ grahs
potato Kartoffel ⓕ kar·to·fel
pottery Töpferwaren ⓕ pl terp·fer·vah·ren
pound (money & weight) Pfund ⓝ pfunt
poverty Armut ⓕ ar·moot
power Kraft ⓕ kraft
practical praktisch prak·tish
prawn Garnele ⓕ gar·nay·le
prayer Gebet ⓝ ge·bayt
prefer vorziehen fawr·tsee·en
pregnancy test kit Schwangerschaftstest ⓜ shvang·er·shafts·test
pregnant schwanger shvang·er
premenstrual tension prämenstruelle Störung ⓕ pray·mens·tru·e·le shter·rung
prepare vorbereiten fawr·be·rai·ten
present (gift) Geschenk ⓝ ge·shengk
present (time) Gegenwart ⓕ gay·gen·vart
president Präsident(in) ⓜ/ⓕ

pre·zi·*dent*/pre·zi·*den*·tin
pressure Druck ⓜ druk
pretty hübsch hüpsh
prevent verhindern fer·*hin*·dern
price Preis ⓜ prais
priest Priester ⓜ *prees*·ter
prime minister Premierminister(in) ⓜ/ⓕ prem·*yay*·mi·nis·ter/ prem·*yay*·mi·nis·te·rin
prime minister (in Germany & Austria) Bundeskanzler(in) ⓜ/ⓕ *bun*·des·kants·ler/*bun*·des·kants·le·rin
print (artwork) Druck ⓜ druk
print (photography) Abzug ⓜ *ap*·tsook
prison Gefängnis ⓝ ge·*feng*·nis
prisoner Gefangene ⓜ&ⓕ ge·*fang*·e·ne
private privat pri·*vaht*
produce produzieren pro·du·*tsee*·ren
profession Beruf ⓜ be·*roof*
profit Gewinn ⓜ ge·*vin*
programme Programm ⓝ pro·*gram*
projector Projektor ⓜ pro·*yek*·tor
promise versprechen fer·*shpre*·khen
proposal Vorschlag ⓜ *fawr*·shlahk
prostitute Prostituierte ⓕ pros·ti·tu·*eer*·te
protect beschützen be·*shü*·tsen
protected geschützte ge·*shüts*·te
protest Protest ⓜ pro·*test*
protest protestieren pro·tes·*tee*·ren
provisions Verpflegung ⓕ fer·*pflay*·gung
prune Backpflaume ⓕ *bak*·pflow·me
psychology Psychologie ⓕ psü·kho·lo·*gee*
pub Kneipe ⓕ *knai*·pe
public telephone öffentliches Telefon ⓝ *er*·fent·li·khes te·le·*fawn*
public toilet öffentliche Toilette ⓕ *er*·fent·li·khe to·a·*le*·te
pull ziehen *tsee*·en
pump (Luft)Pumpe ⓕ (*luft*·)*pum*·pe
pumpkin Kürbis ⓜ *kür*·bis
puncture Reifenpanne ⓕ *rai*·fen·pa·ne
punish bestrafen be·*shtrah*·fen
pure rein rain
purple lila *lee*·la
push schieben *shee*·ben
put (horizontal) legen *lay*·gen
put (vertical) stellen *shte*·len

Q

qualifications Qualifikationen ⓕ pl kva·li·fi·ka·*tsyaw*·nen
quality Qualität ⓕ kva·li·*tayt*
quarantine Quarantäne ⓕ ka·ran·*tay*·ne
quarrel Streit ⓜ shtrait
quarter Viertel ⓝ *feer*·tel
queen Königin ⓕ *ker*·ni·gin
question Frage ⓕ *frah*·ge
queue Schlange ⓕ *shlang*·e
quick schnell shnel
quiet ruhig *roo*·ikh
quit (job) kündigen *kün*·di·gen

R

rabbit Kaninchen ⓝ ka·*neen*·khen
race (sport) Rennen ⓝ *re*·nen
racetrack Rennbahn ⓕ *ren*·bahn
racing bike Rennrad ⓝ *ren*·raht
racism Rassismus ⓜ ra·*sis*·mus
racquet Schläger ⓜ *shlay*·ger
radiator Kühler ⓜ *kü*·ler
radio Radio ⓝ *rah*·di·o
radish Rettich ⓜ *re*·tikh
railway station Bahnhof ⓜ *bahn*·hawf
rain Regen ⓜ *ray*·gen
raincoat Regenmantel ⓜ *ray*·gen·man·tel
raisin Rosine ⓕ ro·*zee*·ne
rally (racing) Rallye ⓕ *re*·li
rape vergewaltigen fer·ge·*val*·ti·gen
rapids Stromschnellen ⓕ pl *shtrawm*·shne·len
rare selten *zel*·ten
rash Ausschlag ⓜ *ows*·shlahk
raspberry Himbeere ⓕ *him*·bey·re

rat Ratte ⓕ *ra*·te
rate of pay Lohn(satz) ⓜ *lawn*(·zats)
raw roh raw
razor Rasierer ⓜ ra·*zee*·rer
razor blades Rasierklingen ⓕ pl ra·*zeer*·kling·en
read lesen *lay*·zen
reading Lesung ⓕ *lay*·zung
ready fertig *fer*·tikh
real estate agent Makler(in) ⓜ/ⓕ *mahk*·ler/*mahk*·le·rin
realistic realistisch re·a·*lis*·tish
reason Grund ⓜ grunt
receipt Quittung ⓕ *kvi*·tung
receive erhalten er·*hal*·ten
recently vor kurzem fawr *kur*·tsem
recharge aufladen *owf*·lah·den
recommend empfehlen emp·*fay*·len
recording Aufnahme ⓕ *owf*·nah·me
recyclable wiederverwertbar *vee*·der·fer·vert·bahr
recycle recyceln ri·*sai*·keln
red rot rawt
referee Schiedsrichter(in) ⓜ/ⓕ *sheets*·rikh·ter/*sheets*·rikh·te·rin
reference (work) Zeugnis ⓝ *tsoyk*·nis
referendum Volksentscheid ⓜ *folks*·ent·shait
reflexology Fußreflexzonenmassage ⓕ foos·ray·*fleks*·tsaw·nen·ma·sah·zhe
refrigerator Kühlschrank ⓜ *kül*·shrangk
refugee Flüchtling ⓜ *flükht*·ling
refund Rückzahlung ⓕ *rük*·tsah·lung
refuse ablehnen *ap*·lay·nen
region Region ⓕ re·*gyawn*
registered mail Einschreiben ⓝ *ain*·shrai·ben
regulation Vorschrift ⓕ *fawr*·shrift
relation (family) Verwandte ⓜ&ⓕ fer·*van*·te
relationship Beziehung ⓕ be·*tsee*·ung
relax sich entspannen zikh ent·*shpa*·nen
relic (religious) Reliquie ⓕ re·*lee*·kvi·e
religion Religion ⓕ re·li·*gyawn*
religious religiös re·li·*gyers*
remote abgelegen *ap*·ge·lay·gen
remote control Fernbedienung ⓕ *fern*·be·dee·nung
rent mieten *mee*·ten
repair reparieren re·pa·*ree*·ren
repeat wiederholen vee·der·*haw*·len
republic Republik ⓕ re·pu·*bleek*
reservation Reservierung ⓕ re·zer·*vee*·rung
reserve reservieren re·zer·*vee*·ren
rest eine Pause machen *ai*·ne *pow*·ze *ma*·khen
restaurant Restaurant ⓝ res·to·*rahng*
resume (CV) Lebenslauf ⓜ *lay*·bens·lowf
retired pensioniert pahng·zyo·*neert*
return zurückkommen tsu·*rük*·ko·men
return (ticket) Rückfahrkarte ⓕ *rük*·fahr·kar·te
review (arts) Kritik ⓕ kri·*teek*
rhythm Rhythmus ⓜ *rüt*·mus
rice Reis ⓜ rais
rich (wealthy) reich raikh
ride Ritt ⓜ rit
ride (horse) reiten *rai*·ten
riding school Reitschule ⓕ *rait*·shoo·le
right (correct) richtig *rikh*·tikh
right (direction) rechts rekhts
right there gleich dort glaikh dort
right-wing rechts(gerichtet) *rekhts*(·ge·rikh·tet)
ring (on finger) Ring ⓜ ring
ring (of phone) klingeln *kling*·eln
rip-off Abzockerei ⓕ ap·tso·ke·*rai*
risk Risiko ⓝ *ree*·zi·ko
river Fluss ⓜ flus
road Straße ⓕ *shtrah*·se
road map Straßenkarte ⓕ *shtrah*·sen·kar·te

rob berauben be·*row*·ben
robbery Raub ⓜ rowp
rock Fels ⓜ fels
rock (music) Rockmusik ⓕ *rok*·mu·zeek
rock climbing Klettern ⓝ *kle*·tern
rock group Rockgruppe ⓕ *rok*·gru·pe
roll (bread) Brötchen ⓝ *brert*·khen
romantic romantisch ro·*man*·tish
roof Dach ⓝ dakh
room Zimmer ⓝ *tsi*·mer
rope Seil ⓝ zail
round rund runt
roundabout Kreisverkehr ⓜ *krais*·fer·kair
route Route ⓕ *roo*·te
rowing Rudern ⓝ *roo*·dern
rubbish Müll ⓜ mül
rug Teppich ⓜ *te*·pikh
rugby Rugby ⓝ *rag*·bi
ruins Ruinen ⓕ pl ru·*ee*·nen
rules Regeln ⓕ pl *ray*·geln
rum Rum ⓜ rum
run laufen *low*·fen
run out of ausgehen *ows*·gay·en

S

Sabbath Sabbat ⓜ *za*·bat
sad traurig *trow*·rikh
saddle Sattel ⓜ *za*·tel
safe (for valuables) Safe ⓜ sayf
safe sicher *zi*·kher
safe sex Safe Sex ⓜ sayf seks
safety Sicherheit ⓕ *zi*·kher·hait
sailing Segeln ⓝ *zay*·geln
saint Heilige ⓜ&ⓕ *hai*·li·ge
salad Salat ⓜ za·*laht*
salami Salami ⓕ za·*lah*·mi
salary Gehalt ⓝ ge·*halt*
sale (Sonder)Angebot ⓝ (*zon*·der·) *an*·ge·bawt
sales tax Umsatzsteuer ⓕ *um*·zats·shtoy·er
salmon Lachs ⓜ laks
salt Salz ⓝ zalts
same gleiche *glai*·khe
sand Sand ⓜ zant
sandals Sandalen ⓕ pl zan·*dah*·len
sanitary napkins Damenbinden ⓕ pl *dah*·men·bin·den
sardine Sardine ⓕ zar·*dee*·ne
Saturday Samstag ⓜ *zams*·tahk
sauce Sauce/Soße ⓕ *zaw*·se
sauna Sauna ⓕ *zow*·na
sausage Wurst ⓕ vurst
save (money) sparen *shpah*·ren
save (someone) retten *re*·ten
say sagen *zah*·gen
scarf Schal ⓜ shahl
scenery Landschaft ⓕ *lant*·shaft
school Schule ⓕ *shoo*·le
science Wissenschaft ⓕ *vi*·sen·shaft
scientist Wissenschaftler(in) ⓜ/ⓕ *vi*·sen·shaft·ler/*vi*·sen·shaft·le·rin
scissors Schere ⓕ *shair*·re
score ein Tor schießen ain tawr *shee*·sen
scoreboard Anzeigetafel ⓕ *an*·tsai·ge·tah·fel
Scotland Schottland ⓝ *shot*·lant
screen (TV/computer) Bildschirm ⓜ *bilt*·shirm
screwdriver Schraubenzieher ⓜ *shrow*·ben·tsee·er
script Drehbuch ⓝ *dray*·bookh
sculpture Skulptur ⓕ skulp·*toor*
sea Meer ⓝ meer
seagull Möwe ⓕ *mer*·ve
seasick seekrank *zay*·krangk
seaside Meeresküste ⓕ *meer*·res·küs·te
season Jahreszeit ⓕ *yah*·res·tsait
seat (car) Sitz ⓜ zits
seat (train/cinema) Platz ⓜ plats
seatbelt Sicherheitsgurt ⓜ *zi*·kher·haits·gurt
second Sekunde ⓕ ze·*kun*·de
second zweite *tsvai*·te
secondhand gebraucht ge·*browkht*
secondhand shop Secondhand-

geschäft ⓝ se·kend·*hend*·ge·sheft
secret Geheimnis ⓝ ge·*haim*·nis
secretary Sekretär(in) ⓜ/ⓕ ze·kre·*tair*(·rin)
see sehen *zay*·en
self-employed selbstständig *zelpst*·shten·dikh
selfish egoistisch e·go·*is*·tish
self-service Selbstbedienung ⓕ *zelpst*·be·dee·nung
sell verkaufen fer·*kow*·fen
send senden *zen*·den
sensible vernünftig fer·*nünf*·tikh
sensual sinnlich *zin*·likh
separate getrennt ge·*trent*
serial Serien- *zair*·ri·en·
series Serie ⓕ *zair*·ri·e
serious ernst ernst
service charge Bedienungszuschlag ⓜ be·*dee*·nungks·tsoo·shlahk
service station Tankstelle ⓕ *tangk*·shte·le
several einige *ai*·ni·ge
sew nähen *nay*·en
sex Sex ⓜ seks
sexism Sexismus ⓜ sek·*sis*·mus
sexy sexy *sek*·si
shade Schatten ⓜ *sha*·ten
shadow Schatten ⓜ *sha*·ten
shampoo Shampoo ⓝ *sham*·poo
shape Form ⓕ form
share (with) teilen (mit) *tai*·len (mit)
shave rasieren ra·*zee*·ren
shaving cream Rasiercreme ⓕ ra·*zeer*·kraym
she sie zee
sheep Schaf ⓝ shahf
sheet (bed) Bettlaken ⓝ *bet*·lah·ken
shelf Regal ⓝ re·*gahl*
ship Schiff ⓝ shif
shirt Hemd ⓝ hemt
shoe shop Schuhgeschäft ⓝ *shoo*·ge·sheft
shoes Schuhe ⓜ pl *shoo*·e
shoot (gun) schießen *shee*·sen
shop Geschäft ⓝ ge·*sheft*
shopping centre Einkaufszentrum ⓝ *ain*·kowfs·tsen·trum
short kurz kurts
short (height) klein klain
shortage Knappheit ⓕ *knap*·hait
shortcut Abkürzung ⓕ *ap*·kür·tsung
shorts Shorts pl shorts
short-sleeved kurzärmelig *kurts*·er·me·likh
shoulder Schulter ⓕ *shul*·ter
shout schreien *shrai*·en
show Show ⓕ shoh
show zeigen *tsai*·gen
shower Dusche ⓕ *doo*·she
shrine Schrein ⓜ shrain
shut (closed) geschlossen ge·*shlo*·sen
shut (close) schließen *shlee*·sen
shy schüchtern *shükh*·tern
sick krank krangk
side Seite ⓕ *zai*·te
sign Schild ⓝ shilt
signature Unterschrift ⓕ *un*·ter·shrift
signpost Wegweiser ⓜ *vayk*·vai·zer
silk Seide ⓕ *zai*·de
silver silbern *zil*·bern
similar ähnlich *ayn*·likh
simple einfach *ain*·fakh
since (May) seit (Mai) zait (mai)
sing singen *zing*·en
Singapore Singapur ⓝ *zing*·a·poor
singer Sänger(in) ⓜ/ⓕ *zeng*·er/ *zeng*·e·rin
single (person) Single ⓜ singl
single (unmarrried) ledig *lay*·dikh
single room Einzelzimmer ⓝ *ain*·tsel·tsi·mer
singlet Unterhemd ⓝ *un*·ter·hemt
sister Schwester ⓕ *shves*·ter
sit sitzen *zi*·tsen
situation Lage ⓕ *lah*·ge
size Größe ⓕ *grer*·se
skate eislaufen *ais*·low·fen
skateboarding Skateboarden ⓝ *skayt*·bor·den
ski skifahren *shee*·fah·ren

ENGLISH–GERMAN S

skiing Skifahren ⓝ *shee*·fah·ren
skimmed milk fettarme Milch ⓕ *fet*·ar·me milkh
skin Haut ⓕ howt
skirt Rock ⓜ rok
sky Himmel ⓜ *hi*·mel
sleep schlafen *shlah*·fen
sleeping bag Schlafsack ⓜ *shlahf*·zak
sleeping car Schlafwagen ⓜ *shlahf*·vah·gen
sleeping pills Schlaftabletten ⓕ pl *shlahf*·ta·ble·ten
sleepy schläfrig *shlayf*·rikh
slippery glatt glat
slope Hang ⓜ hang
slow langsam *lang*·zahm
slowly langsam *lang*·zahm
small klein klain
smell Geruch ⓜ ge·*rookh*
smile lächeln *le*·kheln
smoke rauchen *row*·khen
snack Snack ⓜ snek
snail Schnecke ⓕ *shne*·ke
snake Schlange ⓕ *shlang*·e
snorkelling Schnorcheln ⓝ *shnor*·kheln
snow Schnee ⓜ shnay
snow pea Zuckererbse ⓕ *tsu*·ker·erp·se
snowboarding Snowboarden ⓝ *snoh*·bor·den
snowfield Schneefeld ⓝ *shnay*·felt
soap Seife ⓕ *zai*·fe
soap opera Seifenoper ⓕ *zai*·fen·aw·per
soccer Fußball ⓜ *foos*·bal
social welfare Wohlfahrt ⓕ *vawl*·fahrt
socialist sozialistisch zo·tsya·*lis*·tish
socks Socken ⓕ pl *zo*·ken
soft drink alkoholfreies Getränk ⓝ al·ko·*hawl*·frai·es ge·*trengk*
sold out ausverkauft *ows*·fer·kowft
solid fest fest
some einige *ai*·ni·ge
someone jemand *yay*·mant
something etwas *et*·vas
sometimes manchmal *mankh*·mahl
son Sohn ⓜ zawn
song Lied ⓝ leet
son-in-law Schwiegersohn ⓜ *shvee*·ger·zawn
soon bald balt
sore schmerzhaft *shmerts*·haft
sore throat Halsschmerzen ⓜ pl *hals*·shmer·tsen
soup Suppe ⓕ *zu*·pe
sour cream Schmand ⓜ shmant
south Süden ⓜ *zü*·den
souvenir Souvenir ⓝ zu·ve·*neer*
souvenir shop Souvenirladen ⓜ zu·ve·*neer*·lah·den
soy milk Sojamilch ⓕ *zaw*·ya·milkh
soy sauce Sojasauce ⓕ *zaw*·ya·zaw·se
space Raum ⓜ rowm
spade Spaten ⓜ *shpah*·ten
Spain Spanien ⓝ *shpah*·ni·en
spare tyre Reservereifen ⓜ re·*zer*·ve·rai·fen
speak sprechen *shpre*·khen
special speziell shpe·*tsyel*
specialist Spezialist(in) ⓜ/ⓕ shpe·tsya·*list*/shpe·tsya·*lis*·tin
speed Geschwindigkeit ⓕ ge·*shvin*·dikh·kait
speed limit Geschwindigkeitsbegrenzung ⓕ ge·*shvin*·dikh·kaits·be·gren·tsung
spiced würzig *vür*·tsikh
spicy scharf sharf
spider Spinne ⓕ *shpi*·ne
spinach Spinat ⓜ shpi·*naht*
spokes Speichen ⓕ pl *shpai*·khen
spoon Löffel ⓜ *ler*·fel
sport Sport ⓜ shport
sportsperson Sportler(in) ⓜ/ⓕ *shport*·ler/*shport*·le·rin
sprain Muskelzerrung ⓕ *mus*·kel·tser·rung
spring (coil) Feder ⓕ *fay*·der
spring (season) Frühling ⓜ *frü*·ling
square (town) Platz ⓜ plats

stadium Stadion ⓝ *shtah*·di·on
stage Stadium ⓝ *shtah*·di·um
stage (theatre) Bühne ⓕ *bü*·ne
stairway Treppe ⓕ *tre*·pe
stamp Briefmarke ⓕ *breef*·mar·ke
standby ticket Standby-Ticket ⓝ stend·*bai*·ti·ket
standing room Stehplatz ⓜ *shtay*·plats
star sign Sternzeichen ⓝ *shtern*·tsai·khen
star Stern ⓜ shtern
(four-)star (Vier-)Sterne- (*feer*·) *shter*·ne·
start Beginn ⓜ be·*gin*
start (sport) Start ⓜ shtart
start anfangen *an*·fang·en
state Staat ⓜ shtaht
station Bahnhof ⓜ *bahn*·hawf
stationer Schreibwarenhandlung ⓕ *shraip*·vah·ren·han·dlung
statue Statue ⓕ *shtah*·tu·e
stay (at a hotel) übernachten ü·ber·*nakh*·ten
stay (not leave) bleiben *blai*·ben
steak (beef) Steak ⓝ stayk
steal stehlen *shtay*·len
steep steil shtail
step (stairs) Stufe ⓕ *shtoo*·fe
stereo Stereoanlage ⓕ *shtair*·re·o·an·lah·ge
stingy geizig *gai*·tsikh
stock Vorrat ⓜ *fawr*·raht
stockings Strümpfe ⓜ pl *shtrümp*·fe
stomach Magen ⓜ *mah*·gen
stomachache Magenschmerzen ⓜ pl *mah*·gen·shmer·tsen
stone Stein ⓜ shtain
stoned (drugged) stoned stohnd
stop Halt ⓜ halt
stop anhalten *an*·hal·ten
storm Sturm ⓜ shturm
story Geschichte ⓕ ge·*shikh*·te
stove Herd ⓜ hert
straight gerade ge·*rah*·de
strange fremd fremt
stranger Fremde ⓜ&ⓕ *frem*·de
strawberry Erdbeere ⓕ *ert*·bey·re
stream Bach ⓜ bakh
street Straße ⓕ *shtrah*·se
street kids Straßenkinder ⓝ pl *shtrah*·sen·kin·der
on strike streiken *shtrai*·ken
string Schnur ⓕ shnoor
strong stark shtark
stubborn stur shtoor
student Student(in) ⓜ/ⓕ shtu·*dent*/ shtu·*den*·tin
student card Studentenausweis ⓜ shtu·*den*·ten·ows·vais
studio Studio ⓝ *shtoo*·di·o
studio (art) Atelier ⓝ a·tel·*yay*
study studieren shtu·*dee*·ren
stupid dumm dum
style Stil ⓜ shteel
subtitles Untertitel ⓜ pl *un*·ter·tee·tel
suburb Vorort ⓜ *fawr*·ort
subway U-Bahn ⓕ *oo*·bahn
sugar Zucker ⓜ *tsu*·ker
suitcase Koffer ⓜ *ko*·fer
summer Sommer ⓜ *zom*·mer
sun Sonne ⓕ *zon*·ne
sunblock Sonnencreme ⓕ *zon*·en·kraym
sunburn Sonnenbrand ⓜ *zon*·en·brant
Sunday Sonntag ⓜ *zon*·tahk
sunglasses Sonnenbrille ⓕ *zon*·en·bri·le
sunny sonnig *zon*·nikh
sunrise Sonnenaufgang ⓜ *zo*·nen·owf·gang
sunset Sonnenuntergang ⓜ *zo*·nen·un·ter·gang
supermarket Supermarkt ⓜ *zoo*·per·markt
superstition Aberglaube ⓜ *ah*·ber·glow·be
supporters Anhänger ⓜ pl *an*·heng·er
surf surfen *ser*·fen
surface mail normale Post ⓕ

nor·*mah*·le post
surfboard Surfbrett ⓝ *serf*·bret
surname Nachname ⓜ *nahkh*·nah·me
surprise Überraschung ⓕ ü·ber·*ra*·shung
sweater Pullover ⓜ pu·*law*·ver
Sweden Schweden ⓝ *shvay*·den
sweet süß züs
swim schwimmen *shvi*·men
swimming pool Schwimmbad ⓝ *shvim*·baht
swimsuit Badeanzug ⓜ *bah*·de·an·tsook
Switzerland Schweiz ⓕ shvaits
synagogue Synagoge ⓕ zü·na·*gaw*·ge
synthetic synthetisch zün·*tay*·tish
syringe Spritze ⓕ *shpri*·tse

T

table Tisch ⓜ tish
table tennis Tischtennis ⓝ *tish*·te·nis
tablecloth Tischdecke ⓕ *tish*·de·ke
tail Schwanz ⓜ shvants
tailor Schneider(in) ⓜ/ⓕ *shnai*·der/*shnai*·de·rin
take nehmen *nay*·men
take (to) bringen *bring*·en
take off Abflug ⓜ *ap*·flook
talk sprechen *shpre*·khen
tall groß graws
tampons Tampons ⓜ pl *tam*·pons
tanning lotion Bräunungsmilch ⓕ *broy*·nungks·milkh
tap Wasserhahn ⓜ *va*·ser·hahn
target Ziel ⓝ tseel
tasty schmackhaft *shmak*·haft
tax Steuer ⓕ *shtoy*·er
taxi Taxi ⓝ *tak*·si
taxi stand Taxistand ⓜ *tak*·si·shtant
tea Tee ⓜ tay
teacher Lehrer(in) ⓜ/ⓕ *lair*·rer/*lair*·re·rin
team Mannschaft ⓕ *man*·shaft
teaspoon Teelöffel ⓜ *tay*·ler·fel
technique Technik ⓕ *tekh*·nik
teeth Zähne ⓜ pl *tsay*·ne
telephone Telefon ⓝ te·le·*fawn*
telephone telefonieren te·le·fo·*nee*·ren
telescope Teleskop ⓝ te·les·*kawp*
television Fernseher ⓜ *fern*·zay·er
tell erzählen er·*tsay*·len
temperature (fever) Fieber ⓝ *fee*·ber
temperature (weather) Temperatur ⓕ tem·pe·ra·*toor*
temple Tempel ⓜ *tem*·pel
ten zehn tsayn
tennis Tennis ⓝ *te*·nis
tennis court Tennisplatz ⓜ *te*·nis·plats
tent Zelt ⓝ tselt
tent pegs Heringe ⓜ pl *hay*·ring·e
terminal (transport) Endstation ⓕ *ent*·shta·tsyawn
terrible schrecklich *shrek*·likh
test Test ⓜ test
thank danken *dang*·ken
theatre Theater ⓝ te·*ah*·ter
their ihr eer
there dort dort
thermos Thermosflasche ⓕ *ter*·mos·fla·she
they sie zee
thick dick dik
thief Dieb ⓜ deep
thin dünn dün
think denken *deng*·ken
third dritte *dri*·te
thirsty durstig *durs*·tikh
this (month) diesen (Monat) *dee*·zen (*maw*·nat)
this (one) dieser/diese/dieses ⓜ/ⓕ/ⓝ *dee*·zer/*dee*·ze/*dee*·zes
thousand tausend *tow*·zent
thread Faden ⓜ *fah*·den
throat Hals ⓜ hals
through durch durkh
thrush (condition) Mundfäule ⓕ *munt*·foy·le
thunder Donner ⓜ *do*·ner
Thursday Donnerstag ⓜ *do*·ners·tahk
ticket (bus/metro/train) Fahrkarte ⓕ

fahr·kar·te
ticket (cinema/museum) Eintrittskarte ⓕ *ain*·trits·kar·te
ticket (plane) Flugticket ⓝ *flook*·ti·ket
ticket collector Fahrkartenkontrolleur/in ⓜ/ⓕ *fahr*·kar·ten·kon·tro·ler/*fahr*·kar·ten·kon·tro·ler·rin
ticket machine Fahrkartenautomat ⓜ *fahr*·kar·ten·ow·to·maht
ticket office Fahrkartenverkauf ⓜ *fahr*·kar·ten·fer·kowf
ticket office (theatre) Theaterkasse ⓕ te·*ah*·ter·ka·se
tides Gezeiten pl ge·*tsai*·ten
tight eng eng
time Zeit ⓕ tsait
time difference Zeitunterschied ⓜ *tsait*·un·ter·sheet
timetable Fahrplan ⓜ *fahr*·plahn
tin (can) Dose ⓕ *daw*·ze
tin opener Dosenöffner ⓜ *daw*·zen·erf·ner
tiny winzig *vin*·tsikh
tip (gratuity) Trinkgeld ⓝ *tringk*·gelt
tire ermüden er·*mü*·den
tired müde *mü*·de
tissues Papiertaschentücher ⓝ pl pa·*peer*·ta·shen·tü·kher
toast Toast ⓜ tawst
toaster Toaster ⓜ *taws*·ter
tobacco Tabak ⓜ *ta*·bak
tobacconist Tabakladen ⓜ *ta*·bak·lah·den
tobogganing Rodeln ⓝ *raw*·deln
today heute *hoy*·te
toe Zehe ⓕ *tsay*·e
tofu Tofu ⓜ *taw*·fu
together zusammen tsu·*za*·men
toilet Toilette ⓕ to·a·*le*·te
toilet paper Toilettenpapier ⓝ to·a·*le*·ten·pa·peer
tomato Tomate ⓕ to·*mah*·te
tomato sauce Tomatensauce ⓕ to·*mah*·ten·zaw·se
tomb Grab ⓝ grahp
tomorrow morgen *mor*·gen
tomorrow morning morgen früh *mor*·gen *frü*
tonight heute Abend *hoy*·te *ah*·bent
too (also) auch owkh
too (many) zu (viele) tsoo (*fee*·le)
tools Werkzeug ⓝ *verk*·tsoyk
tooth Zahn ⓜ tsahn
toothache Zahnschmerzen ⓜ pl *tsahn*·shmer·tsen
toothbrush Zahnbürste ⓕ *tsahn*·bürs·te
toothpaste Zahnpasta ⓕ *tsahn*·pas·ta
toothpick Zahnstocher ⓜ *tsahn*·shto·kher
torch (flashlight) Taschenlampe ⓕ *ta*·shen·lam·pe
touch berühren be·*rü*·ren
tour Tour ⓕ toor
tourist Tourist/in ⓜ/ⓕ tu·*rist*/tu·*ris*·tin
tourist office Fremdenverkehrsbüro ⓝ *frem*·den·fer·kairs·bü·raw
towards auf ... zu owf ... tsoo
towel Handtuch ⓝ *hant*·tookh
tower Turm ⓜ turm
town Stadt ⓕ shtat
toxic waste Giftmüll ⓜ *gift*·mül
toy Spielzeug ⓝ *shpeel*·tsoyk
track (path) Weg ⓜ vayk
track (sports) Bahn ⓕ bahn
trade Handel ⓜ *han*·del
traffic Verkehr ⓜ fer·*kair*
traffic lights Ampel ⓕ *am*·pel
trail Pfad ⓜ pfaht
train Zug ⓜ tsook
train station Bahnhof ⓜ *bahn*·hawf
tram Straßenbahn ⓕ *shtrah*·sen·bahn
transit lounge Transitraum ⓜ tran·*zeet*·rowm
translate übersetzen ü·ber·*ze*·tsen
transport Transport ⓜ trans·*port*
travel reisen *rai*·zen
travel agency Reisebüro ⓝ

rai·ze·bü·raw
travel sickness Reisekrankheit ⓕ *rai*·ze·krangk·hait
tree Baum ⓜ bowm
trip Reise ⓕ *rai*·ze
trousers Hose ⓕ *haw*·ze
truck Lastwagen ⓜ *last*·vah·gen
true wahr vahr
trust trauen *trow*·en
try (attempt) versuchen fer·*zoo*·khen
T-shirt T-Shirt ⓝ *tee*·shert
tube (tyre) Schlauch ⓜ shlowkh
Tuesday Dienstag ⓜ *deens*·tahk
tuna Thunfisch ⓜ *toon*·fish
tune Melodie ⓕ me·lo·*dee*
turkey Truthahn ⓜ *troot*·hahn
turn abbiegen *ap*·bee·gen
TV (set) Fernseher ⓜ *fern*·zay·er
TV series Fernsehserie ⓕ *fern*·zay·zair·ri·e
tweezers Pinzette ⓕ pin·*tse*·te
twice zweimal *tsvai*·mahl
twin beds zwei Einzelbetten ⓝ pl tsvai *ain*·tsel·be·ten
twins Zwillinge ⓜ pl *tsvi*·ling·e
type Typ ⓜ tüp
typical typisch *tü*·pish
tyre Reifen ⓜ *rai*·fen

U

ultrasound Ultraschall ⓜ *ul*·tra·shal
umbrella Regenschirm ⓜ *ray*·gen·shirm
uncle Onkel ⓜ *ong*·kel
uncomfortable unbequem *un*·be·kvaym
under unter *un*·ter
underground U-Bahn ⓕ *oo*·bahn
understand verstehen fer·*shtay*·en
underwear Unterwäsche ⓕ *un*·ter·ve·she
unemployed arbeitslos *ar*·baits·laws
unemployment Arbeitslosigkeit ⓕ *ar*·baits·law·zikh·kait
unfair unfair *un*·fair
uniform Uniform ⓕ u·ni·*form*
universe Universum ⓝ u·ni·*vair*·zum
university Universität ⓕ u·ni·ver·zi·*tayt*
unleaded bleifrei *blai*·frai
unsafe nicht sicher *nikht zi*·kher
until (June) bis (Juni) bis (*yoo*·ni)
unusual ungewöhnlich *un*·ge·vern·likh
up nach oben nahkh *aw*·ben
uphill aufwärts *owf*·verts
upstairs oben *aw*·ben
urgent dringend *dring*·ent
USA USA ⓕ pl oo·es·*ah*
useful nützlich *nüts*·likh

V

vacant frei frai
vacation Ferien pl *fair*·i·en
vaccination Schutzimpfung ⓕ *shuts*·im·pfung
vagina Vagina ⓕ va·*gee*·na
validate (ticket) entwerten ent·*ver*·ten
valley Tal ⓝ tahl
valuable wertvoll *vert*·fol
value (price) Wert ⓜ vert
van Lieferwagen ⓜ *lee*·fer·vah·gen
veal Kalbfleisch ⓝ *kalp*·flaish
vegetable Gemüse ⓝ ge·*mü*·ze
vegetarian Vegetarier(in) ⓜ/ⓕ ve·ge·*tah*·ri·er/ve·ge·*tah*·ri·e·rin
vein Vene ⓕ *vay*·ne
venereal disease Geschlechts-krankheit ⓕ ge·*shlekhts*·krangk·hait
venue Veranstaltungsort ⓜ fer·*an*·shtal·tungks·ort
very sehr zair
view Aussicht ⓕ *ows*·zikht
village Dorf ⓝ dorf
vine Rebe ⓕ *ray*·be
vinegar Essig ⓜ *e*·sikh
vineyard Weinberg ⓜ *vain*·berk
virus Virus ⓜ *vee*·rus
visa Visum ⓝ *vee*·zum
visit besuchen be·*zoo*·khen

vitamins Vitamine ⓝ pl *vi·ta·mee·ne*
vodka Wodka ⓜ *vot·ka*
voice Stimme ⓕ *shti·me*
volume (amount) Volumen ⓝ *vo·loo·men*
volume (book) Band ⓜ *bant*
volume (loudness) Lautstärke ⓕ *lowt·shter·ke*
vomit übergeben *oo·ber·gey·ben*
vote wählen *vay·len*

W

wage Lohn ⓜ *lawn*
wait warten *var·ten*
waiter Kellner(in) ⓜ/ⓕ *kel·ner/kel·ne·rin*
waiting room (doctor's) Wartezimmer ⓝ *var·te·tsi·mer*
waiting room (train station) Wartesaal ⓜ *var·te·zahl*
walk gehen *gay·en*
wall (outer) Mauer ⓕ *mow·er*
want wollen *vo·len*
war Krieg ⓜ *kreek*
wardrobe Garderobe ⓕ *gar·draw·be*
warm warm *varm*
warn warnen *var·nen*
wash (oneself) sich waschen *zikh va·shen*
wash (something) waschen *va·shen*
wash cloth (flannel) Waschlappen ⓜ *vash·la·pen*
washing machine Waschmaschine ⓕ *vash·ma·shee·ne*
washing powder Waschpulver ⓝ *vash·pul·ver*
wasp Wespe ⓕ *ves·pe*
watch Uhr ⓕ *oor*
watch beobachten *be·aw·bakh·ten*
watch (TV) fernsehen *fern·zay·en*
water Wasser ⓝ *va·ser*
water (from the tap) Leitungswasser ⓝ *lai·tungks·va·ser*
water bottle Wasserflasche ⓕ *va·ser·fla·she*
waterfall Wasserfall ⓜ *va·ser·fal*
watermelon Wassermelone ⓕ *va·ser·me·law·ne*
waterproof wasserdicht *va·ser·dikht*
waterskiing Wasserskifahren ⓝ *va·ser·shee·fah·ren*
wave Welle ⓕ *ve·le*
way Weg ⓜ *vayk*
we wir *veer*
weak schwach *shvakh*
wealthy reich *raikh*
weapon Waffe ⓕ *va·fe*
wear tragen *trah·gen*
weather Wetter ⓝ *ve·ter*
wedding Hochzeit ⓕ *hokh·tsait*
wedding cake Hochzeitstorte ⓕ *hokh·tsaits·tor·te*
wedding present Hochzeitsgeschenk ⓝ *hokh·tsaits·ge·shengk*
Wednesday Mittwoch ⓜ *mit·vokh*
(this) week (diese) Woche ⓕ *(dee·ze) vo·khe*
weekend Wochenende ⓝ *vo·khen·en·de*
weigh wiegen *vee·gen*
weight Gewicht ⓝ *ge·vikht*
welcome willkommen *vil·ko·men*
welfare Sozialhilfe ⓕ *zo·tsyahl·hil·fe*
welfare state Sozialstaat ⓜ *zo·tsyahl·shtaht*
well gut *goot*
west Westen ⓜ *ves·ten*
wet nass *nas*
what was *vas*
wheel Rad ⓝ *raht*
wheelchair Rollstuhl ⓜ *rol·shtool*
when (adverb) wann *van*
when (conjunction) wenn *ven*
whenever wann immer *van i·mer*
where wo *vaw*
whisky Whisky ⓜ *vis·ki*
white weiß *vais*
who wer *vair*
whole ganz *gants*
why warum *va·rum*
wide breit *brait*

wife Ehefrau Ⓕ *ay*·e·frow
wild wild vilt
win gewinnen ge·*vi*·nen
wind Wind Ⓜ vint
window Fenster Ⓝ *fens*·ter
windscreen Windschutzscheibe Ⓕ *vint*·shuts·shai·be
windsurfing Windsurfen Ⓝ *vint*·ser·fen
windy windig *vin*·dikh
wine Wein Ⓜ vain
— **red** Rotwein Ⓜ *rawt*·vain
— **sparkling** Schaumwein Ⓜ *showm*·vain
— **white** Weißwein Ⓜ *vais*·vain
winery Weinkellerei Ⓕ *vain*·ke·le·rai
wings Flügel Ⓜ pl *flü*·gel
winner Sieger(in) Ⓜ/Ⓕ *zee*·ger/*zee*·ge·rin
winter Winter Ⓜ *vin*·ter
wire Draht Ⓜ draht
wish wünschen *vün*·shen
with mit mit
within (an hour) innerhalb (einer Stunde) *i*·ner·halp (*ai*·ner *shtun*·de)
without ohne *aw*·ne
woman Frau Ⓕ frow
wonderful wunderbar *vun*·der·bahr
wood Holz Ⓝ holts
wool Wolle Ⓕ *vo*·le
word Wort Ⓝ vort
work Arbeit Ⓕ *ar*·bait
work arbeiten *ar*·bai·ten
work permit Arbeitserlaubnis Ⓕ *ar*·baits·er·lowp·nis
workout Training Ⓝ *tray*·ning
workshop Werkstatt Ⓕ *verk*·shtat
world Welt Ⓕ velt
World Cup Weltmeisterschaft Ⓕ *velt*·mais·ter·shaft
worms Würmer Ⓜ pl *vür*·mer
worried besorgt be·*zorkt*
worse schlechter *shlekh*·ter
worship einen Gottesdienst besuchen *ai*·nen *go*·tes·deenst be·*zoo*·khen
write schreiben *shrai*·ben
writer Schriftsteller(in) Ⓜ/Ⓕ *shrift*·shte·ler/*shrift*·shte·le·rin
wrong falsch falsh

Y

(this) year (dieses) Jahr Ⓝ (*dee*·zes) yahr
yellow gelb gelp
yen Yen Ⓜ yen
yes ja yah
yesterday gestern *ges*·tern
yet schon shawn
not yet noch nicht nokh nikht
yoga Joga Ⓝ *yaw*·ga
yoghurt Joghurt Ⓜ *yaw*·gurt
you sg inf du doo
you sg&pl pol Sie zee
young jung yung
your sg inf dein dain
your sg&pl pol Ihr eer
youth hostel Jugendherberge Ⓕ *yoo*·gent·her·ber·ge

Z

zero null nul
zip/zipper Reißverschluss Ⓜ *rais*·fer·shlus
zodiac Sternzeichen Ⓝ *shtern*·tsai·khen
zoo Zoo Ⓜ tsaw
zucchini Zucchini Ⓕ tsu·*kee*·ni

DICTIONARY

German to English

DEUTSCH–ENGLISCH

Nouns in the dictionary, and adjectives affected by gender, have their gender indicated by ⓕ, ⓜ or ⓝ. If it's a plural noun, you'll also see pl. Where a word that could be either a noun or a verb has no gender indicated, it's a verb.

A

abbiegen ap·bee·gen turn
Abend ⓜ ah·bent evening
Abendessen ⓝ ah·bent·e·sen dinner
aber ah·ber but
Aberglaube ⓜ ah·ber·glow·be superstition
abfahren ap·fah·ren leave (depart)
Abfahrt ⓕ ap·fahrt departure
Abfall ⓜ ap·fal rubbish • garbage
Abfertigungsschalter ⓜ ap·fer·ti·gungks·shal·ter check-in (desk)
Abflug ⓜ ap·flook take off
Abführmittel ⓝ ap·für·mi·tel laxatives
abgelegen ap·ge·lay·gen remote
Abgeordnete ⓜ&ⓕ ap·ge·ord·ne·te member of parliament
abgeschlossen ap·ge·shlo·sen locked
abhängig ap·heng·ikh addicted
Abholzung ⓕ ap·hol·tsung deforestation
Abkürzung ⓕ ap·kür·tsung shortcut
ablehnen ap·lay·nen refuse
Abschleppdienst ⓜ ap·shlep·deenst breakdown service
abseits ap·zaits offside
Abstrich ⓜ ap·shtrikh pap smear
Abtreibung ⓕ ap·trai·bung abortion
abwärts ap·verts downhill
Abzockerei ⓕ ap·tso·ke·rai rip-off
Abzug ⓜ ap·tsook print (photography)
Adapter ⓜ a·dap·ter adaptor
Adressanhänger ⓜ a·dres·an·heng·er luggage tag
Adresse ⓕ a·dre·se address
Aerobics pl e·ro·biks aerobics
Afrika ⓝ a·fri·kah Africa
Aftershave ⓝ ahf·ter·shayf aftershave
ähnlich ayn·likh similar
AIDS ⓝ aydz AIDS
Aktentasche ⓕ ak·ten·ta·she briefcase
Aktivist(in) ⓜ/ⓕ ak·ti·vist/ak·ti·vis·tin activist
Aktuelles ⓝ ak·tu·e·les current affairs
Akupunktur ⓕ a·ku·pungk·toor acupuncture
Alkohol ⓜ al·ko·hawl alcohol
alkoholfreies Getränk ⓝ al·ko·hawl·frai·es ge·trengk soft drink

Alkoholiker(in) ⓜ/ⓕ al·ko·haw·li·ker/ al·ko·haw·li·ke·rin alcoholic
alkoholisch al·ko·haw·lish alcoholic
alle a·le all
Allee ⓕ a·lay avenue
allein a·lain alone
Allergie ⓕ a·lair·gee allergy
alles a·les everything
allgemein al·ge·main general
alltäglich al·tayk·likh every day
alt alt old • ancient
Altar ⓜ al·tahr altar
Alter ⓝ al·ter age
Amateur(in) ⓜ/ⓕ a·ma·ter/ a·ma·ter·in amateur
Ameise ⓕ ah·mai·ze ant
Ampel ⓕ am·pel traffic lights
sich amüsieren zikh a·mü·zee·ren enjoy (oneself)
an an at • to
Anarchist(in) ⓜ/ⓕ a·nar·khist/ a·nar·khis·tin anarchist
anbaggern an·ba·gern chat up
andere an·de·re other • different
anfangen an·fang·en start
Anführer ⓜ an·fü·rer leader
Angel ⓕ ang·el fishing rod
Angestellte ⓜ&ⓕ an·ge·shtel·te employee
Angst (haben) angkst (hah·ben) (to be) afraid
anhalten an·hal·ten stop
Anhänger ⓜ pl an·heng·er supporters
ankommen an·ko·men arrive
Ankunft ⓕ an·kunft arrivals
ansehen an·zay·en look at
(an)statt an·shtat instead of
Anti-Atom- an·ti·a·tawm· antinuclear
Antibiotika ⓝ pl an·ti·bi·aw·ti·ka antibiotics
Antiquariat ⓝ an·ti·kva·ri·aht second-hand bookshop
Antiquität ⓕ an·ti·kvi·tayt antique
Antiseptikum ⓝ an·ti·zep·ti·kum antiseptic
Antwort ⓕ ant·vort answer
antworten ant·vor·ten answer
Anzahlung ⓕ an·tsah·lung deposit
Anzeige ⓕ an·tsai·ge advertisement
Anzeigetafel ⓕ an·tsai·ge·tah·fel scoreboard
Apfel ⓜ ap·fel apple
Apfelmost ⓜ ap·fel·most cider
Apotheke ⓕ a·po·tay·ke chemist • pharmacy
Aprikose ⓕ a·pri·kaw·ze apricot
Arbeit ⓕ ar·bait work
arbeiten ar·bai·ten work
Arbeiter(in) ⓜ/ⓕ ar·bai·ter/ ar·bai·te·rin worker • labourer
Arbeitgeber ⓜ ar·bait·gay·ber employer
Arbeitserlaubnis ⓕ ar·baits·er·lowp·nis work permit
arbeitslos ar·baits·laws unemployed
Arbeitslosengeld ⓝ ar·baits·law·zen·gelt unemployment benefit
Arbeitslosigkeit ⓕ ar·baits·law·zikh·kait unemployment
Arbeitsstelle ⓕ ar·baits·shte·le job
archäologisch ar·khe·o·law·gish archaeological
Architektur ⓕ ar·khi·tek·toor architecture
Arm ⓜ arm arm
arm arm poor
Armut ⓕ ar·moot poverty
Arzt ⓜ artst doctor (medical)
Ärztin ⓕ erts·tin doctor (medical)
Aschenbecher ⓜ a·shen·be·kher ashtray
Asien ⓝ ah·zi·en Asia
Asthma ⓝ ast·ma asthma
Asylant(in) ⓜ/ⓕ a·zü·lant/a·zü·lan·tin asylum seeker
Atelier ⓝ a·tel·yay studio (art)
atmen aht·men breathe
Atmosphäre ⓕ at·mos·fair·re atmosphere

Atomenergie ⓕ a·tawm·e·ner·gee nuclear energy
Atommüll ⓜ a·tawm·mül nuclear waste
Aubergine ⓕ aw·ber·zhee·ne aubergine • eggplant
auch owkh too • also
auch nicht owkh nikht neither
auf owf on • at
auf ... zu owf ... tsoo towards
Aufführung ⓕ owf·fü·rung performance
aufheben owf·hay·ben pick up (object)
Aufnahme ⓕ owf·nah·me recording
aufpassen owf·pa·sen mind (object) • pay attention
Auftritt ⓜ owf·trit gig
aufwärts owf·verts uphill
Auge ⓝ ow·ge eye
Augenblick ⓜ ow·gen·blik moment
Augentropfen ⓜ pl ow·gen·trop·fen eye drops
aus ows from • out
aus (Baumwolle) ows (bawm·vo·le) made of (cotton)
Ausbeutung ⓕ ows·boy·tung exploitation
Ausgang ⓜ ows·gang exit
ausgebucht ows·ge·bookht booked out
ausgehen ows·gay·en go out • run out of
mit jemandem ausgehen mit yay·man·dem ows·gay·en date someone
ausgeschlossen ows·ge·shlo·sen excluded
ausgezeichnet ows·ge·tsaikh·net excellent
Auskunft ⓕ ows·kunft information
im Ausland im ows·lant abroad
ausländisch ows·len·dish foreign
Auspuff ⓜ ows·puf exhaust (car)
Ausrüstung ⓕ ows·rüs·tung equipment
Ausschlag ⓜ ows·shlahk rash
außer ow·ser apart from • besides
Aussicht ⓕ ows·zikht view
Aussichtspunkt ⓜ ows·zikhts·pungkt lookout
Ausstellung ⓕ ows·shte·lung exhibition
austeilen ows·tai·len deal (cards)
Auster ⓕ ows·ter oyster
Australien ⓝ ows·trah·li·en Australia
ausverkauft ows·fer·kowft sold out
Ausweis ⓜ ows·vais identification
Auto ⓝ ow·to car
Autobahn ⓕ ow·to·bahn motorway (tollway)
Autokennzeichen ⓝ ow·to·ken·tsai·khen licence plate number
automatisch ow·to·mah·tish automatic
Autor(in) ⓜ/ⓕ ow·tor/ow·taw·rin author
Autoverleih ⓜ ow·to·fer·lai car hire
Avokado ⓕ a·vo·kah·do avocado
Axt ⓕ akst axe

B

Baby ⓝ bay·bi baby
Babynahrung ⓕ bay·bi·nah·rung baby food
Babypuder ⓝ bay·bi·poo·der baby powder
Babysitter ⓜ bay·bi·si·ter babysitter
Bach ⓜ bakh stream
Bäckerei ⓕ be·ke·rai bakery
Backpflaume ⓕ bak·pflow·me prune
Bad ⓝ baht bath
Badeanzug ⓜ bah·de·an·tsook swimsuit
Badetuch ⓝ bah·de·tookh bath towel
Badezimmer ⓝ bah·de·tsi·mer bathroom
Bahn ⓕ bahn track (sports) • railway
Bahnhof ⓜ bahn·hawf railway station

Bahnsteig ⓜ *bahn*·shtaik platform
bald balt soon
Balkon ⓜ bal·*kawn* balcony
Ball ⓜ bal ball
Ballett ⓝ ba·*let* ballet
Banane ⓕ ba·*nah*·ne banana
Band ⓕ bent band (music)
Band ⓜ bant volume (book)
Bank ⓕ bangk bank
Bankauszug ⓜ *bangk*·ows·tsook bankdraft
Bankkonto ⓝ *bangk*·kon·to bank account
Bär ⓜ bair bear
Bargeld ⓝ *bahr*·gelt cash
Batterie ⓕ ba·te·*ree* battery
bauen *bow*·en build
Bauer ⓜ *bow*·er farmer
Bäuerin ⓕ *boy*·e·rin farmer
Bauernhof ⓜ *bow*·ern·hawf farm
Baum ⓜ bowm tree
Baumwolle ⓕ *bowm*·vo·le cotton
Bedienungszuschlag ⓜ be·*dee*·nungks·tsoo·shlahk service charge
bedrohte be·*draw*·te endangered
beenden be·*en*·den finish
Beginn ⓜ be·*gin* beginning
beginnen be·*gi*·nen begin
Begleiter(in) ⓜ/ⓕ be·*glai*·ter/be·*glai*·te·rin companion
Begräbnis ⓝ be·*grayp*·nis funeral
Behinderung be·*hin*·der·ung disability
bei bai at
Beichte ⓕ *baikh*·te confession (religious)
beide *bai*·de both
Bein ⓝ bain leg (body)
Beispiel ⓝ *bai*·shpeel example
Bekleidungsgeschäft ⓝ be·*klai*·dungks·ge·sheft clothing store
Belästigung ⓕ be·*les*·ti·gung harassment
Belichtungsmesser ⓜ be·*likh*·tungks·me·ser light meter
beliebt be·*leept* popular
Benzin ⓝ ben·*tseen* petrol • gas
Benzinkanister ⓜ ben·*tseen*·ka·nis·ter petrol can
beobachten be·*aw*·bakh·ten watch
bequem be·*kvaym* comfortable
berauben be·*row*·ben rob
Berg ⓜ berk mountain
Berghütte ⓕ *berk*·hü·te mountain hut
Bergsteigen ⓝ *berk*·shtai·gen mountaineering
Bergweg ⓜ *berk*·vayk mountain path
Beruf ⓜ be·*roof* occupation • profession
berühmt be·*rümt* famous
berühren be·*rü*·ren touch
beschäftigt be·*shef*·tikht busy (person)
beschützen be·*shü*·tsen protect
sich beschweren zikh be·*shvair*·ren complain
besetzt be·*zetst* busy (phone)
Besitzer(in) ⓜ/ⓕ be·*zi*·tser/be·*zi*·tse·rin owner
besorgt be·*zorkt* worried
besser *be*·ser better
bestätigen be·*shtay*·ti·gen confirm (reservation)
beste *bes*·te best
bestechen be·*shte*·khen bribe
Besteck ⓝ be·*shtek* cutlery
besteigen be·*shtai*·gen board (plane, ship)
bestellen be·*shte*·len order
Bestellung ⓕ be·*shte*·lung order (restaurant)
bestrafen be·*shtrah*·fen punish
besuchen be·*zoo*·khen visit
Betäubung ⓕ be·*toy*·bung anaesthetic
sich beteiligen zikh be·*tai*·li·gen participate
Betrag ⓜ be·*trahk* amount
Betrüger(in) ⓜ/ⓕ be·*trü*·ger/be·*trü*·ge·rin cheat
betrunken be·*trung*·ken drunk

Bett ⓝ *bet* bed
Bettlaken ⓝ *bet*·lah·ken sheet (bed)
Bettler(in) ⓜ/ⓕ *bet*·ler/*bet*·le·rin beggar
Bettwäsche ⓕ *bet*·ve·she linen (bed)
Bettzeug ⓝ *bet*·tsoyk bedding
Beutelmelone ⓕ *boy*·tel·me·law·ne cantaloupe
bezahlen be·*tsah*·len pay
Beziehung ⓕ be·*tsee*·ung relationship
BH ⓜ bay·*hah* bra
Bibel ⓕ *bee*·bel Bible
Bibliothek ⓕ bi·bli·o·*tayk* library
Biene ⓕ *bee*·ne bee
Bier ⓝ *beer* beer
Bildschirm ⓜ *bilt*·shirm screen (TV, computer)
Billard ⓝ *bil*·yart pool (game)
billig *bi*·likh cheap
Birne ⓕ *bir*·ne pear
bis (Juni) bis (*yoo*·ni) until (June)
bis zu ... bis tsoo ... as far as ...
Biss ⓜ bis bite (animal)
ein bisschen ain *bis*·khen a little
bitte *bi*·te please
um etwas bitten um *et*·vas *bi*·ten ask for something
bitter *bi*·ter bitter
Blase ⓕ *blah*·ze blister
Blasenentzündung ⓕ *blah*·zen·en·tsün·dung cystitis
Blatt ⓝ blat leaf
blau blow blue
bleiben *blai*·ben stay (remain)
bleifrei *blai*·frai unleaded
Bleistift ⓜ *blai*·shtift pencil
blind blint blind
Blinddarm ⓜ *blint*·darm appendix
Blindenhund ⓜ *blin*·den·hunt guide dog
Blindenschrift ⓕ *blin*·den·shrift Braille
Blinker ⓜ *bling*·ker indicator
Blitz ⓜ blits lightning • flash
blockiert blo·*keert* blocked
Blume ⓕ *bloo*·me flower
Blumenhändler ⓜ *bloo*·men·hen·dler florist
Blumenkohl ⓜ *bloo*·men·kawl cauliflower
Blut ⓝ bloot blood
Blutdruck ⓜ *bloot*·druk blood pressure
Blutgruppe ⓕ *bloot*·gru·pe blood group
Bluterguss ⓕ *bloot*·er·gus bruise
Bluttest ⓜ *bloot*·test blood test
Boden ⓜ *baw*·den floor
Bohne ⓕ *baw*·ne bean
Bonbon ⓜ bong·*bong* candy
Boot ⓝ bawt boat
an Bord an bort aboard
Bordkarte ⓕ *bort*·kar·te boarding pass
Botanischer Garten ⓜ bo·*tah*·ni·sher *gar*·ten botanic garden
Botschaft ⓕ *bawt*·shaft embassy
Botschafter(in) ⓜ/ⓕ *bawt*·shaf·ter/*bawt*·shaf·te·rin ambassador
Boxen ⓝ *bok*·sen boxing
braten *brah*·ten fry
Bratpfanne ⓕ *braht*·pfa·ne frying pan
brauchen *brow*·khen need
braun brown brown
breit brait wide
Bremsen ⓕ pl *brem*·zen brakes
Bremsflüssigkeit ⓕ *brems*·flü·sikh·kait brake fluid
Brennholz ⓝ *bren*·holts firewood
Brennstoff ⓜ *bren*·shtof fuel
Brett ⓝ bret board (plank)
Brief ⓜ breef letter
Briefkasten ⓜ *breef*·kas·ten mailbox
Briefmarke ⓕ *breef*·mar·ke stamp
Briefumschlag ⓜ *breef*·um·shlahk envelope
brillant bril·*yant* brilliant
Brille ⓕ *bri*·le glasses (spectacles)
bringen *bring*·en bring • take
Brokkoli ⓜ pl *bro*·ko·li broccoli
Bronchitis ⓕ bron·*khee*·tis bronchitis

Broschüre ⓕ *bro·shü·re* brochure
Brot ⓝ *brawt* bread
Brötchen ⓝ *brert·khen* bread roll
Brücke ⓕ *brü·ke* bridge
Bruder ⓜ *broo·der* brother
Brunnen ⓜ *bru·nen* fountain
Brust ⓕ *brust* breast
Brustkorb ⓜ *brust·korp* chest
Buch ⓝ *bookh* book
buchen *boo·khen* book (reserve)
Buchhalter(in) ⓜ/ⓕ *bookh·hal·ter/bookh·hal·te·rin* accountant
Buchhandlung ⓕ *bookh·han·dlung* bookshop
Buddhist(in) ⓜ/ⓕ *bu·dist/bu·dis·tin* Buddhist
Buffet ⓝ *bü·fay* buffet
bügeln *bü·geln* iron (clothes)
Bühne ⓕ *bü·ne* stage (theatre)
Bundeskanzler(in) ⓜ/ⓕ *bun·des·kants·ler/bun·des·kants·le·rin* prime minister (Germany & Austria)
Burg ⓕ *burk* castle
Bürgermeister(in) ⓜ/ⓕ *bür·ger·mais·ter/bür·ger·mais·te·rin* mayor
Bürgerrechte ⓝ pl *bür·ger·rekh·te* civil rights
Büro ⓝ *bü·raw* office
Büroangestellte ⓜ&ⓕ *bü·raw·an·ge·shtel·te* office worker
Bus ⓜ *bus* bus (city)
Busbahnhof ⓜ *bus·bahn·hawf* bus station
Bushaltestelle ⓕ *bus·hal·te·shte·le* bus stop
Butter ⓕ *bu·ter* butter

C

Café ⓝ *ka·fay* cafe
Campingplatz ⓜ *kem·ping·plats* camping ground
Cashewnuss ⓕ *kesh·yoo·nus* cashew
CD ⓕ *tsay·day* CD
Celsius ⓜ *tsel·zi·us* centigrade
Cent ⓜ *sent* cent
Chancengleichheit ⓕ *shahng·sen·glaikh·hait* equal opportunity
charmant *shar·mant* charming
Chef(in) ⓜ/ⓕ *shef/she·fin* boss
chemische Reinigung ⓕ *khay·mi·she rai·ni·gung* dry-cleaner
Chili(sauce) ⓕ *chi·li(·zaw·se)* chili (sauce)
Christ(in) ⓜ/ⓕ *krist/kris·tin* Christian
Computerspiel ⓝ *kom·pyoo·ter·shpeel* computer game
Coupon ⓜ *ku·pong* coupon
Couscous ⓜ *kus·kus* couscous
Cousin(e) ⓜ/ⓕ *ku·zen/ku·zee·ne* cousin
Cracker ⓜ *kre·ker* cracker
Cricket ⓝ *kri·ket* cricket
Curry(pulver) ⓝ *ker·ri(·pul·ver)* curry (powder)

D

Dach ⓝ *dakh* roof
Dachboden ⓜ *dakh·baw·den* attic
Dachs ⓜ *daks* badger
Damenbinden ⓕ pl *dah·men·bin·den* sanitary napkins
Dämmerung ⓕ *de·me·rung* dawn • dusk
danken *dang·ken* thank
Datum ⓝ *dah·tum* date (day)
Decke ⓕ *de·ke* blanket
dein *dain* your sg inf
Demokratie ⓕ *de·mo·kra·tee* democracy
Demonstration ⓕ *de·mon·stra·tsyawn* demonstration
denken *deng·ken* think
Denkmal ⓝ *dengk·mahl* monument
Deo ⓝ *day·o* deodorant
Detail ⓝ *de·tai* detail
Deutsch ⓝ *doytsh* German
Deutschland ⓝ *doytsh·lant* Germany

Diabetis ⓕ *di·a·bay·tis* diabetes
Diät ⓕ *di·ayt* diet
Dichtung ⓕ *dikh·tung* poetry
dick *dik* thick • fat
Dieb ⓜ *deep* thief
Dienstag ⓜ *deens·tahk* Tuesday
dieser ⓜ *dee·zer* this (one)
direkt *di·rekt* direct
Disko(thek) ⓕ *dis·ko(·tayk)* disco
Diskriminierung ⓕ *dis·kri·mi·nee·rung* discrimination
Doktor(in) ⓜ/ⓕ *dok·tor/dok·taw·rin* doctor (title)
Dokumentation ⓕ *do·ku·men·ta·tsyawn* documentary
Dollar ⓜ *do·lahr* dollar
Dolmetscher(in) ⓜ/ⓕ *dol·met·sher/dol·met·she·rin* interpreter
Dom ⓜ *dawm* cathedral
Donner ⓜ *do·ner* thunder
Donnerstag ⓜ *do·ners·tahk* Thursday
Dope ⓝ *dawp/dohp* dope (drugs)
Doppelbett ⓝ *do·pel·bet* double bed
doppelt *do·pelt* double
Doppelzimmer ⓝ *do·pel·tsi·mer* double room
Dorf ⓝ *dorf* village
dort *dort* there
Dose ⓕ *daw·ze* can (tin)
Dosenöffner ⓜ *daw·zen·erf·ner* can opener
Dozent(in) ⓜ/ⓕ *do·tsent/do·tsen·tin* lecturer
Drachenfliegen ⓝ *dra·khen·flee·gen* hang-gliding
Draht ⓜ *draht* wire
draußen *drow·sen* outside
dringend *dring·ent* urgent
dritte *dri·te* third
Droge ⓕ *draw·ge* drug
Drogenabhängigkeit ⓕ *draw·gen·ap·heng·ikh·kait* drug addiction
Drogenhändler ⓜ *draw·gen·hen·dler* drug dealer
Druck ⓜ *druk* pressure • print (art)
Drüsenfieber ⓝ *drü·zen·fee·ber* glandular fever
du *doo* you sg inf
dumm *dum* stupid
dunkel *dung·kel* dark
dünn *dün* thin
durch *durkh* through
Durchfall ⓜ *durkh·fal* diarrhoea
Durchwahl ⓕ *durkh·vahl* direct-dial
durstig *durs·tikh* thirsty
Dusche ⓕ *doo·she* shower
Dutzend ⓝ *du·tsent* dozen

E

Ebene ⓕ *ay·be·ne* plain
Echse ⓕ *ek·se* lizard
Ecke ⓕ *e·ke* corner
egoistisch *e·go·is·tish* selfish
Ehe ⓕ *ay·e* marriage
Ehefrau ⓕ *ay·e·frow* wife
Ehemann ⓜ *ay·e·man* husband
ehrlich *air·likh* honest
Ei ⓝ *ai* egg
Eierstockzyste ⓕ *ai·er·shtok·tsüs·te* ovarian cyst
eifersüchtig *ai·fer·zükh·tikh* jealous
(in) Eile *in ai·le* (in a) hurry
Eimer ⓜ *ai·mer* bucket
ein(s) *ain(s)* one
einfach *ain·fakh* simple
einfache Fahrkarte ⓕ *ain·fa·khe fahr·kar·te* one-way ticket
einige *ai·ni·ge* some • several
einkaufen gehen *ain·kow·fen gay·en* go shopping
Einkaufszentrum ⓝ *ain·kowfs·tsen·trum* shopping centre
Einkommensteuer ⓕ *ain·ko·men·shtoy·er* income tax
einladen *ain·lah·den* invite
einlassen *ain·la·sen* admit (entry)
einlösen *ain·ler·zen* cash (a cheque)
einmal *ain·mahl* once

Einschreiben ⓝ *ain·shrai·ben* registered mail
eintreten *ain·tray·ten* enter
Eintrittsgeld ⓝ *ain·trits·gelt* cover charge
Eintrittskarte ⓜ *ain·trits·kar·te* (admission) ticket
Eintrittspreis ⓜ *ain·trits·prais* admission price
einzeln aufgeführt *ain·tseln owf·ge·fürt* itemised
Einzelzimmer ⓝ *ain·tsel·tsi·mer* single room
Eis ⓝ *ais* ice
Eiscreme ⓕ *ais·kraym* ice cream
Eisdiele ⓕ *ais·dee·le* ice cream parlour
Eisenwarengeschäft ⓝ *ai·zen·vah·ren·ge·sheft* hardware store
Eishockey ⓝ *ais·ho·ki* ice hockey
eislaufen *ais·low·fen* ice skating
Eispickel ⓜ *ais·pi·kel* ice axe
Ekzem ⓝ *ek·tsaym* eczema
Elektrizität ⓕ *e·lek·tri·tsi·tayt* electricity
Elektrogeschäft ⓝ *e·lek·tro·ge·sheft* electrical store
Eltern ⓝ pl *el·tern* parents
emotional *e·mo·tsyo·nahl* emotional
empfehlen *emp·fay·len* recommend
Empfindlichkeit ⓕ *emp·fint·likh·kait* film speed • sensitivity
(am) Ende *(am) en·de* (at the) end
Endstation ⓕ *ent·shta·tsyawn* terminal
Energie ⓕ *e·ner·gee* energy
eng *eng* tight
Englisch ⓝ *eng·lish* English
Enkelkind ⓝ *eng·kel·kint* grandchild
Ente ⓕ *en·te* duck
entscheiden *ent·shai·den* decide
sich entspannen *zikh ent·shpa·nen* relax
entwerfen *ent·ver·fen* design
entwerten *ent·ver·ten* validate (ticket)
Entzündung ⓕ *en·tsün·dung* infection • inflammation
Epilepsie ⓕ *e·pi·lep·see* epilepsy
er *air* he
erbrechen *er·bre·khen* vomit
Erbse ⓕ *erp·se* pea
Erdbeben ⓝ *ert·bay·ben* earthquake
Erdbeere ⓕ *ert·bey·re* strawberry
Erde ⓕ *er·de* Earth
Erdnuss ⓕ *ert·nus* peanut • ground nut
Erfahrung ⓕ *er·fah·rung* experience
erhalten *er·hal·ten* receive
erkältet sein *er·kel·tet zain* have a cold
Erlaubnis ⓕ *er·lowp·nis* permission
ermüden *er·mü·den* tire
ernst *ernst* serious
erstaunlich *er·shtown·likh* amazing
erste *ers·te* first
Erwachsene ⓜ&ⓕ *er·vak·se·ne* adult
erzählen *er·tsay·len* tell
Erziehung ⓕ *er·tsee·ung* education
Essen ⓝ *e·sen* food
essen *e·sen* eat
Essig ⓜ *e·sikh* vinegar
etwas *et·vas* something • anything
Euro ⓜ *oy·ro* euro
Europa ⓝ *oy·raw·pa* Europe
Euthanasie ⓕ *oy·ta·na·zee* euthanasia
Express- *eks·pres·* express
Expresspost ⓕ *eks·pres·post* express mail

F

Fabrik ⓕ *fa·breek* factory
Faden ⓜ *fah·den* thread
fahren *fah·ren* travel by vehicle
Fahrgast ⓜ *fahr·gast* passenger (bus/taxi)
Fahrkarte ⓕ *fahr·kar·te* ticket
Fahrkartenautomat ⓜ *fahr·kar·ten·ow·to·maht* ticket machine
Fahrkartenkontrolleur(in) ⓜ/ⓕ *fahr·kar·ten·kon·tro·ler·(rin)* ticket collector
Fahrkartenverkauf ⓜ *fahr·kar·ten·fer·kowf* ticket office

Fahrplan ⓜ *fahr*·plahn timetable
Fahrrad ⓝ *fahr*·raht bicycle
Fahrradkette ⓕ *fahr*·raht·ke·te bicycle chain
Fahrzeugpapiere ⓝ pl *fahr*·tsoyk·pa·pee·re car owner's title (document)
Fahrzeugzulassung ⓕ *fahr*·tsoyk·*tsoo*·la·sung car registration
Fallschirmspringen ⓝ *fal*·shirm·shpring·en parachuting
falsch falsh false • wrong
Familie ⓕ fa·*mee*·li·e family
Familienname ⓜ fa·*mee*·li·en·nah·me family name
Familienstand ⓜ fa·*mee*·li·en·shtant marital status
Fan ⓜ fen fan (sports)
Farbe ⓕ *far*·be colour
Farben ⓕ pl *far*·ben paints
fast fast almost
Fastenzeit ⓕ *fas*·ten·tsait Lent
faul fowl lazy
Fax ⓝ faks fax
Fechten ⓝ *fekh*·ten fencing (sports)
Feder ⓕ *fay*·der spring (coil)
Fehler ⓜ *fay*·ler mistake
fehlerhaft *fay*·ler·haft faulty
Fehlgeburt ⓕ *fayl*·ge·burt miscarriage
Feier ⓕ *fai*·er celebration
Feige ⓕ *fai*·ge fig
Feinkostgeschäft ⓝ *fain*·kost·ge·sheft delicatessen
Feld ⓝ felt field
Feldfrucht ⓕ *felt*·frukht crop
Fels ⓜ fels rock
Fenster ⓝ *fens*·ter window
Ferien pl *fair*·ri·en holidays • vacation
Fern- *fern*· long-distance
Fernbedienung ⓕ *fern*·be·dee·nung remote control
Fernbus ⓜ *fern*·bus bus (intercity)
Fernglas ⓝ *fern*·glahs binoculars
fernsehen *fern*·zay·en watch TV
Fernseher ⓜ *fern*·zay·er TV set
Fernsehserie ⓕ *fern*·zay·zair·ri·e TV series
fertig *fer*·tikh ready • finished
Fest ⓝ fest festival • party
fest fest solid
fettarme Milch ⓕ *fet*·ar·me milkh skimmed milk
feucht foykht damp
Feuchtigkeitscreme ⓕ *foykh*·tikh·kaits·kraym moisturiser
Feuer ⓝ *foy*·er fire
Feuerzeug ⓝ *foy*·er·tsoyk cigarette lighter
Fieber ⓝ *fee*·ber fever
Filet ⓝ fi·*lay* fillet
Film ⓜ film movie • film (camera)
finden *fin*·den find
Finger ⓜ *fing*·er finger
Firma ⓕ *fir*·ma company
Fisch ⓜ fish fish
Fischen ⓝ *fi*·shen fishing
Fitness-Studio ⓝ *fit*·nes·shtoo·di·o gym
flach flakh flat
Flagge ⓕ *fla*·ge flag
Flasche ⓕ *fla*·she bottle
Flaschenöffner ⓜ *fla*·shen·erf·ner bottle opener
Fleisch ⓝ flaish meat
Fliege ⓕ *flee*·ge fly
fliegen *flee*·gen fly
Flitterwochen pl *fli*·ter·vo·khen honeymoon
Floh ⓜ flaw flea
Flohmarkt ⓜ *flaw*·markt flea market
Flüchtling ⓜ *flükht*·ling refugee
Flug ⓜ flook flight
Flügel ⓜ pl *flü*·gel wings
Fluggast ⓜ *flook*·gast passenger (plane)
Flughafen ⓜ *flook*·hah·fen airport
Flughafengebühr ⓕ *flook*·hah·fen·ge·bür airport tax

Fluglinie ⓕ *flook*·lee·ni·e airline
Flugticket ⓝ *flook*·ti·ket plane ticket
Flugzeug ⓝ *flook*·tsoyk aeroplane
Fluss ⓜ flus river
folgen *fol*·gen follow
Forderung ⓕ *for*·de·rung demand
Form ⓕ form shape
formell for·*mel* formal
Foto ⓝ *faw*·to photo
Fotogeschäft ⓝ *faw*·to·ge·sheft camera shop
Fotograf(in) ⓜ/ⓕ fo·to·*grahf*/fo·to·*grah*·fin photographer
Fotografie ⓕ fo·to·gra·*fee* photograph • photography
fotografieren fo·to·gra·*fee*·ren take a photograph
Foul ⓝ fowl foul
Foyer ⓝ fo·a·*yay* foyer
Frage ⓕ *frah*·ge question
eine Frage stellen *ai*·ne *frah*·ge *shte*·len ask a question
Frankreich ⓝ *frangk*·raikh France
Frau ⓕ frow woman
frei frai free (not bound) • vacant
Freibad ⓝ *frai*·baht (outdoor) swimming pool
Freigepäck ⓝ *frai*·ge·pek baggage allowance
Freitag ⓜ *frai*·tahk Friday
fremd fremt strange
Fremde ⓜ&ⓕ *frem*·de stranger
Fremdenverkehrsbüro ⓝ *frem*·den·fer·kairs·bü·raw tourist office
Freund ⓜ froynt male friend • boyfriend
Freundin ⓕ *froyn*·din female friend • girlfriend
freundlich *froynt*·likh friendly
Frieden ⓜ *free*·den peace
Friedhof ⓜ *freet*·hawf cemetery
frisch frish fresh (not stale)
Frischkäse ⓜ *frish*·kay·ze cream cheese
Friseur(in) ⓜ/ⓕ fri·*zer*/fri·*zer*·rin hairdresser
Frosch ⓜ frosh frog
Frost ⓜ frost frost
Frucht ⓕ frukht fruit
früh frü early
Frühling ⓜ *frü*·ling spring (season)
Frühstück ⓝ *frü*·shtük breakfast
Frühstücksflocke ⓕ *frü*·shtüks·flo·ke breakfast cereal
Frühstücksspeck ⓜ *frü*·shtüks·shpek bacon
fühlen *fü*·len feel
Führer ⓜ *fü*·rer guide • guidebook
Führerschein ⓜ *fü*·rer·shain driving licence
Führung ⓕ *fü*·rung guided tour
füllen *fü*·len fill
Fundbüro ⓝ *funt*·bü·raw lost property office
für für for
Fuß ⓜ foos foot
Fußball ⓜ *foos*·bal football • soccer
Fußgänger(in) ⓜ/ⓕ *foos*·geng·er/*foos*·geng·e·rin pedestrian
füttern *fü*·tern feed

G

Gabel ⓕ *gah*·bel fork
Gang ⓜ gang aisle
Gänge ⓜ pl *geng*·e gears
ganz gants whole
Garage ⓕ ga·*rah*·zhe garage
Garderobe ⓕ gar·*draw*·be wardrobe • cloakroom
Garnele ⓕ gar·*nay*·le prawn • shrimp
Garten ⓜ *gar*·ten garden
Gas ⓝ gahs gas (for cooking)
Gasflasche ⓕ *gahs*·fla·she gas cylinder
Gaskartusche ⓕ *gahs*·kar·tu·she gas cartridge
Gastfreundschaft ⓕ *gast*·froynt·shaf hospitality
Gebäude ⓝ ge·*boy*·de building

geben *gay*·ben give
Gebet ⓝ ge·*bayt* prayer
Gebirgszug ⓜ ge·*birks*·tsook mountain range
gebraucht ge·*browkht* secondhand
Geburtsdatum ⓝ ge·*burts*·dah·tum date of birth
Geburtsort ⓜ ge·*burts*·ort place of birth
Geburtstag ⓜ ge·*burts*·tahk birthday
Geburtsurkunde ⓕ ge·*burts*·oor·kun·de birth certificate
gefährlich ge·*fair*·likh dangerous
Gefangene ⓜ&ⓕ ge·*fang*·e·ne prisoner
Gefängnis ⓝ ge·*feng*·nis prison
gefiltert ge·*fil*·tert filtered
gefrieren ge·*free*·ren freeze
Gefühle ⓝ pl ge·*fü*·le feelings
gegen *gay*·gen against
gegenüber gay·gen·*ü*·ber opposite
Gegenwart ⓕ *gay*·gen·vart present (time)
Gehacktes ⓝ ge·*hak*·tes mince
Gehalt ⓝ ge·*halt* salary
Geheimnis ⓝ ge·*haim*·nis secret
gehen *gay*·en walk
Gehweg ⓜ *gay*·vayk footpath
Geisteswissenschaften ⓕ pl *gais*·tes·vi·sen·shaf·ten humanities
geizig *gai*·tsikh stingy
gelangweilt ge·*lang*·vailt bored
gelb gelp yellow
Geld ⓝ gelt money
Geldautomat ⓜ *gelt*·ow·to·maht automatic teller machine (ATM)
Geldbuße ⓕ *gelt*·boo·se fine (money)
Geldschein ⓜ *gelt*·shain banknote
Geldwechsel ⓜ *gelt*·vek·sel currency exchange
Gelegenheitsarbeit ⓕ ge·*lay*·gen·haits·ar·bait casual work
Gemüse ⓝ ge·*mü*·ze vegetable

Genehmigung ⓕ ge·*nay*·mi·gung permit
genug ge·*nook* enough
Gepäck ⓝ ge·*pek* luggage
Gepäckaufbewahrung ⓕ ge·*pek*·owf·be·vah·rung left luggage
Gepäckausgabe ⓕ ge·*pek*·ows·gah·be luggage claim
gerade ge·*rah*·de straight (direction)
Gerechtigkeit ⓕ ge·*rekh*·tikh·kait justice
Gericht ⓝ ge·*rikht* court (legal)
Geruch ⓜ ge·*rookh* smell
Geschäft ⓝ ge·*sheft* shop • business
Geschäftsfrau ⓕ ge·*shefts*·frow businesswoman
Geschäftsmann ⓜ ge·*shefts*·man businessman
Geschäftsreise ⓕ ge·*shefts*·rai·ze business trip
Geschenk ⓝ ge·*shengk* present (gift)
Geschichte ⓕ ge·*shikh*·te story
Geschlechtskrankheit ⓕ ge·*shlekhts*·krangk·hait venereal disease
geschlossen ge·*shlo*·sen closed
geschützte (Tierarten) ⓕ pl ge·*shüts*·te (*teer*·ar·ten) protected (species)
Geschwindigkeit ⓕ ge·*shvin*·dikh·kait speed
Geschwindigkeitsbegrenzung ⓕ ge·*shvin*·dikh·kaits·be·gren·tsung speed limit
Gesetz ⓝ ge·*zets* law
Gesetzgebung ⓕ ge·*zets*·gay·bung legislation
Gesicht ⓝ ge·*zikht* face
gestern *ges*·tern yesterday
Gesundheit ⓕ ge·*zunt*·hait health
Getränk ⓝ ge·*trengk* drink
Getränkehandel ⓜ ge·*treng*·ke·han·del liquor store
getrennt ge·*trent* separate (distinct)
Gewebe ⓝ ge·*vay*·be fabric

Gewicht ⓝ ge·*vikht* weight
Gewinn ⓜ ge·*vin* profit
gewinnen ge·*vi*·nen win
Gewürznelke ⓕ ge·*vürts*·nel·ke clove (spice)
Gezeiten pl ge·*tsai*·ten tides
giftig *gif*·tikh poisonous
Giftmüll ⓜ *gift*·mül toxic waste
Gin ⓜ dzhin gin
Gipfel ⓜ *gip*·fel peak
Gitarre ⓕ gi·*ta*·re guitar
Glas ⓝ glahs glass • jar
glatt glat slippery
gleich dort glaikh dort right there
gleiche *glai*·khe same
Gleichheit ⓕ *glaikh*·hait equality
Gleis ⓝ glais platform
Gleitschirmfliegen ⓝ *glait*·shirm·flee·gen paragliding
Gletscher ⓜ *glet*·sher glacier
Glück ⓝ glük luck • happiness
glücklich *glük*·likh lucky • happy
Glückwunsch ⓜ *glük*·vunsh congratulations
Glühbirne ⓕ *glü*·bir·ne light bulb
Gold ⓝ golt gold
Golfplatz ⓜ *golf*·plats golf course
Gott ⓜ got god (general)
Gottesdienst ⓜ *go*·tes·deenst church service
Grab ⓝ grahp grave • tomb
Grad ⓜ graht degree
grafische Kunst ⓕ *grah*·fi·she kunst graphic art
Gramm ⓝ gram gram
Gras ⓝ grahs grass • pot (dope)
gratis *grah*·tis free (gratis)
grau grow grey • gray
Grenze ⓕ *gren*·tse border
Grippe ⓕ *gri*·pe influenza
groß graws big • great • tall
Größe ⓕ *grer*·se size (general)
Großeltern ⓝ pl *graws*·el·tern grandparents
Großmutter ⓕ *graws*·mu·ter grandmother
Großvater ⓜ *graws*·fah·ter grandfather
grün grün green
Grund ⓜ grunt reason
Gurke ⓕ *gur*·ke cucumber
Gürtel ⓜ *gür*·tel belt
gut goot good • well
gutaussehend *goot*·ows·zay·ent handsome
Gymnastik ⓕ güm·*nas*·tik gymnastics
Gynäkologe ⓜ gü·ne·ko·*law*·ge gynaecologist
Gynäkologin ⓕ gü·ne·ko·*law*·gin gynaecologist

H

Haar ⓝ hahr hair
Haarbürste ⓕ *hahr*·bürs·te hairbrush
haben *hah*·ben have
Hafen ⓜ *hah*·fen port • harbour
Hafer(flocken) ⓜ pl *hah*·fer(·flo·ken) oats
Hähnchenschenkel ⓜ *hayn*·khen·sheng·kel chicken drumstick
Halal- ha·*lal*· halal
Hälfte ⓕ *helf*·te half
Hallenbad ⓝ *ha*·len·baht (indoor) swimming pool
hallo ha·lo/ha·*law* hello
halluzinieren ha·lu·tsi·*nee*·ren hallucinate
Hals ⓜ hals throat
Halskette ⓕ *hals*·ke·te necklace
Halsschmerzen pl *hals*·shmer·tsen sore throat
Halt ⓜ halt stop
Hammer ⓜ *ha*·mer hammer
Hamster ⓜ *hams*·ter hamster
Hand ⓕ hant hand
Handel ⓜ *han*·del trade
handgemacht *hant*·ge·makht handmade

Handschuh ⓜ *hant*·shoo glove
Handtasche ⓕ *hant*·ta·she handbag
Handtuch ⓝ *han*·tookh towel
Handwerk ⓝ *hant*·verk crafts
Handy ⓝ *hen*·di mobile/cell phone
Hang ⓜ hang slope
Hängematte ⓕ *heng*·e·ma·te hammock
hart hart hard (not soft)
Haschee ⓝ ha·*shay* hash
Haupt- *howpt*· main
Hauptplatz ⓜ *howpt*·plats main square
Haus ⓝ hows house
Hausarbeit ⓕ *hows*·ar·bait housework
nach Hause nahkh *how*·ze (go) home
Hausfrau ⓕ *hows*·frow homemaker
Hausmann ⓜ *hows*·man homemaker
Haut ⓕ howt skin
heilig *hai*·likh holy
Heiligabend ⓜ hai·likh·*ah*·bent Christmas Eve
Heilige ⓜ&ⓕ *hai*·li·ge saint
Heim ⓝ haim home
Heimweh haben *haim*·vay *hah*·ben to be homesick
heiraten *hai*·rah·ten marry
heiß hais hot
Heizgerät ⓝ *haits*·ge·rayt heater
helfen *hel*·fen help
hell hel light (weight)
Helm ⓜ helm helmet
Hemd ⓝ hemt shirt
Herausgeber(in) ⓜ/ⓕ he·*rows*·gay·ber/ he·*rows*·gay·be·rin editor
Herbst ⓜ herpst autumn • fall
Herd ⓜ hert stove
Hering ⓜ *hay*·ring herring
Heringe ⓜ pl *hay*·ring·e tent pegs
Heroin ⓝ he·ro·*een* heroin
Herz ⓝ herts heart
Herzleiden ⓝ *herts*·lai·den heart condition
Herzschrittmacher ⓜ *herts*·shrit·ma·kher pacemaker (heart)
Heuschnupfen ⓜ *hoy*·shnup·fen hay fever • allergies
heute *hoy*·te today
heute Abend *hoy*·te *ah*·bent tonight
hier heer here
Hilfe ⓕ *hil*·fe help
Himbeere ⓕ *him*·bey·re raspberry
Himmel ⓜ *hi*·mel sky
Hindu ⓜ&ⓕ *hin*·du Hindu
hinten *hin*·ten at the back • behind
Hintern *hin*·tern bum (body)
hinüber hi·*nü*·ber across (to)
historisch his·*taw*·rish historical
Hitze ⓕ *hi*·tse heat
HIV-positiv *hah*·ee·fow·*paw*·zi·teef HIV positive
hoch hawkh high (up)
Hochebene ⓕ *hawkh*·ay·be·ne plateau
Hochzeit ⓕ *hokh*·tsait wedding
Hochzeitsgeschenk ⓝ *hokh*·tsaits·ge·shengk wedding present
Hochzeitstorte ⓕ *hokh*·tsaits·tor·te wedding cake
Hockey ⓝ *ho*·ki hockey
Höhe ⓕ *her*·e altitude
Höhle ⓕ *her*·le cave
Holz ⓝ holts wood
homöopathisches Mittel ⓝ haw·mer·o·*pah*·ti·shes *mi*·tel homeopathic medicine
homosexuell haw·mo·zek·su·*el* homosexual
Honig ⓜ *haw*·nikh honey
hören *her*·ren hear • listen
Hörgerät ⓝ *her*·ge·rayt hearing aid
Horoskop ⓝ ho·ros·*kawp* horoscope
Hose ⓕ *haw*·ze trousers
Hotel ⓝ ho·*tel* hotel
hübsch hüpsh pretty

Hüfttasche ⓕ hüft·ta·she bumbag • fanny pack
Hügel ⓜ hü·gel hill
Huhn ⓝ hoon chicken
Hühnerbrust ⓕ hü·ner·brust chicken breast
Hülsenfrucht ⓕ hül·zen·frukht legume
Hund ⓜ hunt dog
hundert hun·dert hundred
hungrig hung·rikh hungry
husten hoos·ten cough
Hustensaft ⓜ hoos·ten·zaft cough medicine
Hut ⓜ hoot hat
Hütte ⓕ hü·te hut
Hüttenkäse ⓜ hü·ten·kay·ze cottage cheese

I

ich ikh I
Idee ⓕ i·day idea
Idiot ⓜ i·di·awt idiot
ihr eer her • their
Ihr eer your polite
illegal i·le·gahl illegal
immer i·mer always • forever
Immigration ⓕ i·mi·gra·tsyawn immigration
in in in • at
inbegriffen in·be·gri·fen included
Indien ⓝ in·di·en India
Industrie ⓕ in·dus·tree industry
Informationstechnologie ⓕ in·for·ma·tsyawns·tekh·no·lo·gee IT
Ingenieuer(in) ⓜ/ⓕ in·zhe·nyer(·rin) engineer
Ingenieurwesen ⓝ in·zhe·nyer·vay·zen engineering
Ingwer ⓜ ing·ver ginger
Injektion ⓕ in·yek·tsyawn injection (medical)
innen i·nen inside
Innenstadt ⓕ i·nen·shtat city centre
innerhalb (einer Stunde) i·ner·halp (ai·ner shtun·de) within (an hour)
Insekt ⓝ in·zekt insect
Insektenschutzmittel ⓝ in·zek·ten·shuts·mi·tel insect repellent
Insel ⓕ in·zel island
Installateur(in) ⓜ/ⓕ in·sta·la·ter/in·sta·la·ter·rin plumber
interessant in·tre·sant interesting
international in·ter·na·tsyo·nahl international
Internet ⓝ in·ter·net internet
Interview ⓝ in·ter·vyoo interview
irgendein ir·gent·ain any
irgendetwas ir·gent·et·vas anything
irgendwo ir·gent·vaw anywhere
Irland ⓝ ir·lant Ireland

J

ja yah yes
Jacke ⓕ ya·ke jacket
Jagd ⓕ yahkt hunting
Jahr ⓝ yahr year
Jahreszeit ⓕ yah·res·tsait season
Japan ⓝ yah·pahn Japan
Jeans ⓕ pl dzheens jeans
jeder yay·der everyone
jeder ⓜ yay·der each • every
jemand yay·mant someone
Jetlag ⓜ dzhet·leg jet lag
jetzt yetst now
Jockey ⓜ dzho·ki jockey
Joga ⓝ yaw·ga yoga
Joggen ⓝ dzho·gen jogging
Joghurt ⓜ yaw·gurt yoghurt
Journalist(in) ⓜ/ⓕ zhur·na·list/zhur·na·lis·tin journalist
Juckreiz ⓜ yuk·raits itch
jüdisch yü·dish Jewish
Jugendherberge ⓕ yoo·gent·her·ber·ge youth hostel
jung yung young
Junge ⓜ yung·e boy
Jura ⓝ yoo·ra law (subject)

K

Kabel ⓝ *kah*·bel cable
Kaffee ⓜ ka·fay coffee
Kakao ⓜ ka·*kow* cocoa
Kakerlake ⓕ *kah*·ker·lah·ke cockroach
Kalbfleisch ⓝ *kalp*·flaish veal
Kalender ⓜ ka·*len*·der calendar
kalt kalt cold
Kamera ⓕ *kah*·me·ra camera
Kamm ⓜ kam comb
Kampf ⓜ kampf fight
Kampfsport ⓜ *kampf*·shport martial arts
Kanada ⓝ *ka*·na·dah Canada
Kanarienvogel ⓜ ka·*nah*·ri·en·faw·gel canary
Kaninchen ⓝ ka·*neen*·khen rabbit
Kantine ⓕ kan·*tee*·ne canteen
Kapelle ⓕ ka·*pe*·le chapel • band (music)
Kapitalismus ⓜ ka·pi·ta·*lis*·mus capitalism
kaputt ka·*put* broken
Karte ⓕ *kar*·te map • ticket
Karten ⓕ pl *kar*·ten cards
Kartoffel ⓕ kar·*to*·fel potato
Karton ⓜ kar·*tong* box • carton
Karwoche ⓕ *kahr*·vo·khe Holy Week
Käse ⓜ *kay*·ze cheese
Kasino ⓝ ka·*zee*·no casino
Kasse ⓕ *ka*·se cash register • checkout • ticket counter
Kassierer(in) ⓜ/ⓕ ka·*see*·rer/ka·*see*·re·rin cashier
Katholik(in) ⓜ/ⓕ ka·to·*leek*/ka·to·*lee*·kin Catholic
Kätzchen ⓝ *kets*·khen kitten
Katze ⓕ *ka*·tse cat
kaufen *kow*·fen buy
Kaugummi ⓝ *kow*·gu·mi chewing gum
Kaviar ⓜ *kah*·vi·ahr caviar
Keilriemen ⓜ *kail*·ree·men fanbelt
keine *kai*·ne none
Keks ⓜ kayks biscuit • cookie
Keller ⓜ *ke*·ler cellar
Kellner(in) ⓜ/ⓕ *kel*·ner/*kel*·ne·rin waiter
kennen *ke*·nen know (a person)
Keramik ⓕ ke·*rah*·mik ceramic
Kerze ⓕ *ker*·tse candle
Kessel ⓜ *ke*·sel kettle
Ketchup ⓜ *ket*·chap ketchup
Kette ⓕ *ke*·te chain
Kichererbse ⓕ *ki*·kher·erp·se chickpea
Kiefer ⓜ *kee*·fer jaw
Kilogramm ⓝ *kee*·lo·gram kilogram
Kilometer ⓜ ki·lo·*may*·ter kilometre
Kind ⓝ kint child
Kinder ⓝ pl *kin*·der children
Kinderbetreuung ⓕ *kin*·der·be·troy·ung childminding
Kindergarten ⓜ *kin*·der·gar·ten kindergarten
Kinderkrippe ⓕ *kin*·der·kri·pe creche
Kindersitz ⓜ *kin*·der·zits child seat
Kino ⓝ *kee*·no cinema
Kiosk ⓜ *kee*·osk convenience store
Kirche ⓕ *kir*·khe church
Kissen ⓝ *ki*·sen pillow
Kissenbezug ⓜ *ki*·sen·be·tsook pillowcase
Kiwifrucht ⓕ *kee*·vi·frukht kiwi fruit
Klasse ⓕ *kla*·se class
klassisch *kla*·sish classical
Klavier ⓝ kla·*veer* piano
Kleid ⓝ klait dress
Kleidung ⓕ *klai*·dung clothing
klein klain little • small• short (height)
Kleingeld ⓝ *klain*·gelt loose change
klettern *kle*·tern climb
Klettern ⓝ *kle*·tern rock climbing
Klima ⓝ *klee*·ma climate
Klimaanlage ⓕ *klee*·ma·an·lah·ge air-conditioning

klingeln *kling*·eln ring (of phone)
Klippe ⓕ *kli*·pe cliff
Kloster ⓝ *klaws*·ter convent • monastery
Knappheit ⓕ *knap*·hait shortage
Kneipe ⓕ *knai*·pe pub
Knie ⓝ knee knee
Knoblauch ⓜ *knawp*·lowkh garlic
Knöchel ⓜ *kner*·khel ankle
Knochen ⓜ *kno*·khen bone
Knopf ⓜ knopf button
Knoten ⓜ *knaw*·ten lump (health)
Koch ⓜ kokh chef • cook
kochen *ko*·khen cook
Kocher ⓜ *ko*·kher camping stove
Köchin ⓕ *ker*·khin chef • cook
Köder ⓜ *ker*·der bait
Koffer ⓜ *ko*·fer suitcase
Kofferraum ⓜ *ko*·fer·rowm boot • trunk
Kohl ⓜ kawl cabbage
Kokain ⓝ ko·ka·*een* cocaine
Kollege ⓜ ko·*lay*·ge colleague
Kollegin ⓕ ko·*lay*·gin colleague
kommen *ko*·men come
Kommunion ⓕ ko·mun·*yawn* communion
Komödie ⓕ ko·*mer*·di·e comedy
Kompass ⓜ *kom*·pas compass
Konditorei ⓕ kon·dee·to·*rai* cake shop
Kondom ⓝ kon·*dawm* condom
König ⓜ *ker*·nikh king
Königin ⓕ *ker*·ni·gin queen
können *ker*·nen be able to • have permission to
konservativ *kon*·zer·va·teef conservative
Konsulat ⓝ kon·zu·*laht* consulate
Kontaktlinsen ⓕ pl kon·*takt*·lin·zen contact lenses
Kontostand ⓜ *kon*·to·shtant balance (account)
Kontrollstelle ⓕ kon·*trol*·shte·le checkpoint
Konzert ⓝ kon·*tsert* concert
Konzerthalle ⓕ kon·*tsert*·ha·le concert hall
Kopf ⓜ kopf head
Kopfsalat ⓜ *kopf*·za·laht lettuce
Kopfschmerzen pl *kopf*·shmer·tsen headache
Kopfschmerztablette ⓕ *kopf*·shmerts·ta·ble·te headache tablets
Korb ⓜ korp basket
Körper ⓜ *ker*·per body
korrupt ko·*rupt* corrupt
koscher *kaw*·sher kosher
kosten *kos*·ten cost
köstlich *kerst*·likh delicious
Kraft ⓕ kraft power
Krampf ⓜ krampf cramp
krank krangk sick
Krankenhaus ⓝ *krang*·ken·hows hospital
Krankenpfleger ⓜ *krang*·ken·pflay·ger nurse
Krankenschwester ⓕ *krang*·ken·shves·ter nurse
Krankenwagen ⓜ *krang*·ken·vah·gen ambulance
Krankheit ⓕ *krangk*·hait disease
Kräuter ⓝ pl *kroy*·ter herbs
Krebs ⓜ krayps cancer
Kreditkarte ⓕ kre·*deet*·kar·te credit card
Kreisverkehr ⓜ *krais*·fer·kair roundabout
Kreuz ⓝ kroyts cross (religious)
Krieg ⓜ kreek war
Kritik ⓕ kri·*teek* review (arts)
Küche ⓕ *kü*·khe kitchen
Kuchen ⓜ *koo*·khen cake
Kuckucksuhr ⓕ *ku*·kuks·oor cuckoo clock
Kugelschreiber ⓜ *koo*·gel·shrai·ber pen (ballpoint)
Kuh ⓕ koo cow
Kühler ⓜ *kü*·ler radiator

Kühlschrank ⓜ *kül·shrangk* refrigerator
sich kümmern um zikh *kü*·mern um look after
Kunde ⓜ *kun*·de client
kündigen *kün*·di·gen resign
Kundin ⓕ *kun*·din client
Kunst ⓕ kunst art
Kunstgalerie ⓕ *kunst*·ga·le·ree art gallery
Kunstgewerbe ⓝ *kunst*·ge·ver·be arts & crafts
Kunsthandwerk ⓝ *kunst*·hant·verk handicrafts
Künstler(in) ⓜ/ⓕ *künst*·ler/*künst*·le·rin artist
Kunstsammlung ⓕ *kunst*·zam·lung art collection
Kunstwerk ⓝ *kunst*·verk work of art
Kupplung ⓕ *kup*·lung clutch (car)
Kürbis ⓜ *kür*·bis pumpkin
kurz kurts short
kurzärmelig *kurts*·er·me·likh short-sleeved
Kuss ⓜ kus kiss
küssen *kü*·sen kiss
Küste ⓕ *küs*·te coast

L

lächeln *le*·kheln smile
lachen *la*·khen laugh
Lachs ⓜ laks salmon
Lage ⓕ *lah*·ge situation
Lager ⓝ *lah*·ger lager
Lamm ⓝ lam lamb
Land ⓝ lant country • countryside
Landschaft ⓕ *lant*·shaft scenery
Landwirtschaft ⓕ *lant*·virt·shaft agriculture
lang lang long
langärmelig *lang*·er·me·likh long-sleeved
langsam *lang*·zahm slow • slowly
langweilig *lang*·vai·likh boring
Laptop ⓜ *lep*·top laptop
Lastwagen ⓜ *last*·vah·gen truck
Lauch ⓜ lowkh leek
laufen *low*·fen run
Läuse ⓕ pl *loy*·ze lice
laut lowt loud • noisy
Lautstärke ⓕ *lowt*·shter·ke volume (loudness)
Lawine ⓕ la·*vee*·ne avalanche
leben *lay*·ben to live
Leben ⓝ *lay*·ben life
Lebenslauf ⓜ *lay*·bens·lowf CV • resume
Lebensmittelhändler ⓜ *lay*·bens·mi·tel·hen·dler greengrocer
Lebensmittelladen ⓜ *lay*·bens·mi·tel·lah·den grocery store
Lebensmittelvergiftung ⓕ *lay*·bens·mi·tel·fer·*gif*·tung food poisoning
Leber ⓕ *lay*·ber liver
Leder ⓝ *lay*·der leather
ledig *lay*·dikh single (of person)
leer lair empty
legen *lay*·gen put (horizontal)
Lehrer(in) ⓜ/ⓕ *lair*·rer/*lair*·re·rin teacher • instructor
leicht laikht easy
Leichtathletik ⓕ *laikht*·at·lay·tik athletics
leihen *lai*·en borrow
Leinen ⓝ *lai*·nen linen (fabric)
Leitungswasser ⓝ *lai*·tungks·va·ser tap water
Lenker ⓜ *leng*·ker handlebar
lernen *ler*·nen learn
Lesbierin ⓕ *les*·bi·e·rin lesbian
lesen *lay*·zen read
letzte *lets*·te last
Licht ⓝ likht light
lieben *lee*·ben love
liebevoll *lee*·be·fol caring
Liebhaber(in) ⓜ/ⓕ *leep*·hah·ber/*leep*·hah·be·rin lover
Lied ⓝ leet song
liefern *lee*·fern deliver

Lieferwagen ⓜ *lee*·fer·*vah*·gen van
liegen *lee*·gen lie (not stand)
Lift ⓜ lift lift • elevator
lila *lee*·la purple
Limonade ⓕ li·mo·*nah*·de lemonade
Limone ⓕ li·*maw*·ne lime
Linie ⓕ *lee*·ni·e line
links lingks left (direction)
linksgerichtet *lingks*·ge·rikh·tet left-wing
Linse ⓕ *lin*·ze lentil
Lippen ⓕ pl *li*·pen lips
Lippenbalsam ⓜ *li*·pen·bal·zahm lip balm
Lippenstift ⓜ *li*·pen·shtift lipstick
Liter ⓜ *lee*·ter litre
Löffel ⓜ *ler*·fel spoon
Lohn ⓜ lawn wage
Lohnsatz ⓜ *lawn*·zats rate of pay
Lokal ⓝ lo·*kahl* bar
Luft ⓕ luft air
Luftkrankheit ⓕ *luft*·krangk·hait airsickness
Luftpost ⓕ *luft*·post airmail
Luftpumpe ⓕ *luft*·pum·pe pump
Luftverschmutzung ⓕ *luft*·fer·shmu·tsung air pollution
Lügner(in) ⓜ/ⓕ *lüg*·ner/*lüg*·ne·rin liar
Lungen ⓕ pl *lung*·en lungs
lustig *lus*·tikh funny
luxuriös luk·su·ri·*ers* luxury

M

machen *ma*·khen make
Mädchen ⓝ *mayt*·khen girl
Magen ⓜ *mah*·gen stomach
Magen-Darm-Katarrh ⓜ *mah*·gen·*darm*·ka·*tar* gastroenteritis
Magenschmerzen ⓜ pl *mah*·gen·shmer·tsen stomachache
Magenverstimmung ⓕ *mah*·gen·fer·shti·mung indigestion
Majonnaise ⓕ ma·yo·*nay*·ze mayonnaise
Makler(in) ⓜ/ⓕ *mahk*·ler/*mahk*·le·rin real estate agent
Maler(in) ⓜ/ⓕ *mah*·ler/*mah*·le·rin painter
Malerei ⓕ mah·le·*rai* painting (the art)
Mama ⓕ *ma*·ma mum • mom
Mammogramm ⓝ ma·mo·*gram* mammogram
manchmal *mankh*·mahl sometimes
Mandarine ⓕ man·da·*ree*·ne mandarin
Mandel ⓕ *man*·del almond
Mann ⓜ man man
Mannschaft ⓕ *man*·shaft team
Mantel ⓜ *man*·tel overcoat • cloak
Margarine ⓕ mar·ga·*ree*·ne margarine
Marihuana ⓝ ma·ri·hu·*ah*·na marijuana
Markt ⓜ markt market
Marktplatz ⓜ *markt*·plats market square
Marmelade ⓕ mar·me·*lah*·de jam
Maschine ⓕ ma·*shee*·ne machine
Masern pl *mah*·zern measles
Massage ⓕ ma·*sah*·zhe massage
Masseur(in) ⓜ/ⓕ ma·*ser*(·rin) masseur/masseuse
Material ⓝ ma·te·ri·*ahl* material
Matratze ⓕ ma·*tra*·tse mattress
Matte ⓕ *ma*·te mat
Mauer ⓕ *mow*·er wall (outer)
Maurer(in) ⓜ/ⓕ *mow*·rer/*mow*·re·rin bricklayer
Maus ⓕ mows mouse
Mechaniker(in) ⓜ/ⓕ me·*khah*·ni·ker/me·*khah*·ni·ke·rin mechanic
Medien pl *may*·di·en media
Meditation ⓕ me·di·ta·*tsyawn* meditation
Medizin ⓕ me·di·*tseen* medicine
Meer ⓝ meer sea
Meeresküste ⓕ *meer*·res·küs·te seaside

Meerrettich ⓜ *meer*·re·tikh horseradish
Mehl ⓝ mayl flour
mehr mair more
nicht mehr nikht mair not any more
mein main mine • my
Meinung ⓕ *mai*·nung opinion
Meisterschaften ⓕ pl *mais*·ter·shaf·ten championships
Melodie ⓕ me·lo·*dee* tune
Melone ⓕ me·*law*·ne melon
Mensch ⓜ mensh person
Menschen ⓜ pl *men*·shen people
Menschenrechte ⓝ pl *men*·shen·rekh·te human rights
menschlich *mensh*·likh human
Menstruation ⓕ mens·tru·a·*tsyawn* menstruation
Menstruationsbeschwerden ⓕ pl mens·tru·a·*tsyawns*·be·shver·den period pain
Messe ⓕ *me*·se mass (Catholic) • trade fair
Messer ⓝ *me*·ser knife
Metall ⓝ me·*tal* metal
Meter ⓜ *may*·ter metre
Metzgerei ⓕ mets·ge·*rai* butcher shop
mieten *mee*·ten rent • hire
Mietvertrag ⓜ *meet*·fer·trahk lease
Migräne ⓕ mi·*gray*·ne migraine
Mikrowelle ⓕ *mee*·kro·ve·le microwave
Milch ⓕ milkh milk
Milchprodukte ⓝ pl *milkh*·pro·duk·te dairy products
Militär ⓝ mi·li·*tair* military
Millimeter ⓜ mi·li·*may*·ter millimetre
Million ⓕ mi·*lyawn* million
Mineralwasser ⓝ mi·ne·*rahl*·va·ser mineral water
Minute ⓕ mi·*noo*·te minute
mischen *mi*·shen mix
mit mit with
Mitglied ⓝ *mit*·gleet member
Mittag ⓜ *mi*·tahk noon
Mittagessen ⓝ *mi*·tahk·e·sen lunch
Mitteilung ⓕ *mi*·tai·lung message
Mitternacht ⓕ *mi*·ter·nakht midnight
Mittwoch ⓜ *mit*·vokh Wednesday
Möbel ⓝ pl *mer*·bel furniture
Modem ⓝ *maw*·dem modem
mögen *mer*·gen to like
möglich *merk*·likh possible
Möhre ⓕ *mer*·re carrot
Monat ⓜ *maw*·nat month
Montag ⓜ *mawn*·tahk Monday
Morgen ⓜ *mor*·gen morning (6am–10am)
morgen *mor*·gen tomorrow
morgen früh *mor*·gen frü tomorrow morning
Moschee ⓕ mo·*shay* mosque
Moskitospirale ⓕ mos·*kee*·to·shpi·rah·le mosquito coil
Moslem ⓜ *mos*·lem Muslim
Moslime ⓕ mos·*lee*·me Muslim
Motor ⓜ *maw*·tor/mo·*tawr* engine
Motorboot ⓝ *maw*·tor·bawt motorboat
Motorrad ⓝ *maw*·tor·raht motorcycle
Möwe ⓕ *mer*·ve seagull
müde *mü*·de tired
Müll ⓜ mül rubbish • garbage
Mülleimer ⓜ *mül*·ai·mer rubbish bin
Mund ⓜ munt mouth
Mundfäule ⓕ *munt*·foy·le thrush (medical condition)
Münzen ⓕ pl *mün*·tsen coins
Muschel ⓕ *mu*·shel mussel
Museum ⓝ mu·*zay*·um museum
Musik ⓕ mu·*zeek* music
Musiker(in) ⓜ/ⓕ *moo*·zi·ker/*moo*·zi·ke·rin musician
Muskel ⓜ *mus*·kel muscle
Muskelzerrung ⓕ *mus*·kel·tser·rung sprain
Müsli ⓝ *müs*·li muesli
mutig *moo*·tikh brave
Mutter ⓕ *mu*·ter mother

N

nach nahkh after • towards
Nachkomme ⓜ *nahkh*·ko·me descendant
Nachmittag ⓜ *nahkh*·mi·tahk afternoon
Nachname ⓜ *nahkh*·nah·me surname
Nachrichten pl *nahkh*·rikh·ten news
nächste *naykhs*·te next • nearest
Nacht ⓕ nakht night
Nadel ⓕ *nah*·del sewing needle • syringe
Nagelknipser ⓜ pl *nah*·gel·knip·ser nail clippers
nahe *nah*·e close (nearby)
in der Nähe in dair *nay*·e nearby
nähen *nay*·en sew
Name ⓜ *nah*·me name
Nase ⓕ *nah*·ze nose
nass nas wet
Natur ⓕ na·*toor* nature
Naturreservat ⓝ na·*toor*·re·zer·vaht nature reserve
neben *nay*·ben next to
neblig *nay*·blikh foggy
Neffe ⓜ *ne*·fe nephew
nehmen *nay*·men take
nein nain no
nett net nice • kind
Netz ⓝ nets net
neu noy new
Neujahrstag ⓜ *noy*·yahrs·tahk New Year's Day
Neuseeland ⓝ noy·*zay*·lant New Zealand
nicht nikht not
Nichte ⓕ *nikh*·te niece
Nichtraucher- *nikht*·row·kher·non-smoking
nichts nikhts nothing
nie nee never
Niederlande pl *nee*·der·lan·de Netherlands
niedrig *nee*·drikh low
noch nicht nokh nikht not yet
Nonne ⓕ *no*·ne nun
Norden ⓜ *nor*·den north
normal nor·*mahl* ordinary
normale Post ⓕ nor·*mah*·le *post* surface mail
Notfall ⓜ *nawt*·fal emergency
Notizbuch ⓝ no·*teets*·bookh notebook
notwendig *nawt*·ven·dikh necessary
Nudeln pl *noo*·deln noodles • pasta
null nul zero
Nummer ⓕ *nu*·mer number
nur noor only
Nuss ⓕ nus nut
nützlich *nüts*·likh useful

O

obdachlos *op*·dakh·laws homeless
oben *aw*·ben upstairs
Objektiv ⓝ op·yek·*teef* lens (camera)
Obsternte ⓕ *awpst*·ern·te fruit picking
oder *aw*·der or
Ofen ⓜ *aw*·fen oven
offen *o*·fen open
offensichtlich o·fen·*zikht*·likh obvious
öffentlich *er*·fent·likh public
öffnen *erf*·nen open
Öffnungszeiten ⓕ pl *erf*·nungks·tsai·ten opening hours
oft oft often
ohne *aw*·ne without
Ohr ⓝ awr ear
Ohrenstöpsel ⓜ *aw*·ren·shterp·sel earplugs
Ohrringe ⓜ pl *awr*·ring·e earrings
Öl ⓝ erl oil
Olive ⓕ o·*lee*·ve olive
Olivenöl ⓝ o·*lee*·ven·erl olive oil
Olympische Spiele ⓝ pl o·*lüm*·pi·she *shpee*·le Olympic Games
Oma ⓕ *aw*·ma grandmother
Onkel ⓜ *ong*·kel uncle
Opa ⓜ *aw*·pa grandfather
Oper ⓕ *aw*·per opera

Operation ⓕ o·pe·ra·*tsyawn* operation
Opernhaus ⓝ *aw*·pern·hows opera house
Optiker(in) ⓜ/ⓕ *op*·ti·ker/*op*·ti·ke·rin optician
orange o·*rahngzh* orange (colour)
Orange ⓕ o·*rahng*·zhe orange
Orangenmarmelade ⓕ o·*rahng*·zhen·mar·me·lah·de marmalade
Orangensaft ⓜ o·*rahng*·zhen·zaft orange juice
Orchester ⓝ or·*kes*·ter orchestra
organisieren or·ga·ni·*zee*·ren organise
Orgasmus ⓜ or·*gas*·mus orgasm
Orgel ⓕ *or*·gel organ (church)
Original- o·ri·gi·*nahl*· original (not copied)
örtlich *ert*·likh local
Osten ⓜ *os*·ten east
der Nahe Osten ⓜ dair *nah*·e *os*·ten Middle East
Ostern ⓝ *aws*·tern Easter
Österreich ⓝ *ers*·ter·raikh Austria
Ozean ⓜ *aw*·tse·ahn ocean
Ozonschicht ⓕ o·*tsawn*·shikht ozone layer

P

Paar ⓝ pahr pair (couple)
ein paar ain pahr a few
Packung ⓕ *pa*·kung packet
Paket ⓝ pa·*kayt* package • parcel
Pampelmuse ⓕ pam·pel·*moo*·ze grapefruit
eine Panne haben *ai*·ne *pa*·ne *hah*·ben break down
Papa ⓜ *pa*·pa dad
Papagei ⓜ pa·pa·*gai* parrot
Papier ⓝ pa·*peer* paper
Papiertaschentücher ⓝ pl pa·*peer*·ta·shen·tü·kher tissues
Paprika ⓕ *pap*·ri·kah paprika • capsicum • bell pepper
Parfüm ⓝ par·*füm* perfume
Park ⓜ park park
Parkplatz ⓜ *park*·plats car park
Parlament ⓝ par·la·*ment* parliament
Partei ⓕ par·*tai* party (politics)
Pass ⓜ pas pass • passport
Passnummer ⓕ *pas*·nu·mer passport number
Pause ⓕ *pow*·ze intermission
eine Pause machen ai·ne *pow*·ze *ma*·khen rest
Pedal ⓝ pe·*dahl* pedal
Penis ⓜ *pay*·nis penis
Pension ⓕ pahng·*zyawn* boarding house • bed & breakfast
pensioniert pahng·zyo·*neert* retired
Person ⓕ per·*zawn* person
Personalausweis ⓜ per·zo·*nahl*·ows·vais identification card
persönlich per·*zern*·likh personal
Petersilie ⓕ pay·ter·*zee*·li·e parsley
Petition ⓕ pe·ti·*tsyawn* petition
Pfad ⓜ pfaht path • trail
Pfanne ⓕ *pfa*·ne pan
Pfeffer ⓜ *pfe*·fer pepper
Pfefferminzbonbons ⓝ pl pfe·fer·*mints*·bong·bongs mints
Pfeife ⓕ *pfai*·fe pipe
Pferd ⓝ pfert horse
Pfirsich ⓜ *pfir*·zikh peach
Pflanze ⓕ *pflan*·tse plant
Pflaster ⓝ *pflas*·ter plaster • Band-Aid
Pflaume ⓕ *pflow*·me plum
pflücken *pflü*·ken pick (flowers)
Pfund ⓝ pfunt pound (weight)
Phantasie ⓕ fan·ta·*zee* imagination
Physik ⓕ fü·*zeek* physics
Picknick ⓝ *pik*·nik picnic
Pilgerfahrt ⓕ *pil*·ger·fahrt pilgrimage
Pille ⓕ *pi*·le pill
die Pille ⓕ dee *pi*·le the Pill
Pilz ⓜ pilts mushroom
Pinzette ⓕ pin·*tse*·te tweezers

Plakat ⓝ pla·*kaht* poster
Planet ⓜ pla·*nayt* planet
Plastik ⓝ *plas*·tik plastic
Platz ⓜ plats place • seat (train, cinema) • square (town) • court (tennis)
Platz ⓜ **am Gang** plats am gang aisle seat
Poker ⓝ *paw*·ker poker (game)
Politik ⓕ po·li·*teek* politics • policy
Politiker(in) ⓜ/ⓕ po·*lee*·ti·ker/ po·*lee*·ti·ke·rin politician
Polizei ⓕ po·li·*tsai* police
Polizeirevier ⓝ po·li·*tsai*·re·veer police station
Pollen ⓜ *po*·len pollen
Pony ⓝ *po*·ni pony
Porto ⓝ *por*·to postage
Post ⓕ post mail
Postamt ⓝ *post*·amt post office
Postkarte ⓕ *post*·kar·te postcard
postlagernd *post*·lah·gernt poste restante
Postleitzahl ⓕ *post*·lai·tsahl postcode
praktisch *prak*·tish practical
prämenstruelle Störung ⓕ *pray*·mens·tru·e·le *shter*·rung premenstrual tension
Präsident(in) ⓜ/ⓕ pre·zi·*dent*/ pre·zi·*den*·tin president
Preis ⓜ prais price
Premierminister(in) ⓜ/ⓕ prem·*yay*·mi·nis·ter/ prem·*yay*·mi·nis·te·rin prime minister
Priester ⓜ *prees*·ter priest
privat pri·*vaht* private
Privatklinik ⓕ pri·*vaht*·klee·nik private hospital
pro praw per
produzieren pro·du·*tsee*·ren produce
Programm ⓝ pro·*gram* programme
Projektor ⓜ pro·*yek*·tor projector
Prosa ⓕ *praw*·za fiction
Prostituierte ⓕ pros·ti·tu·*eer*·te prostitute
Protest ⓜ pro·*test* protest
protestieren pro·tes·*tee*·ren protest
Prozent ⓝ pro·*tsent* percent
prüfen *prü*·fen check
Psychologie ⓕ psü·kho·lo·*gee* psychology
Pullover ⓜ pu·*law*·ver jumper • sweater
Pumpe ⓕ *pum*·pe pump
Punkt ⓜ pungkt point
Puppe ⓕ *pu*·pe doll

Q

Qualifikationen ⓕ pl kva·li·fi·ka·*tsyaw*·nen qualifications
Qualität ⓕ kva·li·*tayt* quality
Quarantäne ⓕ ka·ran·*tay*·ne quarantine
Querschnittsgelähmte ⓜ&ⓕ *kvair*·shnits·ge·laym·te paraplegic
Quittung ⓕ *kvi*·tung receipt

R

Rabatt ⓜ ra·*bat* discount
Rad ⓝ raht wheel
radfahren *raht*·fah·ren cycle
Radfahrer(in) ⓜ/ⓕ *raht*·fah·rer/ *raht*·fah·re·rin cyclist
Radio ⓝ *rah*·di·o radio
Radsport ⓜ *raht*·shport cycling
Radweg ⓜ *raht*·vayk bike path
Rahmen ⓜ *rah*·men frame
Rallye ⓕ *re*·li rally (racing)
Rasiercreme ⓕ ra·*zeer*·kraym shaving cream
rasieren ra·*zee*·ren shave
Rasierer ⓜ ra·*zee*·rer razor
Rasierklingen ⓕ pl ra·*zeer*·kling·en razor blades
Rassismus ⓜ ra·*sis*·mus racism
Rat ⓜ raht advice
raten *rah*·ten advise • guess
Ratte ⓕ *ra*·te rat
Raub ⓜ rowp robbery

rauchen *row*·khen smoke
Raum ⓜ rowm space
realistisch re·a·*lis*·tish realistic
Rebe ⓕ *ray*·be vine
Rechnung ⓕ *rekh*·nung bill • check
rechts rekhts right (direction)
rechtsgerichtet *rekhts*·ge·rikh·tet right-wing
Rechtsanwalt ⓜ *rekhts*·an·valt lawyer
Rechtsanwältin ⓕ *rekhts*·an·vel·tin lawyer
recyceln ri·*sai*·keln recycle
Regal ⓝ re·*gahl* shelf
Regeln ⓕ pl *ray*·geln rules
Regen ⓜ *ray*·gen rain
Regenmantel ⓜ *ray*·gen·man·tel raincoat
Regenschirm ⓜ *ray*·gen·shirm umbrella
Regierung ⓕ re·*gee*·rung government
Region ⓕ re·*gyawn* region
Regisseur(in) ⓜ/ⓕ re·zhi·*ser*/re·zhi·*ser*·rin director
reich raikh wealthy
Reifen ⓜ *rai*·fen tyre
Reifenpanne ⓕ *rai*·fen·pa·ne puncture
rein rain pure
Reinigung ⓕ *rai*·ni·gung cleaning
Reis ⓜ rais rice
Reise ⓕ *rai*·ze journey • trip
Reisebüro ⓝ *rai*·ze·bü·raw travel agency
Reiseführer ⓜ *rai*·ze·fü·rer guidebook
Reisekrankheit ⓕ *rai*·ze·krangk·hait travel sickness
reisen *rai*·zen travel
Reisende(r) ⓜ/ⓕ *rai*·zen·de passenger (train)
Reisepass ⓜ *rai*·ze·pas passport
Reiseroute ⓕ *rai*·ze·roo·te itinerary
Reiseziel ⓝ *rai*·ze·tseel destination
Reißverschluss ⓜ *rais*·fer·shlus zip • zipper
Reiten ⓝ *rai*·ten horse riding
reiten *rai*·ten ride (horse)
Reitweg ⓜ *rait*·vayk bridle path
Religion ⓕ re·li·*gyawn* religion
religiös re·li·*gyers* religious
Reliquie ⓕ re·*lee*·kvi·e relic (religious)
Rennbahn ⓕ *ren*·bahn racetrack
rennen *re*·nen run
Rennen ⓝ *re*·nen race (sport)
Rennrad ⓝ *ren*·raht racing bike
Rentner(in) ⓜ/ⓕ *rent*·ner/*rent*·ne·rin pensioner
reparieren re·pa·*ree*·ren repair
Republik ⓕ re·pu·*bleek* republic
Reservereifen ⓜ re·*zer*·ve·rai·fen spare tyre
reservieren re·zer·*vee*·ren reserve
Reservierung ⓕ re·zer·*vee*·rung reservation
Restaurant ⓝ res·to·*rahng* restaurant
retten *re*·ten save (someone)
Rettich ⓜ *re*·tikh radish
R-Gespräch ⓝ *air*·ge·shpraykh collect call • reverse-charge call
Rhythmus ⓜ *rüt*·mus rhythm
Richter(in) ⓜ/ⓕ *rikh*·ter/*rikh*·te·rin judge
richtig *rikh*·tikh right (correct)
riesig *ree*·zikh huge
Rindfleisch ⓝ *rint*·flaish beef
Ring ⓜ ring ring (on finger)
Risiko ⓝ *ree*·zi·ko risk
Ritt ⓜ rit ride
Rock ⓜ rok skirt
Rockgruppe ⓕ *rok*·gru·pe rock group
Rockmusik ⓕ *rok*·mu·zeek rock (music)
Rodeln ⓝ *raw*·deln tobogganing
Roggenbrot ⓝ *ro*·gen·brawt rye bread
roh raw raw
Rollschuhfahren ⓝ *rol*·shoo·fah·ren in-line skating
Rollstuhl ⓜ *rol*·shtool wheelchair
Rolltreppe ⓕ *rol*·tre·pe escalator

romantisch *ro·man·tish* romantic
rosa *raw·za* pink
Rosenkohl ⓜ *raw·zen·kawl* Brussels sprout
Rosine ⓕ *ro·zee·ne* raisin
rot *rawt* red
Rotwein ⓜ *rawt·vain* red wine
Route ⓕ *roo·te* route
Rubel ⓜ *roo·bel* rouble
Rücken ⓜ *rü·ken* back (body)
Rückfahrkarte ⓕ *rük·fahr·kar·te* return (ticket)
Rucksack ⓜ *ruk·zak* backpack • knapsack
Rückzahlung ⓕ *rük·tsah·lung* refund
Rudern ⓝ *roo·dern* rowing
Rugby ⓝ *rag·bi* rugby
ruhig *roo·ikh* quiet
Ruinen ⓕ pl *ru·ee·nen* ruins
Rum ⓜ *rum* rum
rund *runt* round

S

Sabbat ⓜ *za·bat* Sabbath
Safe ⓜ *sayf* safe (for valuables)
Safe Sex ⓜ *sayf seks* safe sex
Saft ⓜ *zaft* juice
sagen *zah·gen* say
Sahne ⓕ *zah·ne* cream
Salami ⓕ *za·lah·mi* salami
Salat ⓜ *za·laht* salad
Salz ⓝ *zalts* salt
Samstag ⓜ *zams·tahk* Saturday
Sand ⓜ *zant* sand
Sandalen ⓕ pl *zan·dah·len* sandals
Sänger(in) ⓜ/ⓕ *zeng·er/zeng·e·rin* singer
Sardine ⓕ *zar·dee·ne* sardine
Sattel ⓜ *za·tel* saddle
sauber *zow·ber* clean
Sauce ⓕ *zaw·se* sauce
Sauerstoff ⓜ *zow·er·shtof* oxygen
Sauerteigbrot ⓝ *zow·er·taik·brawt* sourdough bread
Sauna ⓕ *zow·na* sauna
Schach ⓝ *shakh* chess
Schaf ⓝ *shahf* sheep
Schaffner(in) ⓜ/ⓕ *shaf·ner/shaf·ne·rin* conductor
Schal ⓜ *shahl* scarf
scharf *sharf* spicy
Schatten ⓜ *sha·ten* shade • shadow
einen Schaufensterbummel machen *ai·nen show·fens·ter·bu·mel ma·khen* go window-shopping
Schaumwein ⓜ *showm·vain* sparkling wine
Schauspiel ⓝ *show·shpeel* play (theatre) • drama
Schauspieler(in) ⓜ/ⓕ *show·shpee·ler/show·shpee·le·rin* actor
Scheck ⓜ *shek* cheque (bank)
einen Scheck einlösen *ai·nen shek ain·ler·zen* cash a cheque
Scheckkarte ⓕ *shek·kar·te* cheque card
Scheinwerfer ⓜ pl *shain·ver·fer* headlights
Schere ⓕ *shair·re* scissors
schieben *shee·ben* push
Schiedsrichter(in) ⓜ/ⓕ *sheets·rikh·ter/sheets·rikh·te·rin* referee
schießen *shee·sen* shoot (gun)
Schiff ⓝ *shif* ship
Schild ⓝ *shilt* sign
Schinken ⓜ *shing·ken* ham
schlafen *shlah·fen* sleep
schläfrig *shlayf·rikh* sleepy
Schlafsack ⓜ *shlahf·zak* sleeping bag
Schlaftabletten ⓕ pl *shlahf·ta·ble·ten* sleeping pills
Schlafwagen ⓜ *shlahf·vah·gen* sleeping car
Schlafzimmer ⓝ *shlahf·tsi·mer* bedroom
Schläger ⓜ *shlay·ger* racquet
Schlamm ⓜ *shlam* mud
Schlange ⓕ *shlang·e* queue • snake

Schlauch ⓜ shlowkh tube (tyre)
schlecht shlekht bad • off (of food)
schlechter *shlekh*·ter worse
schließen *shlee*·sen close (shut)
Schließfächer ⓝ pl *shlees*·fe·kher luggage lockers
Schloss ⓝ shlos lock • palace
Schlucht ⓕ shlukht gorge
Schlüssel ⓜ *shlü*·sel key
schmackhaft *shmak*·haft tasty
Schmalz ⓝ shmalts lard
Schmand ⓜ shmant sour cream
Schmerz ⓜ shmerts pain
schmerzhaft *shmerts*·haft sore • painful
Schmerzmittel ⓝ *shmerts*·mi·tel painkillers
Schmetterling ⓜ *shme*·ter·ling butterfly
Schmiermittel ⓝ *shmeer*·mi·tel lubricant
Schminke ⓕ *shming*·ke make-up
Schmuck ⓜ shmuk jewellery
schmutzig *shmu*·tsikh dirty
Schnecke ⓕ *shne*·ke snail
Schnee ⓜ shnay snow
Schneefeld ⓝ *shnay*·felt snowfield
schneiden *shnai*·den cut
Schneider/in ⓜ/ⓕ *shnai*·der/*shnai*·de·rin tailor
schnell shnel quick
Schnorcheln ⓝ *shnor*·kheln snorkelling
Schnuller ⓜ *shnu*·ler dummy • pacifier
Schnur ⓕ shnoor string
Schokolade ⓕ sho·ko·*lah*·de chocolate
schon shawn yet • already
schön shern beautiful
Schönheitssalon ⓜ *shern*·haits·za·long beauty salon
Schottland ⓝ *shot*·lant Scotland
Schrank ⓜ shrangk cupboard
Schraubenzieher ⓜ *shrow*·ben·tsee·er screwdriver
schrecklich *shrek*·likh terrible
Schreibarbeit ⓕ *shraip*·ar·bait paperwork
schreiben *shrai*·ben write
Schreibwarenhandlung ⓕ *shraip*·vah·ren·han·dlung stationer
schreien *shrai*·en shout
Schrein ⓜ shrain shrine
Schreiner(in) ⓜ/ⓕ *shrai*·ner/*shrai*·ne·rin carpenter
Schriftsteller(in) ⓜ/ⓕ *shrift*·shte·ler/*shrift*·shte·le·rin writer
schüchtern *shükh*·tern shy
Schuhe ⓜ pl *shoo*·e shoes
Schuld ⓕ shult (someone's) fault
schulden *shul*·den owe
schuldig *shul*·dikh guilty
Schule ⓕ *shoo*·le school
Schulter ⓕ *shul*·ter shoulder
Schüssel ⓕ *shü*·sel bowl
Schutzimpfung ⓕ *shuts*·im·pfung vaccination
schwach shvakh weak
schwanger *shvang*·er pregnant
Schwangerschaftserbrechen ⓝ *shvang*·er·shafts·er·*bre*·khen morning sickness
Schwangerschaftstest ⓜ *shvang*·er·shafts·test pregnancy test kit
Schwanz ⓜ shvants tail
schwarz shvarts black
schwarzer Pfeffer ⓜ *shvar*·tser *pfe*·fer black pepper
schwarzweiß shvarts·*vais* B&W (film)
Schwein ⓝ shvain pig
Schweinefleisch ⓝ *shvai*·ne·flaish pork
Schweiz ⓕ shvaits Switzerland
schwer shvair difficult (task) • heavy
Schwester ⓕ *shves*·ter sister
Schwiegermutter ⓕ *shvee*·ger·mu·ter mother-in-law
Schwiegersohn ⓜ *shvee*·ger·zawn son-in-law
Schwiegertochter ⓕ *shvee*·ger·tokh·ter daughter-in-law

Schwiegervater ⓜ shvee·ger·fah·ter father-in-law
schwierig shvee·rikh difficult
Schwimmbad ⓝ shvim·baht swimming pool
schwimmen shvi·men swim
Schwimmweste ⓕ shvim·ves·te life jacket
schwindelig shvin·de·likh dizzy
schwul shvool gay
schwül shvül muggy
Secondhandgeschäft ⓝ se·kend·hend·ge·sheft secondhand shop
See ⓜ zay lake
seekrank zay·krangk seasick
Segeln ⓝ zay·geln sailing
segnen zayg·nen bless
sehen zay·en see • look
sehr zair very
Seide ⓕ zai·de silk
Seife ⓕ zai·fe soap
Seifenoper ⓕ zai·fen·aw·per soap opera
Seil ⓝ zail rope
Seilbahn ⓕ zail·bahn cable car
sein zain his
sein zain be
seit (Mai) zait (mai) since (May)
Seite ⓕ zai·te side • page
Sekretär(in) ⓜ/ⓕ ze·kre·tair/ze·kre·tair·rin secretary
Sekundarschule ⓕ ze·kun·dahr·shoo·le high school
Sekunde ⓕ ze·kun·de second
Selbstbedienung ⓕ zelpst·be·dee·nung self-service
selbstständig zelpst·shten·dikh self-employed
selten zel·ten rare
senden zen·den send
Senf ⓜ zenf mustard
Serie ⓕ zair·ri·e series
Serviette ⓕ zer·vye·te napkin
Sessellift ⓜ ze·se·lift chairlift (skiing)
Sex ⓜ seks sex
Sexismus ⓜ sek·sis·mus sexism
sexy sek·si sexy
Shampoo ⓝ sham·poo shampoo
Shorts pl shorts shorts • boxer shorts
Show ⓕ shoh show
sicher zi·kher safe
Sicherheit ⓕ zi·kher·hait safety
Sicherheitsgurt ⓜ zi·kher·haits·gurt seatbelt
Sicherung ⓕ zi·khe·rung fuse
sie zee she • they
Sie zee you sg&pl pol
Sieger(in) ⓜ/ⓕ zee·ger/zee·ge·rin winner
silbern zil·bern silver
Silvester ⓝ zil·ves·ter New Year's Eve
Singapur ⓝ zing·a·poor Singapore
singen zing·en sing
Single ⓜ singl single (of person)
sinnlich zin·likh sensual
Sitz ⓜ zits seat (car)
sitzen zi·tsen sit
Skateboarden ⓝ skayt·bor·den skateboarding
Skibrille ⓕ shee·bri·le goggles (skiing)
skifahren shee·fah·ren ski
Skulptur ⓕ skulp·toor sculpture
Slipeinlage ⓕ slip·ain·lah·ge panty liner
Snack ⓜ snek snack
Snowboarden ⓝ snoh·bor·den snowboarding
Socken ⓕ pl zo·ken socks
sofort zo·fort immediately
Sohn ⓜ zawn son
Sojamilch ⓕ zaw·ya·milkh soy milk
Sojasauce ⓕ zaw·ya·zaw·se soy sauce
Sommer ⓜ zom·mer summer
Sonne ⓕ zon·ne sun
Sonnenaufgang ⓜ zon·en·owf·gang sunrise
Sonnenbrand ⓜ zon·en·brant sunburn
Sonnenbrille ⓕ zon·en·bri·le sunglasses

Sonnencreme ⓕ *zon·en·kraym* sunblock
Sonnenuntergang ⓜ *zon·en·un·ter·gang* sunset
sonnig *zon·nikh* sunny
Sonntag ⓜ *zon·tahk* Sunday
Soße ⓕ *zaw·se* sauce
Souvenir ⓝ *zu·ve·neer* souvenir
Souvenirladen ⓜ *zu·ve·neer·lah·den* souvenir shop
Sozialhilfe ⓕ *zo·tsyahl·hil·fe* welfare
sozialistisch *zo·tsya·lis·tish* socialist
Sozialstaat ⓜ *zo·tsyahl·shtaht* welfare state
Spanien ⓝ *shpah·ni·en* Spain
sparen *shpah·ren* save (money)
Spargel ⓜ *shpar·gel* asparagus
Spaß ⓜ *shpahs* fun
Spaß haben *shpahs hah·ben* have fun
spät *shpayt* late
Spaten ⓜ *shpah·ten* spade
Speichen ⓕ pl *shpai·khen* spokes
Speisekarte ⓕ *shpai·ze·kar·te* " menu
Speisewagen ⓜ *shpai·ze·vah·gen* dining car
Spezialist(in) ⓜ/ⓕ *shpe·tsya·list/shpe·tsya·lis·tin* specialist
speziell *shpe·tsyel* special
Spiegel ⓜ *shpee·gel* mirror
Spiel ⓝ *shpeel* match (sport)
spielen *shpee·len* play (game) • play (instrument)
Spielzeug ⓝ *shpeel·tsoyk* toy
Spinat ⓜ *shpi·naht* spinach
Spinne ⓕ *shpi·ne* spider
Spitze ⓕ *shpi·tse* lace
Spitzhacke ⓕ *shpits·ha·ke* pickaxe
Spitzname ⓜ *shpits·nah·me* nickname
Sport ⓜ *shport* sport
Sportler(in) ⓜ/ⓕ *shport·ler/shport·le·rin* sportsperson
Sprache ⓕ *shprah·khe* language
Sprachführer ⓜ *shprahkh·fü·rer* phrasebook
sprechen *shpre·khen* speak
springen *shpring·en* jump
Spritze ⓕ *shpri·tse* syringe
spritzen *shpri·tsen* inject
Spülung ⓕ *shpü·lung* conditioner
Staat ⓜ *shtaht* state
Staatsangehörigkeit ⓕ *shtahts·an·ge·her·rikh·kait* nationality
Staatsbürgerschaft ⓕ *shtahts·bür·ger·shaft* citizenship
Stadion ⓝ *shtah·di·on* stadium
Stadium ⓝ *shtah·di·um* stage
Stadt ⓕ *shtat* city • town
Standby-Ticket ⓝ *stend·bai·ti·ket* stand-by ticket
stark *shtark* strong
Start ⓜ *shtart* start (sport)
statt *shtat* instead of
Statue ⓕ *shtah·tu·e* statue
Steak ⓝ *stayk* steak (beef)
Stechmücke ⓕ *shtekh·mü·ke* mosquito
Stecker ⓜ *shte·ker* plug (electricity)
stehlen *shtay·len* steal
Stehplatz ⓜ *shtay·plats* standing room
steil *shtail* steep
Stein ⓜ *shtain* stone
stellen *shte·len* put (vertical)
sterben *shter·ben* die
Stereoanlage ⓕ *shtair·re·o·an·lah·ge* stereo
Sterne ⓜ pl *shter·ne* stars
Sternzeichen ⓝ *shtern·tsai·khen* star sign • zodiac
Steuer ⓕ *shtoy·er* tax
Stich ⓜ *shtikh* bite (insect)
Stickerei ⓕ *shti·ke·rai* embroidery
Stiefel ⓜ *shtee·fel* boot (footwear)
Stil ⓜ *shteel* style
stilles Wasser ⓝ *shti·les va·ser* still water
Stimme ⓕ *shti·me* voice
Stock ⓜ *shtok* floor (storey)
stoned *stohnd* stoned (drugged)
stoppen *shto·pen* stop

Stöpsel ⓜ *shterp·sel* plug (bath)
stornieren shtor·*nee*·ren cancel
Strand ⓜ shtrant beach
Straße ⓕ *shtrah*·se street • road
Straßenbahn ⓕ *shtrah*·sen·bahn tram
Straßenkarte ⓕ *shtrah*·sen·kar·te road map
Straßenkinder ⓝ pl *shtrah*·sen·kin·der street kids
Straßenmusiker(in) ⓜ/ⓕ *shtrah*·sen·moo·zi·ker/ *shtrah*·sen·moo·zi·ke·rin busker
Streichhölzer ⓝ pl *shtraikh*·herl·tser matches
streiken *shtrai*·ken (to be) on strike
Streit ⓜ shtrait quarrel
streiten *shtrai*·ten argue
Strom ⓜ shtrawm current (electricity)
Stromschnellen ⓕ pl *shtrawm*·shne·len rapids
Strümpfe ⓜ pl *shtrümp*·fe stockings
Strumpfhose ⓕ *shtrumpf*·haw·ze pantyhose
Stück ⓝ shtük piece
Student(in) ⓜ/ⓕ shtu·*dent*/ shtu·*den*·tin student
Studentenausweis ⓜ shtu·*den*·ten·ows·vais student card
studieren shtu·*dee*·ren study
Studio ⓝ *shtoo*·di·o studio
Stufe ⓕ *shtoo*·fe step (stairs)
Stuhl ⓜ shtool chair
stumm shtum mute
stur shtoor stubborn
Sturm ⓜ shturm storm
suchen nach *zoo*·khen nahkh look for
Süchtige ⓜ/ⓕ *zükh*·ti·ge addict
Süden ⓜ *zü*·den south
Supermarkt ⓜ *zoo*·per·markt supermarket
Suppe ⓕ *zu*·pe soup
Surfbrett ⓝ *serf*·bret surfboard
surfen *ser*·fen surf
süß züs sweet
Süßigkeiten ⓕ pl *zü*·sikh·kai·ten lollies • candy
Synagoge ⓕ zü·na·*gaw*·ge synagogue
synthetisch zün·*tay*·tish synthetic

T

Tabak ⓜ *ta*·bak tobacco
Tabakladen ⓜ *ta*·bak·lah·den tobacconist
Tag ⓜ tahk day
Tagebuch ⓝ *tah*·ge·bookh diary (journal)
täglich *tayk*·likh daily
Tal ⓝ tahl valley
Tampons ⓜ pl *tam*·pons tampons
Tankstelle ⓕ *tangk*·shte·le service station
Tante ⓕ *tan*·te aunt
tanzen *tan*·tsen dance
Tasche ⓕ *ta*·she bag • pocket
Taschenbuch ⓝ *ta*·shen·bookh paperback
Taschenlampe ⓕ *ta*·shen·lam·pe torch • flashlight
Taschenmesser ⓝ *ta*·shen·me·ser penknife
Taschenrechner ⓜ *ta*·shen·rekh·ner calculator
Tasse ⓕ *ta*·se cup
Tastatur ⓕ tas·ta·*toor* keyboard
taub towp deaf
Tauchen ⓝ *tow*·khen diving
Taufe ⓕ *tow*·fe baptism • christening
tausend *tow*·zent thousand
Taxi ⓝ *tak*·si taxi
Taxistand ⓜ *tak*·si·shtant taxi stand
Technik ⓕ *tekh*·nik technique
Tee ⓜ tay tea
Teelöffel ⓜ *tay*·ler·fel teaspoon
Teil ⓝ tail part
teilen *tai*·len share
Teilzeit ⓕ *tail*·tsait part-time
Telefon ⓝ te·le·*fawn* telephone
Telefonauskunft ⓕ te·le·*fawn*·ows·kunft directory enquiries

telefonieren te·le·fo·*nee*·ren phone
Telefonzelle ⓕ te·le·*fawn*·tse·le phone box
Teleskop ⓝ te·les·*kawp* telescope
Teller ⓜ *te*·ler plate
Tempel ⓜ *tem*·pel temple
Temperatur ⓕ tem·pe·ra·*toor* temperature (weather)
Tennis ⓝ *te*·nis tennis
Tennisplatz ⓜ *te*·nis·plats tennis court
Teppich ⓜ *te*·pikh rug
Termin ⓜ ter·*meen* appointment
Terminkalender ⓜ ter·*meen*·ka·len·der diary (for appointments)
Terrasse ⓕ te·*ra*·se patio
Test ⓜ test test
teuer *toy*·er expensive
Theater ⓝ te·*ah*·ter theatre
Theaterkasse ⓕ te·*ah*·ter·ka·se ticket office (theatre)
Theke ⓕ *tay*·ke counter (at bar)
Thermosflasche ⓕ *ter*·mos·fla·she thermos
Thunfisch ⓜ *toon*·fish tuna
tief teef deep
Tier ⓝ teer animal
Tisch ⓜ tish table
Tischdecke ⓕ *tish*·de·ke tablecloth
Tischtennis ⓝ *tish*·te·nis table tennis
Toast ⓜ tawst toast
Toaster ⓜ *taws*·ter toaster
Tochter ⓕ *tokh*·ter daughter
Tofu ⓜ *taw*·fu tofu
Toilette ⓕ to·a·*le*·te toilet
Toilettenpapier ⓝ to·a·*le*·ten·pa·peer toilet paper
toll tol terrific
Tomate ⓕ to·*mah*·te tomato
Tomatensauce ⓕ to·*mah*·ten·zaw·se tomato sauce
Topf ⓜ topf pot (ceramics)
Töpferwaren ⓕ pl *terp*·fer·vah·ren pottery
Tor ⓝ tawr gate • goal
Torhüterin ⓕ *tawr*·hü·te·rin goalkeeper
Torwart ⓜ *tawr*·vart goalkeeper
tot tawt dead
töten *ter*·ten kill
Tour ⓕ toor tour
Tourist(in) ⓜ/ⓕ tu·*rist*/tu·*ris*·tin tourist
Touristenklasse ⓕ tu·*ris*·ten·kla·se economy class
tragen *trah*·gen carry • wear
Training ⓝ *tray*·ning workout
trampen *trem*·pen hitchhike
Transitraum ⓜ tran·*zeet*·rowm transit lounge
Transport ⓜ trans·*port* transport
trauen *trow*·en trust
träumen *troy*·men dream
traurig *trow*·rikh sad
treffen *tre*·fen meet
Treppe ⓕ *tre*·pe stairway
treten *tray*·ten kick
trinken *tring*·ken drink
Trinkgeld ⓝ *tringk*·gelt tip (gratuity)
trocken *tro*·ken dry
Trockenobst ⓝ *tro*·ken·awpst dried fruit
trocknen *trok*·nen dry (clothes)
Truthahn ⓜ *troot*·hahn turkey
T-Shirt ⓝ *tee*·shert T-shirt
tun toon do
Tür ⓕ tür door
Turm ⓜ turm tower
Türsteher ⓜ *tür*·shtay·er bouncer (club heavy)
Tüte ⓕ *tü*·te carton (milk)
Typ ⓜ tüp type
typisch *tü*·pish typical

U

U-Bahn ⓕ *oo*·bahn subway (underground)
U-Bahnhof ⓜ *oo*·bahn·hawf metro station
Übelkeit ⓕ *ü*·bel·kait nausea
über *ü*·ber about • above • over
Überbrückungskabel ⓝ ü·ber·*brü*·kungks·kah·bel jumper leads
Überdosis ⓕ *ü*·ber·daw·zis overdose
überfüllt ü·ber·*fült* crowded
übergeben *oo*·ber·gey·ben vomit
Übergepäck ⓝ *ü*·ber·ge·pek excess baggage
übermorgen *ü*·ber·mor·gen day after tomorrow
übernachten ü·ber·*nakh*·ten stay (at a hotel)
Überraschung ⓕ ü·ber·*ra*·shung surprise
Überschwemmung ⓕ ü·ber·*shve*·mung flooding
übersetzen ü·ber·ze·tsen translate
Uhr ⓕ oor clock • watch
Ultraschall ⓜ *ul*·tra·shal ultrasound
umarmen um·*ar*·men hug
Umfrage ⓕ *um*·frah·ge polls
Umkleideraum ⓜ *um*·klai·de·rowm changing room
Umsatzsteuer ⓕ *um*·zats·shtoy·er sales tax
umsteigen *um*·shtai·gen change (trains)
Umtausch ⓜ *um*·towsh exchange
Umwelt ⓕ *um*·velt environment
Umweltverschmutzung ⓕ *um*·velt·fer·shmu·tsung pollution
unbequem *un*·be·kvaym uncomfortable
und unt and
unfair *un*·fair unfair
Unfall ⓜ *un*·fal accident
ungefähr un·ge·*fair* approximately
ungewöhnlich *un*·ge·vern·likh unusual
Ungleichheit ⓕ *un*·glaikh·hait inequality
Uniform ⓕ u·ni·*form* uniform
Universität ⓕ u·ni·ver·zi·*tayt* university
Universum ⓝ u·ni·*vair*·zum universe
unmöglich un·*merk*·likh impossible
unschuldig *un*·shul·dikh innocent
unser *un*·zer our
unten *un*·ten down • at the bottom
unter *un*·ter among • below • under
Unterhemd ⓝ *un*·ter·hemt singlet
Unterkunft ⓕ *un*·ter·kunft accommodation
Unterschrift ⓕ *un*·ter·shrift signature
Untertitel ⓜ pl *un*·ter·tee·tel subtitles
Unterwäsche ⓕ *un*·ter·ve·she underwear
Urlaub ⓜ *oor*·lowp holiday

V

Vagina ⓕ va·*gee*·na vagina
Vater ⓜ *fah*·ter father
Vegetarier(in) ⓜ/ⓕ ve·ge·*tah*·ri·er/ ve·ge·*tah*·ri·e·rin vegetarian
Vene ⓕ *vay*·ne vein
Ventilator ⓜ ven·ti·*lah*·tor fan (machine)
Verabredung ⓕ fer·*ap*·ray·dung date (appointment)
Veranstaltungskalender ⓜ fer·*an*·shtal·tungks·ka·len·der entertainment guide
Veranstaltungsort ⓜ fer·*an*·shtal·tungks·ort venue
Verband ⓜ fer·*bant* bandage
Verbandskasten ⓜ fer·*bants*·kas·ten first-aid kit
Verbindung ⓕ fer·*bin*·dung connection (person)
verbrennen fer·*bre*·nen burn
verdienen fer·*dee*·nen earn
Vergangenheit ⓕ fer·*gang*·en·hait past

Vergaser ⓜ fer·*gah*·zer carburettor
vergessen fer·*ge*·sen forget
vergewaltigen fer·ge·*val*·ti·gen rape
Verhaftung ⓕ fer·*haf*·tung arrest
verhindern fer·*hin*·dern prevent
Verhütungsmittel ⓝ fer·*hü*·tungks·mi·tel contraceptives
verkaufen fer·*kow*·fen sell
Verkehr ⓜ fer·*kair* traffic
Verlängerung ⓕ fer·*leng*·e·rung extension (visa)
verlegen fer·*lay*·gen embarrassed
verletzen fer·*le*·tsen hurt
Verletzung ⓕ fer·*le*·tsung injury
verlieren fer·*lee*·ren lose
Verlobte ⓜ&ⓕ fer·*lawp*·te fiancé • fiancée
Verlobung ⓕ fer·*law*·bung engagement (marriage)
verloren fer·*law*·ren lost
Vermieter(in) ⓜ/ⓕ fer·*mee*·ter/fer·*mee*·te·rin landlord/landlady
vermissen fer·*mi*·sen miss (feel absence of)
Vermittlung ⓕ fer·*mit*·lung operator
vernünftig fer·*nünf*·tikh sensible
verpassen fer·*pa*·sen miss (the bus)
Verpflegung ⓕ fer·*pflay*·gung provisions
verrückt fer·*rükt* crazy
Versicherung ⓕ fer·*zi*·khe·rung insurance
Verspätung ⓕ fer·*shpay*·tung delay
versprechen fer·*shpre*·khen promise
verstehen fer·*shtay*·en understand
Verstopfung ⓕ fer·*shtop*·fung constipation
versuchen fer·*zoo*·khen try (attempt)
Vertrag ⓜ fer·*trahk* contract
Verwaltung ⓕ fer·*val*·tung administration
Verwandte ⓜ&ⓕ fer·*van*·te relation (family)
verzeihen fer·*tsai*·en forgive
viel feel a lot (of) • plenty
viele *fee*·le many
vielleicht fi·*laikht* maybe
Viertel ⓝ *feer*·tel quarter
vierzehn Tage ⓝ pl *feer*·tsayn *tah*·ge fortnight
Virus ⓜ *vee*·rus virus (health) • virus (computer)
Visum ⓝ *vee*·zum visa
Vitamine ⓝ pl vi·ta·*mee*·ne vitamins
Vogel ⓜ *faw*·gel bird
Volksentscheid ⓜ *folks*·ent·shait referendum
voll fol full
Vollkornbrot ⓝ *fol*·korn·brawt wholemeal bread
Vollkornreis ⓜ *fol*·korn·rais brown rice
Vollzeit ⓕ *fol*·tsait full-time
Volumen ⓝ vo·*loo*·men volume
von fon from
vor fawr in front of • before
vor kurzem fawr *kur*·tsem recently
vor uns fawr uns ahead
vorbereiten *fawr*·be·rai·ten prepare
vorgestern *fawr*·ges·tern day before yesterday
Vorhängeschloss ⓝ *fawr*·heng·e·shlos padlock
Vormittag ⓜ *fawr*·mi·tahk morning (10am–noon)
Vorname ⓜ *fawr*·nah·me Christian/given name
Vorort ⓜ *fawr*·ort suburb
Vorrat ⓜ *fawr*·raht stock
vorsichtig *fawr*·zikh·tikh careful
Vorwahl ⓕ *fawr*·vahl area code
vorziehen *fawr*·tsee·en prefer

W

wachsen *vak*·sen grow
sich waschen zikh *va*·shen wash (oneself)
Waffe ⓕ *va*·fe weapon
Wagen ⓜ *vah*·gen carriage (train)
wählen *vay*·len choose • vote

Wahlen ⓕ pl *vah*·len elections
Wähltον ⓜ *vayl*·tawn dial tone
wahr vahr true
während *vair*·rent during
Währung ⓕ *vair*·rung currency
Wald ⓜ valt forest
wandern *van*·dern hike
Wanderstiefel ⓜ pl *van*·der·shtee·fel hiking boots
Wanderweg ⓜ *van*·der·vayk hiking route
wann van when
wann immer van *i*·mer whenever
Warenhaus ⓝ *vah*·ren·hows department store
warm varm warm
warnen *var*·nen warn
warten *var*·ten wait
Wartesaal ⓜ *var*·te·zahl waiting room (train station)
Wartezimmer ⓝ *var*·te·tsi·mer waiting room (doctor's)
warum va·*rum* why
was vas what
Wäscheleine ⓕ *ve*·she·lai·ne clothesline
waschen *va*·shen wash (something)
Wäscherei ⓕ ve·she·*rai* laundrette
Waschküche ⓕ *vash*·kü·khe laundry (room)
Waschlappen ⓜ *vash*·la·pen wash cloth (flannel)
Waschmaschine ⓕ *vash*·ma·shee·ne washing machine
Waschpulver ⓝ *vash*·pul·ver washing powder
Wasser ⓝ *va*·ser water
wasserdicht *va*·ser·dikht waterproof
Wasserfall ⓜ *va*·ser·fal waterfall
Wasserflasche ⓕ *va*·ser·fla·she water bottle
Wasserhahn ⓜ *va*·ser·hahn tap • faucet
Wassermelone ⓕ *va*·ser·me·law·ne watermelon
Wasserskifahren ⓝ *va*·ser·shee·fah·ren waterskiing
Watte-Pads pl *va*·te·pedz cotton balls
Wechselgeld ⓝ *vek*·sel·gelt change (coins)
Wechselkurs ⓜ *vek*·sel·kurs exchange rate
wechseln *vek*·seln exchange (money)
Wecker ⓜ *ve*·ker alarm clock
Weg ⓜ vayk track (path) • way
wegen *vay*·gen because of
Wegweiser ⓜ *vayk*·vai·zer signpost
sich weh tun zikh *vay* toon hurt (yourself)
Wehrdienst ⓜ *vair*·deenst military service
Weihnachten ⓝ *vai*·nakh·ten Christmas
Weihnachtsbaum ⓜ *vai*·nakhts·bowm Christmas tree
Weihnachtsfeiertag ⓜ *vai*·nakhts·fai·er·tahk Christmas Day
weil vail because
Wein ⓜ vain wine
Weinberg ⓜ *vain*·berk vineyard
Weinbrand ⓜ *vain*·brant brandy
Weintrauben ⓕ pl *vain*·trow·ben grapes
weiß vais white
Weißbrot ⓝ *vais*·brawt white bread
weißer Pfeffer ⓜ *vai*·ser *pfe*·fer white pepper
weißer Reis ⓜ *vai*·ser *rais* white rice
Weißwein ⓜ *vais*·vain white wine
weit vait far
Welle ⓕ *ve*·le wave
Welt ⓕ velt world
Weltmeisterschaft ⓕ *velt*·mais·ter·shaft World Cup
wenig *vay*·nikh (a) little
wenige *vay*·ni·ge few
weniger *vay*·ni·ger less
wenn ven when • if
wer vair who

Werkstatt ⓕ *verk*·shtat garage (car repair)
Werkzeug ⓝ *verk*·tsoyk tools
Wert ⓜ vert value (price)
wertvoll *vert*·fol valuable
Wespe ⓕ *ves*·pe wasp
Westen ⓜ *ves*·ten west
Wette ⓕ *ve*·te bet
Wetter ⓝ *ve*·ter weather
Whisky ⓜ *vis*·ki whisky
wichtig *vikh*·tikh important
wie vee how
wie viel vee feel how much
wieder *vee*·der again
wiederverwertbar vee·der·fer·vert·bahr recyclable
wiegen *vee*·gen weigh
wild vilt wild
willkommen vil·*ko*·men welcome
Wind ⓜ vint wind
Windel ⓕ *vin*·del nappy • diaper
Windeldermatitis ⓕ *vin*·del·der·ma·tee·tis nappy rash
windig *vin*·dikh windy
Windschutzscheibe ⓕ *vint*·shuts·shai·be windscreen
Windsurfen ⓝ *vint*·ser·fen windsurfing
Winter ⓜ *vin*·ter winter
winzig *vin*·tsikh tiny
wir veer we
wissen *vi*·sen know (something)
Wissenschaft ⓕ *vi*·sen·shaft science
Wissenschaftler(in) ⓜ/ⓕ *vi*·sen·shaft·ler/*vi*·sen·shaft·le·rin scientist
Witz ⓜ vits joke
wo vaw where
Wochenende ⓝ *vo*·khen·en·de weekend
Wodka ⓜ *vot*·ka vodka
Wohlfahrt ⓕ *vawl*·fahrt social welfare
wohnen *vaw*·nen reside
Wohnung ⓕ *vaw*·nung flat • apartment
Wohnwagen ⓜ *vawn*·vah·gen caravan
Wolke ⓕ *vol*·ke cloud
wolkig *vol*·kikh cloudy
Wolle ⓕ *vo*·le wool
wollen *vo*·len want
Wort ⓝ vort word
Wörterbuch ⓝ *ver*·ter·bookh dictionary
wunderbar *vun*·der·bahr wonderful
wünschen *vün*·shen wish
Würfel ⓜ *vür*·fel dice
Würmer ⓜ pl *vür*·mer worms
Wurst ⓕ vurst sausage
würzig *vür*·tsikh spiced
Wüste ⓕ *vüs*·te desert
wütend *vü*·tent angry

Y

Yen ⓜ yen yen

Z

Zahl ⓕ tsahl number
zählen *tsay*·len count
Zahlung ⓕ *tsah*·lung payment
Zahn ⓜ tsahn tooth
Zahnarz ⓜ *tsahn*·artst dentist
Zahnärztin ⓕ *tsahn*·erts·tin dentist
Zahnbürste ⓕ *tsahn*·bürs·te toothbrush
Zähne ⓜ pl *tsay*·ne teeth
Zahnfleisch ⓝ *tsahn*·flaish gum (mouth)
Zahnpasta ⓕ *tsahn*·pas·ta toothpaste
Zahnschmerzen pl *tsahn*·shmer·tsen toothache
Zahnseide ⓕ *tsahn*·zai·de dental floss
Zahnstocher ⓜ *tsahn*·shto·kher toothpick
Zauberer(in) ⓜ/ⓕ *tsow*·be·rer/*tsow*·be·re·rin magician
Zaun ⓜ tsown fence

Zehe ⓕ *tsay*·e toe • clove (of garlic)
zehn tsayn ten
zeigen *tsai*·gen show • point
Zeit ⓕ tsait time
Zeitschrift ⓕ *tsait*·shrift magazine
Zeitung ⓕ *tsai*·tung newspaper
Zeitungshändler ⓜ *tsai*·tungks·hen·dler newsagency
Zeitungskiosk ⓜ *tsai*·tungks·kee·osk newsstand
Zeitunterschied ⓜ *tsait*·un·ter·sheet time difference
Zelt ⓝ tselt tent
zelten *tsel*·ten camp
Zeltplatz ⓜ *tselt*·plats campsite
Zentimeter ⓜ tsen·ti·*may*·ter centimetre
Zentralheizung ⓕ tsen·*trahl*·hai·tsung central heating
Zentrum ⓝ *tsen*·trum centre
zerbrechen tser·*bre*·khen break
zerbrechlich tser·*brekh*·likh fragile
Zertifikat ⓝ tser·ti·fi·*kaht* certificate
Zeugnis ⓝ *tsoyk*·nis reference (work)
Ziege ⓕ *tsee*·ge goat
ziehen *tsee*·en pull
Ziel ⓝ tseel target • finish (sport)
Zigarette ⓕ tsi·ga·*re*·te cigarette
Zigarre ⓕ tsi·*gar*·re cigar
Zimmer ⓝ *tsi*·mer room
Zimmernummer ⓕ *tsi*·mer·nu·mer room number
Zirkus ⓜ *tsir*·kus circus
Zitrone ⓕ tsi·*traw*·ne lemon
Zoll ⓜ tsol customs
Zoo ⓜ tsaw zoo
zu tsoo too • at
zu Hause tsoo *how*·ze (at) home
Zucchini ⓕ tsu·*kee*·ni zucchini • courgette
Zucker ⓜ *tsu*·ker sugar
Zuckererbse ⓕ *tsu*·ker·erp·se snow pea
Zufall ⓜ *tsoo*·fal chance
Zug ⓜ tsook train
zugeben *tsoo*·gay·ben admit (accept as true)
Zukunft ⓕ *tsoo*·kunft future
Zulassung ⓕ *tsoo*·la·sung car registration
zum Beispiel tsum *bai*·shpeel for example
Zündung ⓕ *tsün*·dung ignition
zurück tsu·*rük* back (return)
zurückkommen tsu·*rük*·ko·men return
zusammen tsu·*za*·men together
Zusammenstoß ⓜ tsu·*za*·men·staws crash
zustimmen *tsoo*·shti·men agree
Zutat ⓕ *tsoo*·taht ingredient
zweimal *tsvai*·mahl twice
zweite *tsvai*·te second
Zwerchfell ⓝ *tsverkh*·fel diaphragm
Zwiebel ⓕ *tsvee*·bel onion
Zwillinge ⓜ pl *tsvi*·ling·e twins
zwischen *tsvi*·shen between

INDEX

REGISTER

For topics that are covered in several sections of this book, we've indicated the most relevant page number in bold.

A

abbreviations ... 3
accidents ... 49, **148**
accommodation ... 56, 59
activities ... 114, **136**, 142
addresses ... 47, **53**, 112
addressing people ... 104
adjectives (grammar) ... 14
admission (sightseeing) ... 94
adverbs (grammar) ... 14
aeroplanes ... 38
age ... 108
alcoholic drinks ... 172
allergies ... **157**, 185
alphabet (German) ... 13
ambulances ... 149
amounts ... **31**, 181
appointments ... 91, **127**
area codes (phone) ... 82
art ... 94
articles (grammar) ... 15
assaults ... 150
ATMs ... 87
Austrian German ... 103

B

babies ... 99
baggage ... 43
bags (shopping) ... 70, 72
banking ... 86
bars ... 125, 163, **176**
bargaining ... 73
be (verb) ... 16
beach ... 144
bed & breakfast (accommodation) ... 56
beer ... 8, 172, **174**
beliefs ... 134
bicycles ... **50**, 140
bills ... 86
bills (restaurant) ... 8, 167, **170**
birthdays ... 111, 113
blind travellers ... 97
boats ... 38, **46**
body language ... 91
body parts (diagram) ... 159
booking (accommodation) ... 57, 59
booking (restaurant) ... 164
booking (taxi) ... **46**, 63, 178
booking (tickets) ... 40, 41
books ... 73
border crossings ... 51
breakfast ... 57, 59, 60, **162**
breastfeeding ... 100
buses ... 38, **43**
business ... 90

C

cafes ... 125
calendar ... 33
cameras ... **75**, 78, 85
camping ... 56, **64**
cars ... 47
car parts (diagram) ... 48
cardinal numbers ... 30
careers ... 109
case (grammar) ... 16
casual speech ... 20, 108
CDs ... 74

cell phones 83
changing money 86
checks (restaurant) 8, 167, **170**
checking in 57
checking out 63
chemists 152, 153, **159**
children 40, 94, **99**, 111, 165
cinema **117**, 125
civilities 102, 103
clothes 74
coffee 172
communications 79
compliments (food) 170
computers 77, **84**
concerts **115**, 125, 126
condiments 169
conferences (business) 90
consonant sounds 11
consulates 151
contact details 80, 91, **112**
contraception 157
conversation 105
cooking classes 95
cooking utensils 182
costs (accommodation) 58, 59, 67
costs (banking) 88
costs (food) 164, 167, 168, **170**, 180
costs (general) 86
costs (phone & internet) 81, 84
costs (sightseeing) 94
costs (sport) 140
costs (transport) 47, 50
countries (German-speaking) 6
countries (nationalities) 107
courses (cooking/language) 95
credit cards 8, 70, 86, 89
cultural differences 135
customs (border crossing) 51
customs (traditions) 135
cycling 50

D

dancing 115, 126
dates (calendar) 33
dating (going out) 129
days of the week 33
deaf travellers 97
debit cards 70, 86
declaring items (customs) 52
demonstratives (grammar) 18
dentists 152
dictionary (English–German) 197
dictionary (German–English) 233
diets (special) 184
directions 53
disabilities, travellers with 97
discounts **94**, 99
doctors 149, **152**
drinks 8, 168, **172**
driving 47
drugs (illegal) **128**, 151

E

eating in 179
eating out **162**, 167, 187
elevators 61, 98
email **84**, 112
embassies 151
emergencies 148
entertainment 124
environment 123
etiquette tips 91, 178
exchange rates 88
exhibitions 94

F

family 99, **110**
family discounts 94
farewells 103, **111**
faulty things 72
fauna 146
feelings 119
film (cinema) **117**, 125
flora 146
food (eating in) 179
food (eating out) **162**, 167, 187
food (menu decoder) 187
food (preparation) 168, **179**, 182, 184
food (shopping) 179
football (soccer) 140, 141
foreign exchange office 87

formal speech 20
fractions 31
future (grammar) 25
future (time) 35

G

galleries 94
gas (petrol) 48, **49**
gay travellers 124
gender (grammar) 18
going out 124
goodbyes 103, **111**
grammar 14
greetings 103
guarantees (shopping) 72
guide dogs 97, 98
guides (hiking) 143
guides (sightseeing) 92

H

halal food 184
have (verb) 19
health 152
hiking 142
hire (bicycle) 50
hire (car & motorbike) 47
hire (sports equipment) 140
history (language) 7
hobbies 114
holidays 51, **106**
homestays 68
hospitals 152
hotels 56, 59
hotel room (diagram) 58

I

idioms 122
illnesses 152, **154**
immigration 51
informal speech 20
injuries 139, **148**, 152
insurance 48
interests 114
internet 84
intonation (pronunciation) 12
introductions (meeting people) 102
invitations 91, 124, **125**

J

jobs 109

K

kissing 132
kosher food 184

L

language classes 95
language difficulties 28
language history 7
laundry (hotel) 60, 61
lawyers 151
leaving 103, **111**
lesbian travellers 124
life jackets (boat) 46
lifts (elevators) **61**, 98
literature 73
local expressions 8, 9, 122
local food 164, 166, 180, **187**
locals (staying with) 68
lockers (luggage) 43
lost (items) 43, **151**, 160
lost (way) 144, **149**
love 133
luggage 43

M

mail 79
maps 53, 92, **142**
marriage 111
meals **162**, 177, 184, 187
mechanics (car) 49
medications 154, 155, 156, **159**
meeting people 102
meeting up 124, **127**
meetings (business) 90
menu decoder 187
menus 99, 165, **166**, 167
messages 61, 83
metro 45
misunderstandings (German) 81, 113
mobile phones 83

money ... 86
months ... 33
motorbike ... 47
movies ... **117**, 125
museums ... 94
music ... 74, **115**

N

names ... 104
nationalities ... 107
negatives (grammar) ... 20
nightclubs ... **124**, 125
nonalcoholic drinks ... 172
numbers ... 30

O

occupations ... 109
older people ... 94, **97**
opinions ... 120
optometrists ... 152
ordinal numbers ... 31
organic food ... 180, **186**
outdoors ... 142

P

parking (bicycle) ... 50
parking (car) ... 48
parties (entertainment) ... 126
parties (politics) ... 121
passports ... **51**, 64, 78, 151
past (grammar) ... 24
past (time) ... 35
pastimes ... 114
paying ... 70, **86**, 91, 170
personal pronouns (grammar) ... 20
petrol ... 48, **49**
pharmacists ... 152, 153, **159**
phone ... **80**, 83, 149
photography ... 75
pick-up lines ... 130
planes ... 38
plants ... 146
plurals (grammar) ... 21
police ... 149, **150**
polite speech ... 20
politics ... 121
possessives (grammar) ... 22
post office ... 79
prepositions (grammar) ... 23
prescriptions (medical) ... 154, 159
present (grammar) ... 24
present (time) ... 34
prices ... see *costs*
professions ... 109
pronouns (grammar) ... 20
pronunciation (German) ... 10

Q

quantities ... **31**, 181
questions (grammar) ... 23

R

rape ... 150
reading (books) ... 73
reading German ... 13
receipts ... 62, **72**, 87
recycling ... 123
refunds ... 72, 87
rejections (dating) ... 130
religion ... 134
renting (accommodation) ... 66
repairs (bicycle) ... 50
repairs (car & motorbike) ... 49
repairs (general) ... 78
reservations (accommodation) ... 57, 59
reservations (restaurant) ... 164
reservations (taxi) ... **46**, 63, 178
reservations (tickets) ... 40
responses (invitations) ... 126
restaurants ... 124, 162, **164**, 184, 187
restaurant table (diagram) ... 169
robbery ... 148, 150
romance ... 129
rooms (diagram) ... 58
rooms (hotel) ... 57, 59

S

safe travel ... 147
sausage (*Wurst*) ... 171
scoring (sport) ... 138, 139
seasons ... 34
seating ... 39, 42, 100, 117, 164, 165
self-catering ... 179

senior travellers ... 94, **97**
sex ... 132
shaking hands ... 91
shopping (food) ... 179
shopping (general) ... 69, 71
sightseeing ... 92
signs ... 49, 96, 145, 149, 166
sizes (clothes) ... 74
smoking ... 128, 155, 165
snacks ... 162
soccer ... 140, 141
social issues ... 121
sounds (German) ... 10
souvenirs ... 69, **77**
special diets ... 184
spelling (German) ... 13
sports ... 136
street (diagram) ... 55
studies ... 109
subtitles (cinema) ... 8, 117
swimming ... 139, 144

T

taxis ... **46**, 63, 178
tea ... 172
telephone ... **80**, 83, 149
tennis ... 136, 140
tents ... 64
theatre ... **117**, 125
theft ... 148, 150
tickets ... **40**, 41, 43
time ... 32
titles (addressing people) ... 104
toilets ... 62, 96, 97, **149**
tongue twisters ... 183
tours ... 95
traditional food ... 164, 166, 180, **187**
trains ... 38, **44**
transport ... 38
trekking ... 142

U

underground (metro) ... 45

V

vaccinations ... 153
valuables ... 64, 150, 151
vegetarian food ... 184
verbs (grammar) ... 24
visas ... 52
volunteering ... 118
vowel sounds ... 10

W

walking ... 142
water (drinkable) ... 65, 143, 144, 172
weather ... 145
wheelchairs ... **97**, 98
wine ... **176**, 177
women travellers ... 156
word order (grammar) ... 25
word stress (pronunciation) ... 12
work ... 90, **109**
writing German ... 13
Wurst (sausage) ... 171

10 Ways TO START A SENTENCE

When's (the next flight)?	Wann ist (der nächste Flug)?	van ist (dair *naykhs*·te fl ook)
Where's (the station)?	Wo ist (der Bahnhof)?	vaw ist (dair *bahn*·hawf)
Where can I (buy a ticket)?	Wo kann ich (eine Fahrkarte kaufen)?	vaw kan ikh (*ai*·ne *fahr*·kar·te *kow*·fen)
Do you have (a map)?	Haben Sie (eine Karte)?	*hah*·ben zee (*ai*·ne *kar*·te)
Is there (a toilet)?	Gibt es (eine Toilette)?	gipt es (*ai*·ne to·a·*le*·te)
I'd like (a coffee).	Ich möchte (einen Kaffee).	ikh *merkh*·te (*ai*·nen *ka*·fay)
I'd like (to hire a car).	Ich möchte (ein Auto mieten).	ikh *merkh*·te (ain *ow*·to *mee*·ten)
Can I (enter)?	Darf ich (hereinkommen)?	darf ikh (her·*ein*·ko·men)
Could you please (help me)?	Könnten Sie (mir helfen)?	*kern*·ten zee (meer *hel*·fen)
Do I have to (book a seat)?	Muss ich (einen Platz reservieren lassen)?	mus ikh (*ai*·nen plats re·zer·*vee*·ren *la*·sen)